The
International Critical Commentary
on the Holy Scriptures of the Old and
New Testaments.

UNDER THE EDITORSHIP OF

THE REV. SAMUEL ROLLES DRIVER, D.D., D.LITT.,

Regius Professor of Hebrew, Oxford;

THE REV. ALFRED PLUMMER, M.A., D.D.,

Late Master of University College, Durham;

AND

THE REV. CHARLES AUGUSTUS BRIGGS, D.D., D.LITT.,

Professor of Theological Encyclopædia and Symbolics,
Union Theological Seminary, New York.

THE INTERNATIONAL CRITICAL COMMENTARY

A

CRITICAL AND EXEGETICAL COMMENTARY

ON

THE BOOK OF ECCLESIASTES

BY

GEORGE AARON BARTON, Ph.D.

PROFESSOR OF BIBLICAL LITERATURE AND SEMITIC LANGUAGES
BRYN MAWR COLLEGE, PENNSYLVANIA

EDINBURGH
T. & T. CLARK LTD, 36 GEORGE STREET

PRINTED IN SCOTLAND BY
MORRISON AND GIBB LIMITED
EDINBURGH AND LONDON
FOR

T. & T. CLARK LTD., EDINBURGH

0 567 05014 9

FIRST IMPRESSION . . . 1912
LATEST IMPRESSION . . 1980

PREFACE

THE following pages are a plain commentary on the Book of Ecclesiastes. Those who expect to find here the advocacy of new and startling theories of this fascinatingly perplexing book will be disappointed. In the judgment of the writer there has been something too much of these things in the recent literature on Qoheleth. An endeavour is made in the following pages to examine the important theories concerning the book, both ancient and modern, in an impartial spirit, and, in the formation of judgments, to go whither the evidence points. Obviously, in treating a work which has been studied so many centuries, there is little opportunity for novel discovery. Occasionally the writer has found himself differing from all his predecessors, but much more often the evidence has pointed to a conclusion already anticipated by some previous worker. He cannot hope that his conclusions will commend themselves to all his colleagues, but if this commentary shall have a part, however humble, in recalling criticism to regions in which the evidence is sufficiently objective to give some ultimate promise of a consensus of judgment on the part of scholars concerning the problems involved, the labour expended upon it will be more than rewarded.

In conclusion, I desire to express my thanks to Dr. Hans H. Spoer, of Jerusalem, for placing at my disposal his collation of some MSS. of the Greek Version of Ecclesiastes in the Library of the Church of the Holy Sepulchre; to Professor Paul Haupt, for permitting me, in spite of my disbelief in his metrical theory, to use, while reading my proofs, advance sheets of his *Hebrew Text of Ecclesiastes;* to the Editor, Professor Charles A. Briggs, for his helpful criticisms and many kindnesses while the book has been passing through the press; and to my wife, for her valuable aid in reading the proofs.

GEORGE A. BARTON.

BRYN MAWR, PA.,
    April 2nd, 1908.

CONTENTS

ABBREVIATIONS.

I. TEXTS AND VERSIONS.

𝕬 = The Arabic Version.
'A = Version of Aquila.
Ald. = Aldine text of 𝕲.
AV. = Authorized Version.

BD. = Baer & Delitzsch, Heb. text.

Chr. = The Chronicler, author of Ch. Ezr. Ne.

D. = The Deuteronomist in Dt., in other books Deuteronomic author of Redactor.

E. = Ephraemitic sources of Hexateuch.
EVˢ = English Versions.

𝕲 = Greek Septuagint Version, Vatican text of Swete.
𝕲ᴬ = The Alexandrine text.
𝕲ᴮ = The Vatican text.
𝕲ᶜ = Codex Ephraemi.
𝕲ᴺ = The Sinaitic text.
𝕲ᵛ = Codex Venetus.

𝕳 = Hebrew consonantal text.
H. = Code of Holiness of the Hexateuch.
Hex. = The Hexateuch

J. = Judaic sources of the Hexateuch.
J.C. = Jerome, Commentary.

𝕶 = The Coptic Version.
Kt. = Kᵉthib, the Hebrew text as written.

𝕷 = Old Latin Version.

Mas. = Massora.
MT. = The Massoretic pointed text.
NT. = The New Testament.
OT. = The Old Testament.
P. = The priestly sources of the Hexateuch.

Qr. = Qᵉrê, the Hebrew text as read.

R. = The Redactor, or editor.
RV. = The Revised Version.
RV.ᵐ = The margin of the Revised Version.

𝕾 = The Syriac Peshitto Version.
𝕾ᴴ = Syriac-Hexaplar Version.
Σ = The Version of Symmachus.

𝕿 = The Targum or Aramaic Version.

𝖁 = The Vulgate Version.
Vrss. = Versions, usually ancient.

WL. = The Wisdom Literature of the OT.

Θ = The Version of Theodotian.

ix

II. BOOKS OF THE OLD AND NEW TESTAMENTS.

Am.	= Amos.	Jon.	= Jonah.
		Jos.	= Joshua.
Bar.	= Baruch	Ju.	= Judges.
BS.	= Ecclesiasticus of Ben Sira.		
		1, 2 K.	= 1, 2 Kings.
1, 2 Ch.	= 1, 2 Chronicles.		
Col.	= Colossians.	La.	= Lamentations.
1, 2 Cor.	= 1, 2 Corinthians.	Lk.	= Luke.
Ct.	= Canticles = The Song of	Lv.	= Leviticus.
	Songs.	Mal.	= Malachi.
Dn.	= Daniel.	1,2 Mac.	= 1, 2 Maccabees.
Dt.	= Deuteronomy.	Mi.	= Micah.
		Mk.	= Mark.
Ec.	= Ecclesiastes.	Mt.	= Matthew.
Est.	= Esther.		
Eph.	= Ephesians.	Na.	= Nahum.
Ex.	= Exodus.	Ne.	= Nehemiah.
Ez.	= Ezekiel.	Nu.	= Numbers.
Ezr.	= Ezra.		
		Ob.	= Obadiah.
Gn.	= Genesis.	Phil.	= Philippians.
Gal.	= Galatians.	Pr.	= Proverbs.
		Ps.	= Psalms.
Hb.	= Habakkuk.		
Heb.	= Hebrews.	Q.	= Qoheleth or Ecclesiastes.
Hg.	= Haggai.	Qoh.	= Qoheleth or Ecclesiastes.
Ho.	= Hosea.		
		Rev.	= Revelation.
Is.	= early parts of Isaiah.	Rom.	= Romans.
Is.[2]	= exilic parts of Isaiah.	Ru.	= Ruth.
Is.[3]	= post-exilic parts of Isaiah.	1, 2 S.	= 1, 2 Samuel.
Jb.	= Job.	1, 2 Thes.	= 1, 2 Thessalonians.
Je.	= Jeremiah.	1, 2 Tim.	= 1, 2 Timothy.
Jn.	= John.	Zc.	= Zechariah.
Jo.	= Joel.	Zp.	= Zephaniah.

III. AUTHORS AND WRITERS.

AE.	= Aben Ezra.		Briggs. The editor
Aug.	= Augustine.		specially referred to
			is designated by
BDB.	= Hebrew and English		*B*DB. F. Brown,
	Lexicon of the OT.,		B*D*B. S. R. Driver,
	edited by F. Brown,		BD*B*. C. A. Briggs.
	S. R. Driver, C. A.	Bar Heb.	= Bar Hebræus.

Be.	= G. Beer.	Ew.	= H. Ewald.
Bick.	= G. Bickell, *Das Buch Kohelet.*	Ew.[§]	= his *Lehrb. der Heb. Sprache.*
Bö.	= F. Böttcher.		
Br.	= C. A. Briggs.	Fü.	= J. Fürst.
Br.[MA]	= Messiah of the Apostles.	Gen.	= Genung, *Words of Koheleth.*
Br.[MG]	= Messiah of the Gospels.	Ges.	= Gesenius, *Thesaurus.*
Br.[MP]	= Messianic Prophecy.	Ges.[Bu.]	= Gesenius, *Wörterbuch,* 13th ed.
Br.[SHS]	= Study of Holy Scripture.	Ges.[K.]	= his Heb. Gram., ed. Kautzsch.
Br.[HEX.]	= Higher Criticism of the Hexateuch.	Ges.[L]	= his *Lehrgebäude.*
		Gins.	= Ginsburg, *Coheleth.*
Calv.	= John Calvin.	Gr.	= Grätz, *Kohelet.*
Che.	= T. K. Cheyne.	Grot.	= Grotius.
ChWB.	= Levy, *Chald. Wörterbuch.*		
Co.	= C. H. Cornill.	H.	= W. R. Harper, *Hebrew Syntax.*
CT.	= *Cuneiform Texts from Babylonian Tablets in the British Museum.*	Ha.	= P. Haupt, *Koheleth* and *Ecclesiastes.*
		Heil.	= Heiligstedt, *Ecclesiastes.*
Da.	= Davidson, *Hebrew Syntax.*	Heng.	= Hengstenberg.
Dat.	= Dathe, *Ecclesiastes.*	Hit.	= F. Hitzig, *Ecclesiastes.*
DB.	= Hastings' Dictionary of the Bible.	Houb.	= C. F. Houbigant.
Del.	= Franz Delitzsch, *Das Buch Koheleth.*	Ja.	= Jastrow, *Dict.* of the Targ., Talm. and Midrashic Lit.
Död.	= Döderlein, *Ecclesiastes*	JBL.	= Journal of Biblical Literature.
Dr.	= S. R. Driver, *Ecclesiastes* in Kittel's *Biblia Hebraica.*	JE.	= Jewish Encyclopædia.
		Jer.	= Jerome.
Dr.[§]	= Heb. Tenses.	Jos.[Ant.]	= Fl. Josephus, *Antiquities.*
Dr.[Intr.]	= Introduction to Literature of OT.	Jos.BJ.	= Fl. Josephus, *Wars of the Jews.*
EB.	= Encyclopædia Biblica.	JQR.	= Jewish Quarterly Review.
Elst.	= Elster.		
Eph. Syr.	= Ephraem Syrus.		
Eur.	= Euringer, *Masorahtext des Koheleth.*	Kam.	= A. S. Kamenetzky.
		Kau.	= E. Kautzsch.

Kenn.	= Benj. Kennicott, *Vetus Testamentum Hebraicum cum variis lectionibus*.	Rö.	= E. Rödiger
		Rob.	= E. Robinson, *Biblical Researches*.
		Ros.	= Rosenmüller.
Ki.	= Daniel Kimchi (Qamchi).	RS.	= W. Robertson Smith.
Kn.	= A. W. Knobel, *Das Buch Qoheleth*.	Sieg.	= D. C. Siegfried, *Prediger und Hoheslied*.
Kö.	= F. E. König, *Lehrgebäude der Heb. Sprache*.	Siev.	= E. Sievers.
		Sm.	= R. Smend.
		SS.	= Siegfried and Stade's *Heb. Wörterbuch*.
Kue.	= A. Kuenen.		
		Sta.	= B. Stade.
Lag.	= P. de Lagarde.		
Lag.*BN*	= his *Bildung der Nomina*.	Talm.	= The Talmud.
Luz.	= S. D. Luzzato.	Tisch.	= C. Tischendorf.
		Tr.	= Tristram, *Natural History of the Bible*.
Marsh.	= Marshall, *Ecclesiastes*.		
M.	= Müller's *Hebrew Syntax*.	Ty.	= T. Tyler, *Ecclesiastes*.
MA.	= W. Muss-Arnold, *Assyr. Dictionary*.	Van d. P.	= van der Palm.
		Vl.	= W. Vlock.
McN.	= A. H. McNeile, *Introd. to Ecclesiastes*.	Vaih.	= J. C. Vaihinger.
Mich.	= J. D. Michaelis.	Wang.	= Dr. Wangemann.
Mish.	= The *Mishna*.	We.	= J. Wellhausen.
		Wild.	= Wildeboer.
NHWB.	= Levy, *Neuhebr. Wörterbuch*.	Wr.	= C. H. H. Wright, *Ecclesiastes*.
No.	= W. Nowack, *Pr. Solom.*		
		Zap.	= V. Zapletal, *Metrik d. Kohelet*.
Pl.	= E. H. Plumtre, *Ecclesiastes*.	Zö.	= O. Zöckler, *Prediger in Lange's Bibelwerk*.
R.	= Rawlinson's *Cuneiform Inscriptions of Western Asia*, IV. R. = Vol. IV. of it.		
		ZAW.	= *Zeitschrift f. alttest. Wissenschaft*.
Ra.	= Rashi.		
Re.	= E. Renan, *L'Ecclésiaste*.	*ZMG*.	= *Z. d. deutsch. Morgenländ. Gesellschaft*.
Ri.*HWB*	= Riehm's *Handwörterbuch*.	*ZPV*.	= *Z. d. deutsch. Pal. Vereins*.

IV. GENERAL, ESPECIALLY GRAMMATICAL.

abr.	= abbreviation.
abs.	= absolute.
abstr.	= abstract.
acc.	= accusative.
acc. cog.	= cognate acc.
acc. pers.	= acc. of person.
acc. rei	= acc. of thing.
acc. to	= according to.
act.	= active.
adj.	= adjective.
adv.	= adverb.
α.λ.	= ἅπαξ λεγόμενον, word or phr. used once.
al.	= *et aliter*, and elsw.
alw.	= always.
antith.	= antithesis, antithetical.
apod.	= apodosis.
Ar.	= Arabic.
Aram.	= Aramaic.
art.	= article.
As.	= Assyrian.
Bab.	= Babylonian.
B. Aram.	= Biblical Aramaic.
c.	= *circa*, about; also *cum*, with.
caus.	= causative.
cod., codd.	= codex, codices.
cf.	= confer, compare.
cog.	= cognate.
coll.	= collective.
comm.	= commentaries.
comp.	= compare.
concr.	= concrete.
conj.	= conjunction.
consec.	= consecutive.
contr.	= contract, contracted.
cstr.	= construct.
d.f.	= daghesh forte.
def.	= defective.
del.	= *dele*, strike out.
dittog.	= dittography.
dub.	= dubious, doubtful.

elsw.	= elsewhere.
esp.	= especially.
emph.	= emphasis, emphatic.
Eth.	= Ethiopic.
exc.	= except.
exil.	= exilic.
f.	= feminine.
fig.	= figurative.
fpl.	= feminine plural.
fr.	= from.
freq.	= frequentative.
fs.	= feminine singular.
gent.	= gentilic.
gl.	= gloss, glossator.
gen.	= genitive.
haplog.	= haplography.
Heb.	= Hebrew.
Hiph.	= Hiphil of verb.
Hithp.	= Hithpael of verb.
impf.	= imperfect.
imv.	= imperative.
indef.	= indefinite.
inf.	= infinitive.
i.p.	= in pause.
i.q.	= *id quod*, the same with.
intrans.	= intransitive.
J.Ar.	= Jewish Aramaic.
juss.	= jussive.
lit.	= literal, literally.
loc.	= local, locality.
m.	= masculine.
Mand.	= Mandæan.
metaph.	= metaphor, metaphorical.
mng.	= meaning.
mpl.	= masculine plural.
ms.	= masculine singular.

n.	= noun.
n. p.	= proper name.
n. pr. loc.	= proper noun of place.
n. unit.	= noun of unity.
Nab.	= Nabathean.
NH.	= New Hebrew.
Niph.	= Niphal of verb.
obj.	= object.
opp.	= opposite, as opposed to or contrasted with.
p.	= person.
parall.	= parallel with.
part.	= particle.
pass.	= passive.
pf.	= perfect.
Ph.	= Phœnician.
phr.	= phrase.
Pi.	= Piel of verb.
pl.	= plural.
post-B.	= post-Biblical.
postex.	= postexilic.
pred.	= predicate.
preëx.	= preëxilic.
preg.	= pregnant.
prep.	= preposition.
prob.	= probable.
pron.	= pronoun.
ptc.	= participle.
Pu.	= Pual of verb.

qu.	= question.
q.v.	= *quod vide.*
rd.	= read.
refl.	= reflexive.
rel.	= relative.
Sab.	= Sabæan.
sf.	= suffix.
sg.	= singular.
si vera	= *si vera lectio.*
sim.	= simile.
sq.	= followed by.
st.	= *status*, state, stative.
str.	= strophe.
subj.	= subject.
subst.	= substantive.
s.v.	= *sub voce.*
syn.	= synonymous.
synth.	= synthetic.
Syr.	= Syriac.
t.	= times (following a number).
tr.	= transfer.
trans.	= transitive.
txt.	= text.
txt. err.	= textual error.
v.	= *vide*, see.
vb.	= verb.
vs.	= verse.

V. OTHER SIGNS.

‖ parallel, of words or clauses chiefly synonymous.

= equivalent, equals.

+ plus denotes that other passages might be cited.

[ ] indicates that the form enclosed is not in the Hebrew, so far as known.

√ = the root, or stem.

′ = sign of abbreviation in Hebrew words.

″ = Yahweh.

( ) = Indicates that Massoretic text has not been followed, but either Vrss. or conjectural emendations.

INTRODUCTION.

§ 1. NAME.

The name *Ecclesiastes* (Latin, *Ecclesiastes*, Greek Ἐκκλεσιασ-τὴς) is apparently a translation of the unique Hebrew word, *Qoheleth*. The meaning of this word is uncertain, but it probably signifies "one who addresses an assembly," or "an official speaker in an assembly," (see critical note on ch. 1¹, where the various meanings which have been supposed to attach to the term are reviewed).

§ 2. PLACE IN THE HEBREW BIBLE.

In the Hebrew Bible Ecclesiastes stands in the third division of the canon among the *K^etubim*, or Hagiography, where it now follows Lamentations and precedes Esther. It forms one of the so-called *Megilloth*, or "Rolls," the only parts of the Hagiography which were publicly read at the Jewish festivals. At what period Ecclesiastes was admitted to its present position is uncertain. In the list of books given in *Baba Batra*, 13, 14, the *Megilloth* are not even grouped together. *Qoheleth* is included, and it immediately follows Proverbs and precedes Canticles, as in our English Bibles. In the Talmudic treatise *Soferim*, which reached its final redaction about the middle of the eighth century, Ruth, Canticles, Lamentations and Esther are mentioned twice (14². ⁸), but Ecclesiastes is omitted from both passages. (JE., XI, p. 427ᵇ and W. R. Smith, OT. in JC., 2d ed., p. 173n.) In the *Mahzor*, edited by Samuel of Vitry at the beginning of the twelfth century, it is said that at the feast of tabernacles the congregation, seated, read the "book" Ecclesiastes. It is not here called a "roll" and was, perhaps, not then included in the *Megilloth*. (Cf. JE.,

VIII, 429.) In the extant MSS. of the Bible the *Megilloth* are usually grouped together, though the order varies, especially in Spanish MSS. (*Cf.* the table in Ryle's *Canon*, 281 *ff.*)

Soon after the twelfth century, apparently, the present order (Ruth, Lamentations, Ecclesiastes) was established in French and German MSS., and has been maintained ever since. Before the first printed editions of the Hebrew Bible were made, Ecclesiastes had, at all events, taken its present position as one of the five *Megilloth*. This is true of the first printed Hagiography, 1486–1487, as well as Bomberg's great *Biblia Rabbinica* of 1517, which contained three Targums and a Rabbinic commentary.

§ 3. CANONICITY.

Ecclesiastes is not mentioned in any canonical writing of the Old Testament. Evidence has, however, come to light in recent years which proves quite conclusively that it was known in an edited form to the author of *Ecclesiasticus*, or *the Wisdom of Jesus Son of Sirach*, who wrote about 180–175 B.C. This evidence is given in detail below in §11; but Nöldeke's article in ZAW., XX, 90 *ff.*, and McNeile's *Introduction to Ecclesiastes*, 34 *ff.*, may also be compared. There is no reason to suppose, however, that Ecclesiastes had been canonized at the time of Ben Sira; on the contrary, the very opposite would seem to be the fact, for Ecclesiastes was also known to a later extra-canonical writer, the author of the *Wisdom of Solomon*, who probably wrote in the first century B.C. The author of this last-mentioned book, in his second chapter, sets himself to correct the sinful utterances of certain ungodly men, and there can be no question but that in verses 1–9 he includes among the sayings of the ungodly a number of the utterances of *Qoheleth* (for details, see below, §12). Whether *Qoheleth* was known to the author of *Wisdom* in the Hebrew or in a Greek translation is unknown; and the fact, if known, would have no bearing on the question of canonicity, for uncanonical books were often translated. (See, however, below, §4, (2) and (3). The tone of the attack upon *Qoheleth*, which is made in *Wisdom*, indicates that to him the book was not yet Scripture. The earnestness of the attack makes rather the impression that the book was a candidate for canonical regard—that it was so esteemed in some quarters—and that the writer wished to open the eyes of his readers to the true character of its sentiments.

A Talmudic story, to which McNeile calls attention, Talm. Jerusalem, *Berakoth*, 11b (vii, 2), would, if any weight can be attached to it, indicate that in the first century B.C. canonical authority was by some assigned to the book. The story is concerning an incident in the reign of Alexander Jannæus (104–79 B.C.). It says, "The king (Jannæus) said to him (Simon ben Shetach, the king's brother-in-law), 'Why didst thou mock me by saying that nine hundred sacrifices were required, when half would have been sufficient?' Simon answered, 'I mocked thee not; thou hast paid thy share and I mine . . . as it is written. For the protection of wisdom is as the protection of money,'" thus making a literal quotation from Eccl. 7¹².

Another Talmudic story quoted by Wright (*Baba Batra*, 4a) relates to the time of Herod. That monarch, having put to death members of the Sanhedrin and deprived Baba ben Buta of his sight, visited the latter in disguise and endeavored to betray him into some unguarded expression with reference to Herod's own tyranny. Ben Buta steadily refused to utter an incautious word, and in his replies he quotes from all three parts of the Biblical canon—from the Pentateuch, Ex. 22²⁷, from the Prophets, Isa. 2², and from the K⁰*tubim*, Pr. 6²³, and in three different parts Eccl. 10²⁰—introducing each quotation with the formula for quoting canonical Scripture. The passage from *Qoheleth* which is thus quoted is:

> Do not even in thy thought curse the king,
> Nor in thy bedchamber curse a rich man ;
> For the bird of heaven shall carry the voice,
> And the owner of wings shall tell a thing.

Wright (p. 21 *ff.*) also gives in full another Talmudic story, to which Bloch had called attention—a story relating to the great Rabbi Gamaliel I (*c.* 44 A.D.). According to this tale (*Sabbath*, 30b), Gamaliel had a dispute with a brilliant pupil, whom Bloch believed to be the Apostle Paul, and in the course of the dispute, the pupil quoted as Scripture twice Eccl. 1⁹: "There is nothing new under the sun."

If these Talmudic tales came from a contemporary source, they would prove that Ecclesiastes had been admitted into the canon by the first century B.C. In fact, all that the passages prove is that the Rabbis of the Talmudic period—the third to the fifth centuries A.D.—had traditions which they apparently believed to be authentic that *Qoheleth* had been recognized as Scripture at the dates mentioned.

The New Testament affords us no help in tracing the canonicity of Ecclesiastes. There is in the NT. no quotation from Ecclesiastes. When, however, the character of the book is taken into account, it is not strange that no reference is made to it. This silence cannot fairly be made an argument against the canonicity of our book. (See Br.ˢᴴˢ, pp. 131–132.)

McNeile, however, goes farther than the evidence will warrant when he argues (*op. cit.*, p. 6 *ff.*) from the New Testament use of the word Scripture (ἡ γραφή, αἱ γραφαί), that the canon was definitely so closed to the writers of the New Testament that another book could not find its way into it. As is well known the three divisions of the canon are mentioned in the prologue to the Greek Ecclesiasticus, proving that they existed when that work was translated, *c.* 130 B.C., and are also referred to in the Gospel of Luke (ch. 24⁴⁴). There is absolutely nothing, however, to show us exactly what the New Testament writers had in the third division of their canon. It is quite possible, as McNeile claims, that ἡ γραφή meant to them a definite body of writings, but that that body was so fixed that no additions could be made to it, is an unproved assumption, and the "impression that 'Scripture' meant to the Apostolic writers the same body of Old Testament writings that it means to us," if it is to be understood that their canon could not have differed from ours by even one book, rests on no adequate evidence whatever. (See Br.ˢᴴˢ, pp. 124 *ff.*, 131.)

Some scholars find quotations from Ecclesiastes in the New Testament. Thus Plumtre thinks that Paul may have had Qoheleth in mind when he wrote "The creation was subjected to vanity" (Rom. 8²⁰); and that the Epistle of James alludes to it: "For ye are a vapor which ap-

peareth for a little time and then vanisheth away" (ch. 4¹⁴). Such parallels are, however, too vague to be convincing. Neither writer may
have been thinking of Qoheleth at all. Haupt believes that Jesus alludes
to Ecclesiastes with the purpose of combating its sentiments in the parable of the rich man who pulled down his barns to build greater,
Lk. 12¹⁶⁻²¹. He sees in Lk. 12¹⁸ an allusion to Eccl. 2⁴ and in 12²⁰ᵇ, to
Eccl. 2¹⁸ᵇ. Again, the allusions are too vague to be convincing. The
view of J. Rendel Harris, that the parable is an elaboration of BS. 5¹ᶠ,
is much more probable. Haupt also holds that Lk. 12²⁷=Matt. 6²⁹,
(*Solomon in all his glory*) is "above all" an allusion to Ecclesiastes, but
again one must say that the likeness is not convincing. It is quite as probable that the account of Solomon in 1 Kings was in the mind of Jesus.

Philo, like the New Testament, makes no reference to *Qoheleth*,
but, as in the case of the New Testament, no argument is to be
drawn from this silence, as he makes no reference to a number of
other books—Ezekiel, Daniel, Canticles, Ruth and Lamentations.

The suggestion made above, that *Qoheleth* was in some quarters
regarded as canonical, but was not universally received, receives
confirmation from one or two famous passages in the Mishna,
which reached its final form about 200 A.D. In the terminology
of the Mishna the way of calling a book canonical is to say that it
"defiles the hands." In the Tract *Yadaim*, 3⁵, we read: "All the
Holy Scriptures defile the hands. The Song of Songs and *Qoheleth* defile the hands. Rabbi Judah says, 'The Song of Songs
defiles the hands, but *Koheleth* is disputed.' Rabbi Jose says,
'*Qoheleth* does not defile the hands, and the Song of Songs is
disputed.' Rabbi Simeon says, '*Qoheleth* belongs to the light
things of the school of Shammai, but to the weighty things of the
school of Hillel.' Rabbi Simeon ben Azzai says, 'I received from
the mouth of the seventy-two elders on the day when they placed
Rabbi Eliezer ben Azariah in the president's chair, that the Song
of Songs and *Qoheleth* defile the hands.' Rabbi Aqiba said, 'Far
be it and peace! No man of Israel has ever doubted concerning
the Song of Songs that it defiled the hands, for there is not a day
in all the world like the day on which the Song of Songs was given
to Israel, because all the *Kᵉtubim* are holy, but the Song of Songs
is most holy. And if they had doubts, they only doubted concerning *Qoheleth*.' Rabbi Johanan, son of Joshua, son of the

father-in-law of Rabbi Aqiba says, 'so they differed and so they concluded.'"

Again, *Eduyoth*, 5³, says: "*Qoheleth* does not defile the hands according to the school of Shammai, but according to the school of Hillel it does defile the hands." These passages are echoed in the Talmud and in later Jewish writings. Now it seems very clear from these statements that down to the end of the first century A.D. Ecclesiastes was among the "Antilegomena" of the Old Testament canon. Ryle is quite right in saying (*Canon*, 174), that it would be difficult after the first century B.C., when the antipathy between the Pharisees and Sadducees became so marked and their contentions so virulent, for a new book to be introduced into the canon. It seems clear that, if *Qoheleth* had not begun to gain a foothold before that in some influential quarter, its chances of canonicity would have been slight, but it seems equally clear that it was not universally accepted as a part of Scripture until after the great council of Jabne (Jamnia), at the end of the first century A.D. (See Br.ᔆᴴˢ, p. 130.)

The book probably won its way at last, because as these passages show it had a part of the Pharisaical influence in its favor. It was not a question of Pharisee against Sadducee. The Sadducees would find no fault with the book. The line of cleavage was between the schools of Shammai and Hillel, and ultimately, probably because the work passed under the great name of Solomon, the school of Hillel won and Ecclesiastes became a part of the Scriptures.

> The view arrived at above agrees substantially with that of W. R. Smith, OT. in J.C., 2d ed., 185 *ff*. Wildeboer, *Origin of the Old Testament Canon*, 147 *ff.*; and McNeile, *Ecclesiastes*. For attempts to explain away this evidence, see Ginsburg, *Coheleth*, 15 *ff*.

The statement of Josephus (*Contra Apion*, 1²²) that the Jewish canon contained 22 books might be significant, if we knew how the 22 books were reckoned. The same is true of the statement in 2 (4) Esdras 14⁴⁵· ⁴⁶, which, according to the Oriental versions, makes the Jewish canon consist of 24 books. In neither case do we know how the number was made up. Different scholars have their theories, but, as positive evidence, both passages are too indefinite either to confirm or to refute the conclusion we have reached. (See Br.ᔆᴴᔆ, p. 127 *ff.*) The canonicity of *Qoheleth* was soon accepted by Christians as well as Jews, for Hermas, *Mand.*, VII, quotes Eccl. 12¹³ and Justin Martyr, in his dialogue with Trypho, ch. 6, seems to recall *Qoheleth* 12⁷. Clement of Alex. quotes by name, in *Stromata*, 1¹³, Eccl. 1¹⁶⁻¹⁸ 7¹³; Tertullian quotes Eccl. 3¹ three times, (*Adv. Marc.* 5⁴, *De Monog.* 3, *De Virg. Vel.* 3); while Origen has several quotations from it.

§ 4. TEXT.

(1). HEBREW TEXT.

The text of the book of Ecclesiastes was written in a late form of the Hebrew language—a form which evinces considerable decay from the earlier tongue, and a considerable approach to the language of the Mishna. Aramaic must have been largely employed by the Jews of the period, for there are many Aramaisms both of vocabulary and construction in Ecclesiastes. (See below, §10.)

> We do not know whether Ecclesiastes was written in the older Hebrew character, in the square Aramaic character, or in a modified form intermediate between the two. The last is probably the fact, for we know from many documents that the older characters of the Moabite Stone had undergone much modification. It is possible that the square character had come in at the time Ecclesiastes was written. The oldest inscription in the square character is that of Arak-el-Amir, which dates from about 180 B.C. (*Cf.* Lidzbarski in JE., I, 443.) This was probably slightly later than the date of our book (see below §13). It is possible, therefore, that the square character may have been employed by the author of Ecclesiastes, but it may have been a form intermediate between the old Hebrew and the square character, such as is found in the Jewish papyri recently discovered in Egypt. (See Sayce and Cowley's *Aramaic Papyri Discovered at Assuan*, London, 1906.) As these papyri are some two hundred years older than Ecclesiastes, the alphabet used by the Jews had probably during the period undergone considerable development towards the square form. (See Br.ᔆᴴᔆ, pp. 172–3.)

A manuscript of the Pentateuch exists in St. Petersburg which

some Jewish scholars think was written before 604 A.D., but so
far as I know no manuscript is known that contains *Qoheleth*
which is older than the eleventh century. These MSS., of course,
contain the text of the Massorets only. They do, however, exhibit some variations.

> The Massorets consulted a number of MSS. which are known by name,
> but which have long ago disappeared, such as Codex Muggeh, Codex
> Hilleli, Codex Sanbuki, Codex Jerusalami, Codex Jericho, Codex
> Sinai, Codex Great Mahzor, Codex Ezra, and Codex Babylon. (For
> description, see Broydè in JE., III, 473 *ff*., esp. Br.^{SHS}, pp. 183–4.)

Many of these MSS. exist in the various libraries of Europe,
and have been studied and employed by scholars. Benjamin
Kennicott, in his *Vetus Testamentum Hebraicum cum variis lec-
tionibus*, Oxford, 1776–1780, noted the variants as they appear in
several hundred MSS. His text of the Megilloth rests on the
collations of 350 of these. Among the texts of Ecclesiastes,
edited in recent years, those of Baer, Ginsburg and Driver (the
last in Kittel's *Biblia Hebraica*) rest on a collation of varying numbers of MSS. Driver's text is the fruit of a collation of
a considerable number of these, and the kind of variation which
they exhibit is well illustrated in his notes.

(2). THE SEPTUAGINT VERSION.

Most important for the history of the text of Ecclesiastes is the
Greek version, which, because of the legend that it was trans-
lated by seventy-two men, is commonly called the Septuagint.
This version is in the following pages designated by 𝕲.

The Greek translation of the Old Testament was not all made
at one time, or by one hand. The Pentateuch was apparently
translated in the third century B.C., and the other parts at various
later dates. The *K^etubim* were naturally translated last of all.
It is probable that the Psalter existed in Greek as early as 130 B.C.,
but there is reason to think that the version of Ecclesiastes now
found in 𝕲 was not made till the end of the first century A.D.,
and that it was made by Aquila, a native of Pontus, who was a
convert first to Christianity and then to Judaism, and who is said

by Jerome to have been a pupil of Aqiba. The reasons for this
view are that the version of *Qoheleth* in 𝔊 exhibits many of the
most marked peculiarities of the style of Aquila's version as preserved by Origen in his famous *Hexapla*—peculiarities which
occur to the same extent in the Septuagint version of no other
Old Testament book. This view was set forth by Graetz (*Geschichte d. Juden*, IV, 437, and *Kohelet*, 173–179). It was opposed
by Dillmann in a characteristically thorough paper in the *Sitzungs-
berichte d. kg. preus. Akad. d. Wiss. zu Berlin*, 1892, I, 3–16; but
Dillman has been ably and successfully answered by McNeile in
his *Introduction to Ecclesiastes*, 115–134. (See Br.[SHS], p. 192.)

Some of the Aquilan marks of style which appear in the Ecclesiastes
of 𝔊 are as follows: the rendering of אֵת, the sign of the acc., by σύν;
גם and וגם by καί γε; לְ, with an infinitive, by τοῦ with an infinitive,
even where it forms simply the complement of a verbal expression as
in 1[8] 8[17] 4[13] 10[15] 3[12] 5[17] 8[15] 11[7], etc., as in Aquila (*cf.* Burkitt's
Aquila, 13), where the Hebrew noun is preceded by לְ, and it would be
inappropriate to render it by εἰς; it is rendered by the article, *e.g.* 2[16]
τοῦ σοφοῦ = לֶחָכָם, 2[26] τῷ ἀνθρώπῳ = לָאָדָם, 3[17] τῷ παντὶ πράγματι =
לְכָל חֵפֶץ, 4[11] καὶ ὁ εἷς = וְלֹאחָר, 9[4] ὁ κύων = לְכֶלֶב, etc.; מִן used in comparison, rendered by ὑπέρ with acc. more than twenty times, as *e.g.*,
in 2[13]; the rendering of פְּעָמִים by καθόδους, 6[6] 7[22. (23)]; of בְּעֵל by παρά,
with a Gen., 5[10. 12] 7[12. (13)] 8[8] 12[11]; טוֹב by ἀγαθωσύνη, 4[9] 5[10. 17] 6[3. 6] 7[14. 15]
9[18]. These are but a few of the examples. Many more will be
found in the work of McNeile already cited. Jerome mentions twice
(*Opera*, V, 32 and 624) Aquila's second edition, which the Hebrews
call κατ᾽ ἀκρίβειαν, and Graetz and McNeile have made it altogether probable that Aquila's first edition is that embodied in 𝔊. Thus only can
one account for the marked approach to Aquila's style and peculiarities,
combined with some equally striking differences from the fragments of
Aquila, preserved by Origen. Dillman had urged these differences as
an objection to the theory that Aquila translated our 𝔊, but as Mc-
Neile observes, a second edition presupposes differences, and it is difficult
to think that a later hand adapted 𝔊 to Aquila's later work without
doing it in a more thorough-going manner.

Whether there had been an earlier translation of *Qoheleth* than
Aquila's first edition is uncertain, but on the whole we conclude
that there probably had not been. The work had only recently
been approved as canonical beyond dispute (see above §3), and

it is probable that shortly afterward Aquila undertook its translation. The translation which we have in 𝕲 was at all events made from a text which differed a good deal from our present Hebrew, and was therefore made from a text that Aqiba had not revised. Possibly it was, as McNeile thinks, in part, because his first edition was made from a text that Aqiba, his teacher, did not approve, that Aquila undertook his revision which resulted in his "second edition."

If these views are correct, the translation of *Qoheleth* which we have in 𝕲 was made in the second quarter of the second century A.D.

The text of 𝕲 for the book of Ecclesiastes has been preserved in five uncial MSS. and in fifteen cursives, which have been studied, though of the cursives three contain only a part of the book. The uncial MSS. are: (1) The famous *Codex Vaticanus* (𝕲ᴮ) in the Vatican Library at Rome, usually cited as B, which dates from the fourth century. The labors of Westcott and Hort on the New Testament vindicated the text of this MS. as on the whole the best for that part of the Bible, and the labors of Swete on the Greek text of the Old Testament tend to confirm these results for the older part of the Canon. (2) The famous *Codex Sinaiticus* (𝕲ᴺ), found by Tischendorf on Mount Sinai, 1844–1859, and now preserved in the Library at St. Petersburg. It is sometimes cited by scholars as ℵ, sometimes as S. It was also written in the fourth century and as an authority for the text falls little short of B. (3) The *Codex Alexandrinus* (𝕲ᴬ), written in the fifth century, now in the British Museum cited as A. (4) *Codex Ephraemi* (𝕲ᶜ), also of the fifth century—a fine palimpsest MS. now in the National Library at Paris, cited as C. (5) *Codex Venetus* (𝕲ⱽ), written in the eighth or ninth century, now in St. Mark's Library, Venice. It is usually cited as ⱽ, and often allies itself with ᴮᴺ.

Of the cursive MSS., 68, written in the fifteenth century, one of the treasures of the Library of St. Marks at Venice, deserves especial mention. It often allies itself with B. McNeile considers it especially important when it differs from B, and holds it to be the most important Greek MS. of Ecclesiastes extant (see his *Ecclesiastes*, 136).

For fuller accounts of the MSS., see Swete's *Introduction to the Old Testament in Greek*, 122–170; Gregory's *Prolegomena* to Tischendorf's *Novum Testamentum Græce*, also his *Textkritik des Neuen Testaments*, and Scrivener's *Plain Introduction to the Criticism of the New Testament*, 4th ed. by Miller, Vol. I. Br.ˢᴴˢ, p. 195 *ff*.

It is possible from the extant witnesses to the text of 𝕲 to detect in its text recensions or types, kindred to those which Westcott and Hort

have identified for the New Testament.   It is for this reason that often
in citing the evidence of 𝕲 the Symbols of MSS. are affixed as 𝕲ᴮ,
𝕲ᴮᴺ, etc.   For analyses of the text of 𝕲, see Klostermann's *De Libri
Coheleth Versione Alexandrina*, Kiel, 1892, and McNeile's *Introduction
to Ecclesiastes*, Cambridge, 1904, pp. 115–168.

(3). THE GREEK VERSION OF AQUILA.

Aquila was a native of Pontus, and a connection of the emperor
Hadrian, who employed a relative of Aquila's to build Ælia
Capitolina on the site of Jerusalem.   Aquila accompanied him,
and while there was converted to Christianity.   As he refused to
abandon the heathen practice of astrology, he was excommuni-
cated, and in disgust joined the Jews.   He undertook a translation
of the Scriptures into Greek in order to set aside the renderings
of the Septuagint which seemed to support the Christians.   Of
Jerome's testimony to his second edition of his rendering of
Qoheleth, we have already spoken, and have shown that in all
probability the version which Origen preserved as Aquila's was
this second edition.   This second edition was probably made from
the text revised by Aquila, for it differs far less widely than 𝕲 from
the Massoretic Text.   If we are right in thinking that there was
no Greek version of Ecclesiastes until Aquila's first edition, then
both his editions have survived, the first entire as 𝕲 and the
second in fragments as 'Α, the symbol by which Aquila is quoted
below.   These fragments have been collated by Montfauçon in
his *Hexaplorum Originis quæ supersunt*, 1713, and by Field in his
Originis Hexaplorum quæ supersunt, Oxford, 1875, and cover
practically the whole book.

For fuller accounts of Aquila's version, *cf.* Swete, *op. cit.*, 31–42
and 55; McNeile, *op. cit.*, 115–134; Burkitt's *Fragments of the
Books of Kings according to the Translation of Aquila*, 1897;
C. Taylor's *Cairo-Genizah Palimpsests*, 1900, and Schürer's *Geschichte des jüdischen Volkes*, etc., 3d ed., Vol. III, 318–321.

(4). THE VERSION OF THEODOTIAN.

Another version was made in the second century A.D. by Theodotian, who seems to have lived at Ephesus.   His work was

known to Irenæus (d. 202 A.D.), who calls him a native of Pontus, and says that he became a convert to Judaism in mature life. It is thought that in some of these details Irenæus confused Theodotian with Aquila. It is hardly likely that two different men who learned Hebrew in mature life should make translations of the Scriptures for the Jews in the same century. Irenæus is, however, probably right in saying that Theodotian lived at Ephesus. Theodotian's version of Daniel seems to have found its way into the Septuagint, as we have supposed that Aquila's first translation of Ecclesiastes did. The work of Theodotian is otherwise known to us only through the Hexapla of Origen, and that has survived only in fragments. Theodotian's renderings do not differ so widely from the Septuagint as do those of Aquila, nor so often from MT. as those of 𝕮. But Dr. Swete says: "He seems to have produced a free revision of the Septuagint rather than an independent version." Theodotian's renderings of *Qoheleth* which have survived afford interesting variants to every chapter of the book. They are contained in the works of Montfauçon and Field cited above.

For a fuller account of Theodotian see Swete, *op. cit.*, pp. 42–49; Gwynn, "Theodotian," in Smith and Wace's *Dict. of Christian Biog.*, and Schürer, *Geschichte*, etc., Vol. III, 321–324.

(5). THE VERSION OF SYMMACHUS.

A fourth translation of the Hebrew into Greek was made by Symmachus near the end of the second or the beginning of the third century A.D. Eusebius and Jerome say that Symmachus was an Ebionite Christian, but according to Epiphanius he was a Samaritan who embraced Judaism. Epiphanius was a blunderer, however, and the probability is that even if Symmachus was of Jewish or Samaritan parentage, he became an Ebionite. Jerome correctly declares that the aim of Symmachus was to express the sense of the Hebrew rather than to follow the order of its words. His version shows that he aimed to set himself free from the influence of the Septuagint as well as to write good Greek. Swete thinks that Symmachus had before him the three other Greek

versions when he made his own, and that he exhibits his indepen-
dence of them all and sometimes of the Hebrew as well. In spite
of this charge it is often true that he has caught the meaning of the
Hebrew and correctly expressed it in Greek. His version was
employed by Origen as early as 228 A.D., and was so highly regarded by that ancient scholar, that he gave it a place in his
Hexapla. His translation of Ecclesiastes affords numerous
interesting variants for every chapter of the book. They are
presented by Montfauçon and Field in the works cited above.

For a fuller account of Symmachus see Swete, *op. cit.*, 40-53;
Gwynn, *op. cit.*; Harnack, *Geschichte der altchristlichen Litera-
ture*, I, 209 *ff.*, and *Chronologie der altchr. Literatur*, II, 164 *ff.*, and
Perles, "Symmachus," in JE., XI, 619.

(6). THE COPTIC VERSION.

The Bible is thought to have been translated into the Egyptian
dialects before the end of the second century. This translation
was made from the Septuagint version, so that the various Egyptian versions—Bohairic, Memphitic, and Sahidic—are in reality
witnesses for the text of the Septuagint. Accounts of these versions are given in Swete, *op. cit.*, 104-108, and in the works of
Gregory and Scrivener cited above. In *S. Bibliorum Fragmenta
Copto-Sahidica Musei Borgiani*, edited by Ciasca, 1880, Vol. II,
pp. 195-254, the whole of *Qoheleth* in a Sahidic translation, except 9^4-10^3, is included. This text was collated by Euringer for
his work *Der Masorahtext des Koheleth kritisch untersucht*, 1890.
These readings usually support the readings of 𝕲. This version
is cited below as 𝕶.

(7). THE SYRIAC PESHITTA.

The origin of this version is involved in much obscurity. Theo-
dore of Mopsuestia declared that no one knew who the translator
was. (*Cf.* Migne, P. G., LXVI, 241.) The version was, however,
made during the early centuries of the Christian era. The Pentateuch was translated from the Hebrew, though in Isaiah, the
Minor Prophets, and the Psalms the Septuagint has had consid-

erable influence. A study of the Peshitta text of *Qoheleth* with a view of determining its relation to the Massoretic text on the one hand and the Septuagint on the other was made by Kamenetzky in *ZAW.*, XXIV (1904), 181–239. Kamenetzky's conclusion, with which my own use of the Peshitta leads me to agree, is that for the most part the Syriac was translated from a Hebrew text which in most places agreed with MT., though in some places it differed from it and at some points it has been influenced by 𝕲. This version is represented in the following pages by the symbol 𝕾. Fuller accounts of the Peshitta will be found in the works of Swete, Gregory and Scrivener, already frequently referred to.

(8). THE SYRO-HEXAPLAR VERSION.

This translation was made by Paul of Tella in 616 and 617 A.D. from the Septuagint column of Origen's *Hexapla*. It is in reality, therefore, a witness for the text of the Septuagint. It is cited below as 𝕾ᴴ. For a fuller account of it and the literature see Swete, *op. cit.*, 112–116. The standard edition of it for Ecclesiastes is still Middledorpf's *Codex Syraco-Hexaplaris*, etc., 1835.

(9). OLD LATIN VERSION.

The origin of the early Latin version or versions of the Bible is involved in as much obscurity as that of the Syriac or Egyptian versions. It is clear that a translation was made into Latin at an early date, and that by the end of the fourth century there were wide variations in its MSS. Samples of these variations are furnished by Swete, *op. cit.*, pp. 89–91. This early translation appears to have been made from the Septuagint. Our sources for the text of this Old Latin are in large part Patristic quotations of the Old Testament. These were collected with great care and fulness by Peter Sabatier in his *Bibliorum sacrorum Latinæ versiones antiquæ*, Rheims, 1743, which was employed by Euringer and is frequently quoted in his *Masorahtext des Koheleth*. Sabatier's work, however, was published more than a century and a half ago, and his quotations now need to be tested by later editions of the Fathers. Some readings for Ecclesiastes from a MS. of

St. Gall may be found in S. Berger's *Notices et extraits*, p. 137 *ff.*
I have attempted to make little use of this version, but it is cited
below a few times as 𝕷. The works of Swete, Gregory and Scrivener contain discussions of this translation.

(10). THE LATIN VULGATE.

The basis of this translation was made by St. Jerome (Eusebius
Hieronymus) between 383 and 420 A.D. It was Jerome's plan
to translate from the Hebrew, but his version was made with a
full knowledge of the material which Origen had collected in the
Hexapla. His Ecclesiastes was made from a text which generally
agreed with MT., though it sometimes departs from it in most
suggestive ways. Full accounts of Jerome's work are given in
the works of Gregory and Scrivener referred to above, and in
Smith and Wace's *Dict. of Christian Biography*. This version is
designated by the symbol 𝕳.

(11). THE ARABIC VERSION.

In the commentary which follows the Arabic version is sometimes quoted. This is the Arabic version which was published
in the London *Polyglot* of 1656 and the Paris *Polyglot* of 1630.
It is believed to be the translation of Saadia Gaon, who died
in 942.

The Hexateuch seems to have been translated from the Hebrew;
Judges, Ruth, parts of Kings, Nehemiah and Job from the Peshitta; while the other poetical books and the prophets seem to
be dependent on the Septuagint. In Qoheleth the Arabic, where
it departs from MT., usually allies itself with 𝕲. It is referred to
below by the symbol 𝔸. Possibly only the Hexateuch was translated by Saadia, as that was made from the Hebrew text. For
accounts of the Arabic version, see Swete, *op. cit.*, 110 *ff.*, and
Gottheil, in JE., III, 189.

(12). THE TARGUM.

As the *Kᵉtubim* were not interpreted in the synagogue services,
Targumim of them (*i.e.*, interpretations into the Aramaic spoken

by the people) were not written as early as the rest of the Bible.
That on the Psalter was not made in its present form before the
ninth century. No Targum of the *Megilloth* is mentioned in any
work older than the *Aruk* (Dictionary) of Nathan ben Jehiel,
which was completed in 1101 A.D. These Targumim are probably, therefore, in their present form, not earlier than the tenth
century, though they may go back to oral interpretations which
are much earlier.

The Targum of *Qoheleth* is a free paraphrase combined with a
midrashic interpretation. Occasionally the text is followed
closely, but more often the interpretation freely departs from it,
for the sake of covering up sceptical expressions which were obnoxious to orthodox Jews. These expressions are often turned
so as to commend the study of the law and support the most
orthodox doctrines and devout course of life. Solomon is believed to be the author of *Qoheleth*, and many allusions in it are
interpreted to refer to events in his life and that of his son Rehoboam. Nevertheless, the Targum is frequently an important
witness to the text, and helps us to correct MT. It is cited as 𝕿.
In addition to the publication of the Targum of *Qoheleth* accessible
in the Polyglots a recension has recently been published from
South Arabic MSS. by Alfred Levy, entitled *Das Targum zu
Koheleth nach südarabischen Handschriften*, Breslau, 1905. For
a more complete account of the *Targumim* and the literature upon
them, see Bacher's article ".Targum," in JE., XIII, *ff*.

(13). QUOTATIONS IN THE TALMUD.

The Jewish writers of the first seven centuries of the Christian
era frequently quoted the OT. These quotations ought to perform for the text-criticism of the OT. the same service that patristic quotations perform for the NT. Euringer in his *Masorahtext*, already referred to, has collected these quotations for *Qoheleth*
from the *Mishna*, and the parts of the Babylonian and Jerusalem
Talmuds which were made up to the seventh century. Of the
221 verses in *Qoheleth*, a part or all of 122 are quoted in these
Jewish writings, and some of them many times. These quotations

have too often been assimilated to MT., to be of much service, but they sometimes present interesting variations from it. Where quoted below, they are designated by the name of the Talmudic tract in which the quotation is made.

An idea of the sort of textual variation presented in these Talmudic quotations may be seen in the following examples. In Qoh. 1¹⁵ לְהֹן is written defectively. The passage is quoted twice in the Mishna, *Khagiga*, 1⁶, *Sukkah*, 2⁶, and twice in the Talmud, *Yebamoth*, 22ᵇ, *Berakoth*, 26ᵃ, and in all cases but the last it is written fully, לְתְקָן. Qoh. 4¹⁷ has רגליך, but the Qr. רגלך. Bab. *Berakoth*, 23ᵃ, Jer. *Berak.*, 4⁴, 13³, and *Megill.*, 71³, all read רגלך, *Tosephta*, 17², only supporting רגליך. In the same verse MT. has כאשר in which it is supported by *Berakoth*, 23ᵃ, but the other Talmudic quotations of the verse (just given) read באשר, as do 𝕲 and Θ. In Qoh. 5⁸ the Kt. is היא, the Qr. הוא. *Sifre* 60ᵃ reads היא with Kt.

Qoh. 12⁶ has as Kt. ירחק; as Qr. ירחק. *Sabbath*, 151ᵇ, and *Semakhot*, 44ᵃ, support the Qr. ירחק.

(14). RECENSIONS OF THE TEXT.

There are persistent and probably trustworthy traditions that Rabbi Aqiba, who had such an influence in systematizing and perfecting the Jewish oral law and system of hermeneutics, also with the aid of Aquila, his pupil, attempted to fix the text of the Bible. He was the creator in a sense of the Rabbinical Bible. (See Ginsburg's article "Akiba," JE., I, 306.) That the first Greek translation of *Qoheleth*, commonly called the Septuagint version, was probably made by Aquila, has been shown above, where it also was pointed out that the differences between the Hebrew underlying the Septuagint and the Hebrew text of later times indicates that Aquila made the Septuagint version of *Qoheleth* before Aqiba had revised the text. McNeile is, therefore, right in holding that by a right critical use of 𝕲 we can obtain a pre-Aqiban recension of *Qoheleth*.

Some of the readings which Aqiba adopted in the Hebrew text underwent alterations by later hands, as McNeile has shown (*Ecclesiastes*, 153–156). In the history of the text of our book, we may then discern three recensions. Leaving out of account the eddies and side currents of corruption and transmission which inevitably manifest themselves in MSS. and versions, these recensions are the pre-Aquilan recension, the Aquilan recension and the Massoretic recension. A careful study of the text on those sane principles which Tischendorf and Westcott and Hort have established for the New Testament, reveals the fact that the text of *Qoheleth* has been transmitted, on the whole, with great fidelity. These recensions differ from one another far less than one would expect, and affect comparatively few passages.

> The best text-critical work hitherto done on Ecclesiastes is that of McNeile in his *Introduction to Ecclesiastes*, to which reference has several times been made. The more drastic work of Bickell, based on his theory of dislocations, as well as that of Zapletal and Haupt, based on a metrical theory of the book, are in most cases conjectures which rest on unproven premises. A criticism of their metrical theories will be found in §9. Winckler's emendations (*Altorientalische Forschungen*, IV) (1896), 351–355, are also usually too conjectural.

With the exception of a few interpolations and a very little editorial material (see below, §7), the work of *Qoheleth* has come down to us modified by design or error far less than is the case with most of the Old Testament books. This is due, undoubtedly, to the fact that it had undergone no long history of transmission and frequent copying before Aqiba set those forces to work which made further serious alterations in the text well-nigh impossible.

§ 5. HISTORY OF THE INTERPRETATION.

It is possible in the space at our disposal to treat the history of the interpretation of *Ecclesiastes* only in outline. We cannot, as Ginsburg has done in his *Coheleth*, go into the merits and demerits of all the commentaries of *Qoheleth*, that have ever been written, whether Jewish or Christian. Those who are interested in such curious details are referred to the "Introduction" of Ginsburg's work, pp. 30–245. It will be possible here to treat in detail only a few of the more important works of recent years, the theories set forth in which are living issues of present-day exegesis.

The earliest commentaries on Ecclesiastes are probably represented in the Jewish *Midrashim*, the beginnings of which go back to the period when the canonicity of the book was first fully recognized, if not to a date even earlier. These works were composed for the edification of congregations, and while the literal sense of a passage was not ignored, if that sense was at all edifying, or would not give offense by its unorthodox character, nevertheless the greatest liberties were taken with the text when it seemed necessary to find edification or orthodoxy in a passage which obviously contained none. The general view of these *Midrashim* was that Solomon wrote *Qoheleth* in his old age, when weary of life, to "expose the emptiness and vanity of all worldly pursuits and carnal gratifications, and to show that the happiness of man consists in fearing God and obeying his commands."

As was pointed out above (p. 15 *ff.*), the Targum of *Qoheleth* is such a midrashic interpretation. In it unspiritual passages are treated as follows:

Ch. 2²⁴—"There is nothing better for a man than that he should eat and drink and enjoy himself," etc.—runs in the Targum: "There is nothing that is more beautiful in man than that he should eat and drink and show his soul good before the children of men, to perform the commandments and to walk in the ways which are right before Him, in order that he may gain good from his labors."

Again 5¹⁸—"A good that is beautiful is it to eat and drink and see good," etc.—the Targum converts into: "Good is it for the children of men and beautiful for them to work in this world that they may eat and drink from their labor so as not to stretch out a hand in violence or plunder, but to keep the words of the law and to be merciful to the poor in order to see good in their labor in this world under the sun."

Similarly 9⁷—"Go eat thy bread with joy and drink thy wine with a glad heart, for already God has accepted thy works" is changed into—"Said Solomon by the spirit of prophecy from before Jah, 'The Lord of the world shall say to all the righteous one by one, Go taste with joy thy bread which has been given to thee on account of the bread which thou hast given to the poor and the unfortunate who were hungry, and drink with good heart thy wine which is hidden for thee in the Garden of Eden, for the wine which thou hast mingled for the poor and needy who were thirsty, for already thy good work has been pleasing before Jah.'"

To men who could read thus into an obnoxious text whatever they liked, every difficulty disappeared. Under the alchemy of allegory and spiritualizing all became easy. Nevertheless sometimes these *Midrashim* found a way of anticipating the theses of modern criticism that parts of the book refer to the exile or later. Thus the Targum says of 1^2—"Vanity of vanities," etc.—"When Solomon, the king of Israel, saw by the spirit of prophecy, that the kingdom of Rehoboam, his son, would be divided with Jeroboam, the son of Nebat, and Jerusalem and the sanctuary would be destroyed and that the people of Israel would go into captivity, he spoke saying, 'Vanity of vanities is this world, vanity of vanities is all for which I and David my father have labored—all is vanity.'"

Meantime, among Christians, the book of Ecclesiastes was being interpreted by similar methods. The earliest Christian commentator on *Qoheleth* was Gregory Thaumaturgus, who died in 270 A.D., whose *Metaphrasis in Ecclesianten Solomonis* gives an interpretative paraphrase of the book. The genuineness of this work has been questioned, some assigning it to Gregory Nazianzen, but Harnack still assigns it to Thaumaturgus. (*Geschichte der altchristlichen Literatur*, I, 430, and *Chronologie*, II, 99.) Gregory regards Solomon as a prophet, holding that his purpose was "to show that all the affairs and pursuits of man which are undertaken in human things are vain and useless, in order to lead us to the contemplation of heavenly things." Gregory of Nyssa and Jerome followed in good time with commentaries on the book, and each pursued a similar strain. The allegorical method was employed in its most developed form, especially by Jerome, who wrote his commentary to induce Basilica, a Roman lady, to embrace the monastic life. According to him, the purpose of the book is "to show the utter vanity of every sublunary enjoyment, and hence the necessity of betaking one's self to an ascetic life, devoted entirely to the service of God!"

Started both among Jews and Christians in such paths as these, the interpretation of Ecclesiastes meandered with various windings through the Middle Ages. The Jewish commentators, Tobia ben Eleazar, Rashi, Rashbam, Ibn Ezra, and others often followed more sober and sane methods than many, on account of the rise of a grammatical school of exegesis among the Jews in the eleventh and twelfth centuries, yet even from them allegory and fanciful interpretations did not disappear. Sometimes a Jew, sometimes a Christian, grasped fairly well the purpose of *Qoheleth*, but most of those who wrote upon it, followed either in the footsteps of the Targum or of Jerome.

Martin Luther was the first to perceive that Solomon cannot have been the author of Ecclesiastes. He says in his "Table Talk": "Solomon himself did not write the book of Ecclesiastes, but it was produced by Sirach at the time of the Maccabees. . . . It is a sort of Talmud, compiled from many books, probably from the library of King Ptolemy Euergetes of Egypt."

This opinion of Luther waited, however, more than a century before it found corroboration. Hugo de Groot, the father of international law, better known as Grotius, published, in 1644, his commentary on the Old Testament. He regarded Ecclesiastes as a collection of opinions of different sages, originally spoken to different peoples. He says: "I believe that the book is not the production of Solomon, but was written in the name of this king, as being led by repentance to do it. For it contains many words which cannot be found except in Ezra, Daniel and the Chaldee paraphrasts."

In the next century the work of Grotius began to produce results both in Germany and England. Thus, in the former country, J. D. Michaelis (*Poetischer Entwurf der Gedanken des Prediger-Buchs Solomons*), in 1751, maintained that a prophet who lived after the exile wrote Ecclesiastes in the name of Solomon, in order that he might be able, in the person of a king so happy and wise, to philosophize all the more touchingly about the vanity of human happiness, while in the latter country, in 1753, Bishop Lowth declared that in Ecclesiastes "the vanity of the world was exemplified by the experience of Solomon, who is introduced in the character of a person investigating a very difficult question" (cf. *Lectures on the Sacred Poetry of the Hebrews*, xxiv) —thus practically admitting the non-Solomonic authorship of the book.

After this the belief that Solomon did not write the book found increasingly abundant expression. Eichhorn, 1779; Döderlein, 1784; Spohn, 1785; Dathe, 1789; Jahn, 1793, and during the nine-

teenth century an increasing number of scholars have maintained
the same view. Döderlein and Dathe dated the book about the
time of the Babylonian exile. Since the dawn of the nineteenth
century scholarly opinion has gradually brought the date of the
book down, first to the Persian, and then to the Greek, period.
The following list is not exhaustive, but it indicates in a general
way how scholars have grouped themselves with regard to date.
Those who hold to the Persian period are Ewald, Knobel, Hengstenberg, Heiligstedt, De Wette, Vaihinger, Ginsburg, Zöckler,
Moses Stuart (*Commentary on Ecclesiastes*), Delitzsch, No-
wack, Wright, Cox, Vlock and Driver. On the other hand, the
following have assigned it to the Greek period, varying from 330
B.C. (Noyes, *Job, Eccl.* and *Cant.*) to 100 B.C. (Renan), viz.:
Zirkel, Noyes, Hitzig, Tyler, Plumtre, Renan, Kuenen (*Poet.
Bücher des A. T.*), Strack (*Einleitung*), Bickell, Cheyne, Dillon,
Wildeboer, Siegfried, Davidson (*Eccl.* in EB.), Peake (*Eccl.* in
DB.), Cornill (*Einleitung*), Bennett (*Introduction*), Winckler
(*Altorientalische Forschungen*, 2d ser., 143–159), A. W. Sterne
(*Ecclesiastes or the Preacher*, London, 1900), Margouliouth
(*Eccl.* in JE.), Genung, Haupt and McFadyen (*Introduction*).
Of the nineteenth century commentators whom I have studied,
Wangemann (1856) alone holds to the Solomonic date, although
Dale (1873) is non-committal with reference to it. Two recent
writers, Marshall and McNeile (both 1904), are unable to decide
between the Persian and Greek periods. One scholar, Graetz
(1871), holds that it belongs to the Roman period and was directed
against Herod the Great. Briggs says that it "is the latest writing
in the Old Testament, as shown by its language, style and theology" (SHS. 321).

It is clear from the above sketch that an increasing consensus
of opinion places our book in the Greek period. The linguistic
argument for the non-Solomonic authorship, which Grotius began
to appreciate, has been worked out to a complete demonstration
by the masterly hand of the late Franz Delitzsch.

The disconnected character of the book of Ecclesiastes impressed
Martin Luther, as we have seen, and led him to regard the work
as a compilation. This fact was taken up and advanced by others

and, finally, in the hands of Yeard (*A Paraphrase upon Ecclesiastes*, London), (1701), Herder (1778) and Eichhorn (1779), led to the view that *Qoheleth* is a dialogue between a refined sensualist and a sensual worldling, who interrupts him, or between a teacher and pupil. A similar view was entertained by Kuenen. Döderlein explained these inconcinnities as the record of the discussions of an "Academy," or group of learned men. Bickell explains them by the supposition that the leaves of an early MS. became disarranged, while Siegfried, McNeile and Haupt explain them on the supposition of later interpolations. Some of these views will be examined more in detail below.

On the other hand, the unity of the book has been strenuously maintained by such scholars as Ginsburg, Zöckler, Delitzsch, Plumtre, Wright, Briggs, Wildeboer, Cornill and Genung. Briggs classes *Koheleth* with Job as a type of moral heroism wrestling with foes to the soul, and winning moral victories over doubt and error (SHS., pp. 425–426). Cornill declares that "Old Testament piety nowhere enjoys a greater triumph than in the book of *Qoheleth*" (*Introduction to Can. Bks. of OT.*, 1907, p. 451). Plumtre, Briggs, Cornill *et al.* before them, regard the contradictory expressions of the book as the varying moods of the writer, as his childhood's faith struggles with the mass of doubt and pessimism which fills his mind.

Zirkel, in 1792, *Untersuchungen über den Prediger*, propounded the theory that *Qoheleth* evinces the formative influence of Greek thought and the Greek language—that its idiom betrays the presence of Greek forms of speech, and that the influence of Stoic philosophy is no less evident.

Zirkel's view was revived and maintained by Hitzig (*Comm.*, 1847), Kleinert (*Der Prediger Solomo*, 1864), and by Thomas Tyler in his *Ecclesiastes—A Contribution to its Interpretation*, London, 1874, who finds in the book evidences of Greek linguistic influence, as well as the traces both of Stoic and Epicurean thought. Tyler maintained that the Sadducees represented Epicurean influence, and the Pharisees Stoic influence, that the Talmud gives proof of the existence of Jewish schools, or academies, and that the mingling of contradictory ideas in the book is accounted for by supposing that the work is a record of the discussions of one of these academies.

Plumtre maintains (*Ecclesiastes in Cambridge Bible*, 1881), as does Tyler, that there are two streams of Greek Philosophical influence, one Stoic and one Epicurean, but, as previously remarked, attributes the contradictions to the varying moods of the author, whose mind gives house-room now to one set of opinions and now to another. Pfleiderer (*Die Philosophie des Heraklit von Eph., nebst Koheleth und besonders im Buch der Weisheit*, 1886) maintained the existence of traces of Greek influence in *Qoheleth*, but traced them to Heraclitus.

Siegfried (*Prediger und Hoheslied*, in Nowack's *Handkommentar*, 1898) and Haupt (*Koheleth, oder Weltschmerz in der Bible*, Leipzig, 1905, the *Book of Ecclesiastes*, Baltimore, 1905) both hold to this Greek influence (though Haupt confines it to the thought, denying any linguistic influence from Greek), but both account for the different philosophic strains by supposing that different parts of the work are from different writers. These theories will be set forth in greater detail below. From this general view of the course of the criticism of Ecclesiastes we pass to examine in detail some of the more important theories concerning it, which have been produced within the last forty years.

Graetz, in his *Koheleth* (1871), notes that Qoheleth directs his remarks in several instances against a *tyrannical* king, whom he also calls a slave (so Graetz understood נער). Graetz remarks that none of the Asmonæans were tyrants, and argues that these characteristics suit Herod the Great alone, whom the Talmud (*Baba Bathra*, 3b, and *Ketuboth*, 24) called the "slave of the Asmonæans." To this period he thought the language of the book, with its mingling of late Hebrew and Aramaic forms, also pointed. The book on this view is a kind of political satire. Graetz denies that the author was a Sadducee, and regards him as a young Jew of the mild, strenuosity-abjuring school of Hillel.

Graetz did regard the author, however, as an out and out sensualist, and finds as he interprets *Qoheleth* many allusions to the gratifications of desire. These interpretations have been shown by many later commentators to be in most cases unwarranted.

Qoheleth was no advocate of debauchery, as is proven by an intelligent interpretation of his utterances in detail. As to Graetz's Herodian date for Koheleth recent commentators find it too late. The external evidence, as is shown below (§13), makes it impossible that the book should be so late.

The contradictions of the book Graetz sought to soften by a theory of dislocations. Such a theory had first been suggested by J. G. van der Palm, in his *Ecclesiastes philologice et critice illustratus*, Leyden, 1784. Graetz placed ch. 7[11, 12] after ch. 5[6], removing ch. 5[7] to take their place after ch. 7[10]; 10[4] he removed to come after 8[4], and 7[19] he placed after 9[17]. Later commentators, however, have not found these changes sufficient to harmonize the contents of the book.

Graetz denied that the last six verses of the book (12[9-14]), formed a part of the original work. Moreover, he held that these were to be divided between two hands. Vv.[12-14] were, Graetz held, a colophon to the whole Hagiography, written at the time *Qoheleth* was received into the canon, as Krochmal had previously suggested. How much of this position is right, and what part of it is untenable, will appear as we proceed.

A more radical theory of dislocations was put forth by the late Professor Bickell of Vienna in 1884 in his little book, *Der Prediger über den Wert des Daseins*, also set forth in more popular form in 1886 in his *Koheleth's Untersuchung über den Wert des Daseins*. Bickell declared that the book is unintelligible as it stands, and that this lack of clearness was produced in the following way. *Qoheleth* was written in book form on fascicles consisting of four leaves once folded, or four double leaves. Each single leaf contained about 525 letters. *Qoheleth* was a part of a book which contained other works written on an unknown number of such fascicles.

> *Qoheleth* began on the sixth leaf of one fascicle and ended on the third leaf of the fourth succeeding fascicle. On the first three leaves (the end of the first fascicle) stood ch. 1[2]–2[11], on the fourth and fifth leaves, 5[9]–6[7]; on the sixth and seventh leaves, 3[9]–4[8]; on the eighth and ninth leaves, 2[12]–3[8]; on the tenth and eleventh leaves (the end of the second fascicle), 8[6]–9[3] and 8[15]; on the twelfth leaf, 9[11]–10[1]; on the thirteenth and fourteenth

leaves, 6^8–7^{22} and [20]; on the fifteenth and sixteenth, 4^9–5^8; on the seventeenth, 10^{16}–11^6 and [5]; on the eighteenth, 7^{23}–8^{5a}; on the nineteenth (end of the third fascicle), 10^{2-15} and 14^b; on the twentieth, 9^{3-10}; on the twenty-first and probably the twenty-second, 11^7–12^8.

The string which held these fascicles together broke and the middle fascicle fell out. The leaves were found by some one not qualified to put them together, who took the inner half of the second fascicle, folded it inside out, and then laid it in the new order immediately after the first fascicle. Next came the inner sheet of the third fascicle, followed by the outside half of the second, into the middle of which the two double leaves, 13, 18, 14, 17 had already been inserted. Although the fourth fascicle kept its place, it did not escape confusion, for between its leaves the first two leaves of the remaining sheet of the third fascicle found a place. Finally, leaf 17, becoming separated from its new environment, found a resting place between 19 and 21. This dislocation removed from the work all traces of its plan.

In the new form it frequently happened that some of the edges did not join properly—a fact which led in time to the insertion of glosses. From this dislocated archetype all extant texts of *Qoheleth* have descended.

If now the original order of the leaves be restored and the glosses removed, the work falls into two distinct halves, a speculative and a practical, each distinguished from the other by its own appropriate characteristics. According to Bickell this first half consisted of the following: Ch. 1^1–2^{11} 5^9–6^7 3^9–4^8 2^{12b}. $^{18-26}$. ^{12a} $^{13-17}$ 3^{1-8} 8^{6-14}. ^{16a}. ^{17a}. ^{16b}. ^{17b} 9^{1-3} 8^{15} 9^{11-18} 10^1 6^8. $^{10-12}$. In this part it is demonstrated that life is an empty round, and that wisdom only serves to make its possessor modest, so that he does not get on as well as the vainly boasting fool.

Part two consisted of the following: Ch. 7^{1a} 10^1 7^{1b-6} 6^9 7^{7-10}. $^{13-19}$. ^{11}. ^{12}. ^{21}. ^{22}. ^{20}. 4^{9-17} 5^{1-8} 10^{16-20} 11^{1-3}. ^{6}. ^{4}. ^{5} 7^{23-29} 8^{1-4} 10^{2-13} 11^{15} (𝕲), 10^{14a}. ^{15}. ^{14b} 9^{3-10} 11^{7-10a} 12^{1a} 11^{10b} 12^{1b-6}. ^{8}.

In this part the advice of Qoheleth is, in view of the fact that life offers no positive good, to make the best of such advantages as we have, to live modestly before the ruler and before God, and to expect everything to be vanity.

The epilogue Bickell thought was from a later hand. This elaborate theory, rejected by most scholars, as too ingenious and improbable, has been accepted in full by Dillon, who sought in his *Skeptics of the Old Testament*, 1895, to commend it to English readers. The theory is not only intricate and elaborate to a degree which creates doubts that, if it were true, a modern scholar would ever have divined it, but it breaks down archæologically in its fundamental assumption that the book form had succeeded the roll form in literary libraries at a date sufficiently early for it to have played the part in the history of Qoheleth supposed by Bickell.

If an accident, such as Bickell supposed, had happened to the exemplar of Ecclesiastes, it must have been earlier than the Greek translation of the book, for the same confusion which Bickell supposes is present in the Greek as well as in the Hebrew text. Even if the Greek translation were made as late as we have supposed above, that was at a date in all probability too early for a literary work to have been written in book form. An examination of the published papyri, found in such large numbers in Egypt by Grenfell and Hunt in recent years, tends to prove that literary works were written in roll form until after the first century A.D., and that the book form did not supersede the roll for more than another hundred years. For evidence, see *e.g.*, *the Archæological Report* of the Egypt Exploration Fund, 1905–1906, p. 10 *ff.*, where literary rolls written in the second and third centuries A.D. are described. See also Gregory, *Canon and Text of the New Testament*, 1907, p. 317 *ff.*, who holds that the book form did not come in until ± 300 A.D. The fundamental assumption of Bickell's theory is accordingly improbable.

In presenting this theory to English readers, Dillon has added a new element to the study of the book. Being an Aryan scholar, he declares (*op. cit.*, 122 *ff.*) that Buddhism is the only one of the world-religions in which such practical fruits as we see exhibited in *Qoheleth* are manifested. Instead of going to Epicureanism to explain these, he accordingly declares that they are due to Buddhistic influence. King Açoka tells us (see V. A. Smith's *Açoka, the Buddhist Emperor of India*, Oxford, 1901) in one of his inscriptions, that in the early part of the third century B.C. he had sent Buddhistic missionaries to the court of the Seleucidæ at Antioch and the court of the Ptolemies at Alexandria. Dillon, accordingly, declares that by 205 B.C. Qoheleth, even if he lived in Jerusalem, might have known Buddhism, though Dillon thinks it more probable that he lived in Alexandria.

In 1894 Professor Paul Haupt, in a paper entitled "The Book

of Ecclesiastes," published in the *Oriental Studies of the Oriental Club of Philadelphia*, declared, "There is no author to the book of Ecclesiastes, at any rate not of the book in the form in which it has come down to us. . . . It reminds me of the remains of a daring explorer, who has met with some terrible accident, leaving his shattered form exposed to the encroachments of all sorts of foul vermin. . . . In some cases there are half a dozen parallel strata of glosses."

This hint of Haupt's was taken up by D. C. Siegfried, who in his *Prediger und Hoheslied*, 1898, in Nowack's *Handkommentar* elaborated it into the theory that five different hands contributed to the contents of *Qoheleth*, and two different epilogists and two different editors in addition have taken part in bringing the work into its present form.

> According to Siegfried the original work was composed by a man who was imbued with an un-Hebraic spirit of pessimism, but who cannot be shown to have been influenced by Stoic philosophy. To this writer (Q[1]) belong the following sections: Eccl. 1^2–2^{12} 2^{14b-24} $3^{1-9. \ 12. \ 15. \ 16.}$ $^{18-21}$ $4^{1-4. \ 6-8. \ 13-16}$ $5^{10-12. \ 13-17}$ 6^{1-7} $7^{1b-4. \ 15. \ 26-28}$ $8^{9. \ 10. \ 14. \ 16. \ 17}$ $9^{2. \ 3. \ 5. \ 6}$ 10^{5-7}. To this work a Sadducee (Q[2]), who had come under the influence of Epicureanism added the following: Ch. 3^{22} 5^{18-20} 7^{14} 8^{15} $9^{4. \ 7-10. \ 12}$ 10^{19} $11^{7. \ 8a. \ 9a}$ 12^{1b-7a}. Another hand (Q[3]), a *Hokma* glossator, contributed the following: $2^{13. \ 14a}$ 4^5 $6^{8. \ 9a}$ $7^{11. \ 12. \ 19}$ 8^1 9^{13-18} $10^{1-3. \ 12-15}$. Still another writer (Q[4]), the *Chasid* glossator, added: $2^{24b-26a}$ $3^{11. \ 13. \ 14. \ 17}$ $5^{1-2. \ 4-6. \ 7b-8}$ 6^{10-12} $7^{13. \ 17. \ 23-25. \ 29}$ $8^{2-8. \ 11-13}$ 9^1 $11^{5. \ 9b}$ $12^{1a. \ 7b}$. Under Q[5] Siegfried classifies the work of glossators whose work cannot be individualized, assigning to them the following: 4^{9-12} $5^{3. \ 7a. \ 9. \ 12}$ $7^{1a. \ 5. \ 6a. \ 7-10. \ 18. \ 20-22}$ 9^{11} $10^{4. \ 8-11. \ 16-18. \ 20}$ $11^{1-4. \ 6}$. To this compound work the first epilogist (E[1]), added ch. $12^{9. \ 10}$, a second epilogist (E[2]), $12^{11. \ 12}$. A first editor (R[1]) prefixed 1^1 and added 12^8, while a second editor (R[2]) added ch. $12^{13. \ 14}$. Thus Siegfried thinks he can discern nine different hands in the composition of the book, and one of these stands for an indefinite number more.

This theory of Siegfried greatly overworks an undoubted fact, *viz.*:—that different hands have had a part in making the book of Ecclesiastes. It is built upon the supposition that absolutely but one type of thought can be harbored by a human mind while it is composing a book. In periods of transition, on the contrary, one can give house-room to widely divergent thoughts. While this fact should not lead us to think that a writer who has penned a sentence is likely flatly to contradict himself in the next, it should prevent us from carrying analysis to the extent which Siegfried has done.

Zapletal, in 1904, in his little book, *Die Metrik des Buches Kohelet*, maintained the thesis that *Qoheleth* is (or was) metrical throughout, and that this fact enables the critic to reject a number of later glosses, which mar the metrical form.

In 1905 Haupt, in two publications, *Koheleth*, published in Leipzig, and *The Book of Ecclesiastes*, published in Baltimore, developed still further the view that he had set forth in 1894. Independently of Zapletal, he also set forth the theory that the book was written in metrical form, and in a way much more thorough-going than Zapletal has revised the text to make it conform to metre.

Haupt has in these works carried out the idea expressed eleven years before that the original work of *Qoheleth* has been piled with glosses. Of the 222 verses of the book, he retains but 124 as genuine—barely more than half—and even from these many small glosses have been subtracted. The most radical feature of Haupt's work is, however, his rearrangement of the material which he regards as genuine. The material is transposed and rejoined in an even more radical way than Bickell had done, and without Bickell's palæographical reason for it. Few verses are left in the connection in which we find them in our Bibles, so that an index becomes necessary to find a passage in the book. On any theory (except Haupt's), no ancient editor took such liberties with the text as Haupt himself has taken. He has practically rewritten the book, basing his changes partly on his metrical theory, but in larger measure on his own inner sense of what the connections ought to be.

As to the date, Haupt believes that the original Ecclesiastes was written by a prominent Sadducæan physician in Jerusalem, who was born at the beginning of the reign of Antiochus Epiphanes (175–164) and died in the first decade of the reign of Alexander Jannæus (104–79 B.C.). The author may have been a *king* in

Jerusalem, if king be taken as in *Gittin*, 62a, and *Berakoth*, 64a, to mean the head of a school. The genuine portions of Ecclesiastes are Epicurean, while in the Pharisaic interpolations Stoic doctrines are found. The original writer may have completed the book about 100 B.C., when he was 75 years old.

This view of the date ignores the important testimony of the book of Ecclesiasticus, which will be presented in detail below. Its testimony makes the interpretation of ch. 4^{13-16}, which Haupt applies to Alexander Balas, and on which he mainly relies for his date, impossible, tempting as that interpretation is. The idea that Qoheleth was a physician, rests upon no more substantial basis than the anatomical interpretation of ch. 12^{2-6}, and to freeze the poetic metaphors of that passage into anatomy, is no more justified than to freeze the poetic metaphors of the Psalms into theology. Ingenious and brilliant as Haupt's work is, it contributes little to the real understanding of Qoheleth, as in almost every feature it rests, as it seems to me, on assumptions which are incapable of proof and do not commend themselves. Meantime, in 1904, the Cambridge University Press had issued McNeile's *Introduction to Ecclesiastes*, to which reference has already been made. This work is important from the higher critical as well as from the text-critical point of view. McNeile recognizes with Haupt and Siegfried that the book has been interpolated, but in his view the interpolated portions are far smaller than they suppose, and the process of interpolation much simpler.

McNeile recognizes two glossators, a *Chasid* glossator and a *Hokma* glossator. To the former he assigns ch. 2^{26} (exc. last clause), $3^{14b.\ 17}$ $4^{17}\ 5^{1-6}\ 7^{18b.\ 26b.\ 29}\ 8^{2b.\ 3a.\ 5.\ 6a.\ 11-13}\ 11^{9b}\ 12^{1a.\ 13.\ 14}$. To the latter, ch. $4^{5.\ 9-12}\ 6^{7.\ 9}\ 7^{1a.\ 4-6a.\ 7-12.\ 19}\ 8^{1}\ 9^{17.\ 18}\ 10^{1-3.\ 8-14a.\ 15.\ 18.\ 19}\ 12^{11.\ 12}$. To an editor he assigns: $1^{1.\ 2}\ 2^{26}$ (last clause), $7^{6b}\ 12^{8-10}$. While reasons will be given below for dissenting from this analysis in a few points, the present writer has again and again found himself in agreement with McNeile. The reasons for this agreement will be set forth below.

McNeile also differs radically from Haupt and Siegfried as regards the influence of Greek philosophical thought on *Qoheleth*, maintaining that there is no clear trace of it. McNeile adduces strong reasons for supposing that the point of view expressed in the book of

Ecclesiastes is the natural product of Semitic, or, more specifically, of Jewish thought, in the conditions which prevailed in late post-exilic time, that this thought resembles Stoicism in a general way because Stoicism was a similar product of Semitic thought, Zeno, the founder of the Stoics, being a Phœnician born at Kition in Cyprus.

In the same year, 1904, Professor Genung of Amherst published his *Words of Koheleth*, in which he essays an interpretation more from the point of view of a student of literature than from that of a text-critic or an ordinary exegete. Genung argues earnestly for the unity of Ecclesiastes and exhibits little patience with any divisive theory. He regards *Qoheleth* as the first in Hebrew thought to follow the inductive method, and explains many of the seeming contradictions of the book by the supposition that the grafting of the inductive method onto the ordinary forms of expression employed by the "Wisdom" writers would necessarily in its first attempt betray the "prentice" hand and leave much in the way of literary harmony to be desired. Qoheleth, says Genung, "frequently reverts to a *mashal* to clinch his argument." Genung overlooks the fact that the larger part of the proverbs in the book do not clinch, but interrupt the argument.

In Genung's view the purpose of *Qoheleth* was to recall the religious spirit of the time back to reality, and that the result of his reasoning is to make life issue, not in religiosity, but in character. There is an element of truth in this, but Genung has greatly overworked it.

On one point Genung speaks with the authority of a literary expert. He declares that *Qoheleth* is essentially a prose book, having the prose temper and the prose work to do. "It contains little, if any, of that lyric intensity which riots in imagery or impassioned eloquence." He also justly observes that the form of Hebrew poetry is largely absent from the book, declaring that for the sake of continuity of thought the writer has abandoned the hampering form of poetry, which would compel returns of the thought to former utterances. In this it must appear even to a superficial reader of the book that, with some exceptions, Genung is right.

§ 6. THE RELATION OF "QOHELETH" TO GREEK THOUGHT.

There are two regions in which traces of Greek influence might conceivably be detected in *Qoheleth, viz.:*—its language and its thought.

1. The contention of Zirkel, Tyler, Plumtre, Siegfried and Wildeboer that Græcisms are to be found in the language of *Qoheleth*, has been ably answered by Delitzsch, Nowack, McNeile and others. Not more than one such linguistic characteristic can be detected in the book, and that belongs to the language of common life, and might be employed by anyone living in Palestine after the Macedonian conquest.

In ch. 1³ the phrase תחת השמש occurs. It is found also 28 times elsewhere in the book. Plumtre and Wildeboer (the latter hesitatingly) regard it as= ὑφ ἡλίῳ. Kleinert and McNeile rightly hold that this is unnecessary. It alternates with תחת השמים, 1¹³ 2³ 3¹ and על הארץ, 8¹⁴. ¹⁶ 11². The phrase also occurs in two Phœnician inscriptions dating from about 300 B.C.—those of Tabnith and Eshmunazer (*cf.* CIS., I, 3 and G. A. Cooke, *North Semitic Inscriptions*, pp. 26, 30). It may easily have been a phrase characteristic of the period without any reference to the Greeks. Zirkel's claim that הוא in the phrase הוא ענין רע (ch. 1¹³) corresponds to the Homeric use of the article as a demonstrative pronoun, has been deemed by none of his successors worthy of serious consideration. פרדס in ch. 2⁶, although the same as παράδεισος, is not derived from it. Both are derived from the Persian *pairi-dieza*, which furnished the word to Semitic-Babylonian, Aramaic, Arabic and Armenian as well. (See *B*DB.) It is also found in Cant. 4¹³ and Ne. 2⁸. מקרה, ch. 2¹⁴ 3¹⁹ 9². ³, was by van der Palm connected with συμφορή, but it occurs in a kindred sense in 1 Sam. 6⁹, where no Greek influence can be suspected. אז יתר, ch. 2¹⁵, Zirkel renders ἔτι μᾶλλον, but as rightly taken by Ginsburg, Wildeboer and McNeile אז="then," "under those circumstances," as in Jer. 22¹⁵. עשות טוב, ch. 3¹², is regarded by Kleinert, Tyler and Siegfried as a literal translation of εὖ πράττειν. It is true that the context excludes an ethical meaning, and shows that it means "be prosperous," or "fare well," but since עשה רעה occurs in the opposite meaning of "vex one's self" or "be in a bad way" in 2 S. 12¹⁸, Greek influence is not necessary to account for the usage. הילד השני, ch. 4¹⁵, was explained by Zirkel from the Greek phrase δεύτερος τοῦ Βασιλέως, and by Delitzsch and Wright from ἕτερος τῶν Μαθητῶν (Mt. 8²¹). Bickell and Siegfried, however, regard השני as a gloss.

If genuine, it is used in a straightforward way to refer to a second youth who became king. אהב כסף, 5⁹, was regarded by Zirkel as = φιλάργυρος, but as McNeile has said one could as well take אהב חכמה (Pr. 29³) as a Græcism=φιλόσοφος. טוב אשר יפה, ch. 5¹⁷, is taken by Graetz, Plumtre, Pfleiderer, Siegfried and Wildeboer as a translation of Καλὸν Κἀγαθόν. That, however, would be טוב ויפה. Del., who is followed by Wr., McN., Kö. (§§414n, 393a), pointed to a parallel in עָוֹן אֲשֶׁר חֵטְא, Ho. 12⁵. There can be no suspicion of Greek influence in Hosea. מענה, ch. 5¹⁹, has, according to Zirkel, the sense of *remunerari*. The use of ענה in this sense he explained through the Gr. ἀμείβεσθαι, which can mean both *remunerari* and *respondere*. ענה is, however, an Aramaic loan word="to occupy" (BDB., see note); but even if it were from ענה, "answer," McN. points to a parallel usage in 1 K. 18²⁴, for which Greek influence could not be responsible. הלך נפש, ch. 6⁹, Zirkel compares with ὁρμὴ τῆς ψυχῆς in Marc. Aurelius 3¹⁵. If there were influence here, it must have been from the Hebrew to the Greek. McN. has called attention to the fact that Ez. 11²¹ and Job 3¹ use הלך in the same sense as Qoh. ויעשם, ch. 6¹², is the one instance wherein Zirkel was right, explaining it by the Greek ποιεῖν χρόνον. McN. would alter the text to avoid this explanation, but on the whole it seems most probable. See notes. יום טובה, ch. 7¹⁴, Kleinert declared was connected with εὐημερία, but others, even those who hold to Græcisms in Qoh., regard it as doubtful. McN. pertinently asks: "What other expression could possibly be chosen as a contrast to יום רעה? יצא את כלם, Zirkel claims, is equal to the Greek μέσην βαδίζειν, but as Del. and others point out יצא has here the sense of "be quit from" or "guiltless of," as in Mishna, *Berakoth*, 2¹, *Sabbath*, 1⁸. This is, then, not a Greek idiom, but NH. מה שהיה Kleinert explains as τὸ τί ἐστιν="the essence of the thing," but, as McN. notes, the expression is found in 1⁹ 3¹⁵ 6⁹, in all of which such a meaning is impossible. It means simply "that which is." אדם, ch. 7²⁸, Graetz takes as equal to איש, owing to the influence of the Greek ἄνθρωπος, but as McN. notes it is simply opposed to אשה as in Gen. 2²². ²³. ²⁵ 3⁸. ¹². ¹⁷. ²⁰. ²¹, and does not correspond to Greek usage at all. פתגם, ch. 8¹¹, which Zirkel takes for the Gr. φθέγμα and others for ἐπίταγμα, is, as Delitzsch pointed out, a Persian word; see notes. הכל, ch. 12¹³, Tyler, who is followed by Sieg., compares with the formula of the Mishna, זה הכלל="this is the general rule," and thinks there is "a pretty clear trace of the influence of Greek philosophical terminology." He compares τὸ καθόλον or τὸ ὅλον, which in Plato is used in the sense of "the Universal." Such a view imports into the phrase a meaning foreign to the context. The word simply means "all," and means that either the whole book, or all that the editor wished to say, has been heard. These points are more fully discussed by McNeile, *op. cit.*, pp. 30–43.

2. As to the possibility that Qoheleth was influenced by Greek philosophical thought, it can be shown that there is even less trace in *Qoheleth* of Greek philosophical, than of Greek linguistic, influence. Renan and McNeile are right in thinking that everything in *Qoheleth* can be accounted for as a development of Semitic thought, and that the expressions which have been seized upon to prove that its writer came under the influence of Greek schools of philosophy only prove at most that Qoheleth was a Jew who had in him the making of a Greek philosopher. (*Cf.* McNeile, *op. cit.*, p. 44.)

Many attempts have been made to prove the contrary. Pfleiderer (*Cf. Jahrbücher für protestantische Theologie*, 1887, 177–180, and his *Die Philosophie des Heraklit von Eph., nebst einem Anhang über heraklitische Einflusse im alttestamentlichen Koheleth, und besonders im Buch der Weisheit*, 1886) tries to show that ch. $3^{1\cdot 9}$ is dependent upon Heraclitus, not only for its thought, but for many of its expressions; but this view has been justly discarded by others. Friedländer (*Griechische Philosophie im alten Testament*, 1904) seeks to prove that Qoheleth was written in the Greek period, assuming that in that case Greek philosophy influenced it. He makes no specific argument for such influence beyond the contention that ch. 7^{19} (= Pr. 21^{22} 24^5) is an echo of Euripides. Sellin (*Spuren griechischer Philosophie im alten Testament*, 1905) has answered him.

The attempt of Tyler, which is followed by Plumtre, Siegfried, and Haupt, to prove that Qoheleth was influenced by the Stoics, deserves more serious attention. Tyler (*Ecclesiastes*, p. 11 *ff.*) finds in the catalogue of times and seasons in ch. $3^{1\cdot 9}$ a setting forth of the great principle of Stoic ethics, that one should live according to nature. He thinks that in vv. 2–8 we have a compendious statement that for every event of human life "Nature" has an appointed season. He finds confirmation of this in ch. 3^{17} where the word "there" according to the Massoretic pointing seems to him to refer to nature. With reference to this last point it may be observed that ch. 3^{17} in all probability is one of the *Chasid* glossator's interpolations to Qoheleth's work, and that the word "there" is a Massoretic mistake (see Commentary, *ad loc.*, for reasons).   The Stoic ethics, too, which Tyler sees in ch. 3^{2-8}, do not appear, on a close examination, to be there.   Qoheleth is not in these verses expressing an ethical standard, but is rather breathing a sigh (see vv. 9, 11) over the fact that all human life with its varied activities is caught in the meshes of an inexorable fate.   This consciousness of the iron grip of fate Qoheleth possesses in common with the Stoics, it must be confessed, but, as Zeller (*Stoics, Epicureans and Sceptics*, London, 1892, p. 332 *ff.*) perceived, the Stoics did not invent this conception, but shared it with nearly all the thinkers of the period.   In an age when first the Persian, then the Macedonian, and finally the Roman conquerer quenched all over the civilized world the torch of freedom, and powerful nations were crushed like egg-shells, it is no wonder that the fact that man is powerless before the onward sweep of things should have impressed the thoughtful minds of the time regardless of nationality.   The fact that this conception appears in Qoheleth is, therefore, a mark of date, rather than evidence of Stoic influence.   Ch. 3^{13-15}, upon which Tyler relies for confirmation of his argument, is obviously open to the same explanation. The writer is simply saying: Man is powerless in the presence of God.

Tyler then argues (*op. cit.*, p. 14 *ff.*) that the picture which Qoheleth draws in ch. 1 of the endless repetitions of nature clearly betrays the influence of the Stoic theory of cycles.   Tyler overlooks, however, the fact that the differences between the Stoics and Qoheleth are really greater than their agreements.   Qoheleth (ch. 1^{4-11}) alludes only to the fact that the generations of men, the sun, the winds, the rivers, and all human affairs, run again and again the same course.   He betrays no consciousness of the Stoic theory of larger world-cycles, at the end of which everything would be destroyed by flood or fire only to be recreated and to start upon a new world-course, in which every detail of its former history would be repeated.   (See Zeller, *op. cit.*, ch. viii.)   Indeed, it is clear that Qoheleth did not hold this view, for his constant plaint is that "man cannot find out what will be after him," or "know what God hath done from the beginning to the end" (*cf.* 3^{11} 6^{12} 7^{14} 11^{5}).   Qoheleth's confession of ignorance is in striking contrast to the dog-

matic certainty of the Stoics.   When one notes these contrasts, it
is hardly possible longer to maintain that Qoheleth betrays in ch. 1
any Stoic influence.   He appears rather as an acute observer of
life, whose bitter experiences have led him to look beneath the surface, and who has thus become conscious of the seemingly futile
repetitions of life, and whose thirst for knowledge of life's mystery
refuses, though baffled, to be satisfied by dogmatism.

Tyler further urges (*op. cit.*, 15 *ff.*) that Qoheleth's oft repeated
dictum "all is vanity" is best explained by Stoic influence, because
Marcus Aurelius declares that "worldly things are but as smoke,
as very nothingness."   On any theory of the date of Ecclesiastes,
however, it might with greater plausibility be urged that the stream
of influence, if influence there was, was in the other direction.
The coincidence that both Qoheleth and the Stoics regarded folly
as madness is also to Tyler an argument for his theory.   If, however, his other arguments are invalid, this fact can be regarded as
no more than a coincidence.

Not only do these alleged evidences of Stoic influence appear to
be unreal, but on many other points the positions of Qoheleth and
the Stoics are in such striking contrast as to render the theory of
Stoic influence most improbable.   The Stoics were materialists,
and most dogmatic in their materialism (Zeller, *op. cit.*, ch. vi),
but there is no trace in Ecclesiastes either of their materialism or
their dogmatism.   The Stoics regarded God as pure reason, and
were as positive and dogmatic about the divine nature as about
the universe; Qoheleth, on the other hand, regarded both God and
his works as unknowable.   God is infinitely above man (*cf.* 5²),
and even what he does man cannot hope to understand (*cf.* 11⁵).
The Stoics thought they understood how the soul was formed in
the unborn child (Zeller, *op. cit.*, pp. 212–213); Qoheleth, on
the other hand, declared that the formation even of the bones
of the unborn infant was a mystery the secret of which is undis-
coverable (ch. 8¹⁷ 11⁵).   There is a great contrast, too, between
the idea of good as presented by Qoheleth and the Stoics respectively.   To Qoheleth there is no absolute good.   A good is a
relative thing; it consists of the satisfaction of the animal appetites
during the period of life when such satisfaction gives enjoyment.

It has no absolute value, but there is in life nothing better (*cf.* ch. 2²⁴ 3¹². ¹³ 5¹⁸. ¹⁹ 9⁷⁻¹⁰ 11⁹ᵃ. ¹⁰). To the Stoics, on the contrary, nothing could be considered a good which did not have an absolute value. (Zeller, *op. cit.*, pp. 231–233.) A similar contrast exists between Qoheleth's idea of the relative position of wise and foolish men and that entertained by the Stoics. Qoheleth has an innate liking for wisdom; he admires it, and at times follows it (ch. 1¹³ 7²⁵. ¹¹⁶ 9¹⁶), but, on the other hand, he cannot rid himself of the feeling that the wise man toils in vain (9¹⁶), that his labor is a fruitless endeavor, and that a fœtus born dead is in reality happier than the wise man (ch. 6³ᵇ⁻⁸). It is true that in another mood he declares that it is better to know that one will die than to know nothing (ch. 9⁵); but on the whole Qoheleth's verdict is that wisdom, like all other things mundane, is vanity. The wise man has no real advantage, except that he suffers what he suffers with his eyes open; in the end he dies like the fool, and goes to the same place (*cf.* 9¹ᶠ). The Stoics, on the other hand, regarded the wise man as the only perfect man, free from passion and want and absolutely happy, falling short in no respect of the happiness of Zeus. (Zeller, *op. cit.*, pp. 270–271.)

Again, the Stoics made distinctions between degrees of goodness. Virtue was an absolute good; other goods were secondary, and certain things were indifferent. (Zeller, *op. cit.*, ch. XI.) Of such distinctions we find no trace in Ecclesiastes. The one kind of good which he knows is to eat and drink and enjoy the full round of physical life while it lasts. This is not an absolute good —Qoheleth knows none—but it is to him the only good within the reach of man. The Stoics also developed theories of applied morals, in which political theories and the duties of the individual were set forth. These culminated in the Roman period in the conception of a citizenship of the world. (Zeller, *op. cit.*, ch. XII.) None of these ideas finds expression in Qoheleth, though it would, of course, be unfair to look for some of them, as they were later developments of Stoicism. The Stoics, too, were great allegorizers (*cf.* Zeller, *op. cit.*, p. 355 *ff.*), and made much of divination (*cf.* Zeller, *op. cit.*, p. 370 *ff.*), traces of neither of which appear anywhere in Ecclesiastes.

Upon a candid comparison of the thought of Ecclesiastes, then, with the philosophy of the Stoics, the supposed dependence of the one on the other turns out to be unreal. The resemblances are not really likenesses but surface coincidences, and the differences are fundamental.

Tyler (*op. cit.*, 18 *ff.*) endeavors to show that Qoheleth also exhibits traces of Epicurean thought. In this argument he relies mainly upon two passages: 3^{18-22} and 5^{18-20}. The former of these teaches, he holds, the Epicurean doctrine of the mortality of the soul, and the latter the Epicurean doctrine of pleasure, or tranquillity, as the essential principle of life. With reference to the first of these points it should be noted that Qoheleth's denial of immortality differs from the Epicurean denial. His is but a passing doubt: it is not dogmatically expressed, and at the end (12^7) his doubt has vanished and he reasserts the older Jewish view (Gn. 2^7). This older view was not an assertion of immortality, but the primitive conception that the breath comes from God and goes back to him. The Epicureans, on the other hand, dogmatically argued for the non-immortality of the soul, and possessed well-assured theories about it. (*Cf.* Zeller, *op. cit.*, pp. 453–456.) As to Tyler's second point, it will be presently shown that this is a Semitic point of view older than Epicurus by many centuries.

Siegfried confesses that neither thorough-going Stoicism nor Epicureanism can be found in the book, but he, nevertheless, distinguishes two authors in the book, the one of whom shows, he thinks, kinship to the Stoics, and the other to the Epicureans.

Haupt, on the other hand, believes that the original *Qoheleth* was strongly imbued with the Epicurean philosophy. He says (*The Book of Ecclesiastes*, 1905, p. 6), "Like Epicurus (341–270 B.C.), Ecclesiastes commends companionship (4^9), and cheerfulness (9^7), but also contentment (6^9), and moderation in sensual pleasures to avoid painful consequences (11^{10}). He warns against wrong-doing, since it entails punishment (7^{17}, 5^6). He does not deny the existence of God (5^2), but he disbelieves a moral order of the universe: divine influence on this world where there is so much imperfection and evil seems to him impossible. In the same way he doubts the immortality of the soul (3^{21}); death ends all consciousness (9^{10}). He by no means commends nothing but eating and drinking and pleasure (8^{15} 2^{24} 5^{18}, cf. 3^{12}); he also preaches the gospel of work (3^{22} 9^{10})."

The part of this argument which relates to immortality has already been considered. Unfortunately for the Epicurean theory, an old Babylonian parallel to Eccl. $9^{7 \cdot 9}$—a parallel which contains the heart of this supposed Epicurean philosophy—has been discovered. It occurs in a fragment of the Gilgamesh epic found on a tablet written in the script of the Hammurabi dynasty (about 2000 B.C.), and was published by Meissner in the *Mitteilungen der Vorderasiatischen Gesellschaft*, 1902, Heft 1. On p. 8, col. iii, l. 3, we read:

> SINCE the gods created man,
> Death they ordained for man,
> Life in their hands they hold,
> Thou, O Gilgamesh, fill indeed thy belly,
> Day and night be thou joyful,
> Daily ordain gladness,
> Day and night rage and make merry,
> Let thy garments be bright,
> Thy head purify, wash with water,
> Desire thy children which thy hand possesses,
> A wife enjoy in thy bosom,
> Peaceably thy work (?) . . .

As Hubert Grimme pointed out (*Orientalische Literaturzeitung*, Vol. VIII, col. 432 *ff.*), this is a most striking parallel to Eccl. $9^{6 \cdot 9}$.

Also their (the dead's) love as well as their hate and their jealousy have already perished, and they have again no portion in all that is done under the sun. Come eat thy bread with joy and drink thy wine with a glad heart, for already God hath accepted thy works. At all times let thy garments be white, and let not oil be lacking on thy head. Enjoy life with a woman whom thou lovest all the days of thy vain life which he gives thee under the sun, for it is thy lot in life and thy toil which thou toilest under the sun.

These passages are not only strikingly similar, but in parts the Hebrew seems to be a translation of the Babylonian (see Commentary). The existence of the influential Jewish colony called the "*Gouliouth*" in Babylonia and its great influence on the Jews of Palestine is well known. There can be little doubt that it was through this channel that this Babylonian philosophy of life became known to Qoheleth and influenced him.

This old Babylonian philosophy, too, it should be noted, contains the heart of all that has been considered Epicurean in Qoheleth. The eating and drinking, the enjoyment of one's labor, the cheerfulness, the delight in pleasure, the feeling that death ends all—all these are contained in it. The script in which it is written attests the existence of these sentiments as early as 2000 B.C., at a time when there is no reason to doubt that they are a product of purely Semitic thought. Qoheleth was, in all probability, acquainted with the Babylonian poem. It is not likely that his whole point of view came from Babylonia, but he adopted the sentiment of the poem, because it expressed a point of view which he had himself reached, while his own thought was made possible by some phases of Jewish thought in the particular period when he lived. Semitic thought in Babylonia had, almost two millennia before Qoheleth, traversed the cycle which Jewish thought was in his person treading.

The point of immediate interest is that the discovery of this parallelism effectually disposes of the theory that Qoheleth was indebted to the thought of Epicurus. Epicurean influence was exceedingly problematical even before this discovery, for Epicureanism was in its way as dogmatic and austere as Stoicism. Qoheleth betrays no trace of the Epicurean dogma that all knowledge comes from sensation, no trace of Epicurean canonic, or natural science, or theology, or morals. Such likenesses as may be discovered are cast in a thoroughly Semitic mould of thought, and are mere coincidences. It may, of course, be urged that it would not be necessary for Qoheleth to adopt the peculiarly Greek characteristics of either Stoicism or Epicureanism in order to be influenced by some of the fundamental conceptions of these systems; but it may be said in reply that no Hebrew could probably be influenced by them without adopting on some points their peculiar methods or dogmatism. St. Paul, Philo, and Justin

Martyr, for example, adopted the allegorizing method, and probably Qoheleth would betray some non-Semitic trait were such influence real.

McNeile (*Ecclesiastes*, pp. 44 *ff.*) has pointed out that Zeno, the founder of Stoicism, was of Phœnician stock, and that, though Ecclesiastes contains some of the seed-thoughts of Stoicism, it only means that another Semite under the influences of the same period in the world's history developed under a somewhat different environment some of the same ideas.   Our present knowledge makes it possible to contend concerning the resemblances between Qoheleth and Epicurus, not that the former borrowed from the latter, but that Epicurus was indebted for his seed-thought to Qoheleth's great forerunner, the Babylonian poet, and that this thought he worked up metaphysically and dogmatically, thus giving it a setting in accordance with the prevailing genius of the Greek philosophy of the period.   In favor of such a thesis a strong argument could be made without harboring any of the extravagant fancies of the contemporary pan-Babylonian school of Germany, but the problem belongs rather to the history of Greek philosophy than to a commentary on Ecclesiastes.

For full descriptions of the teachings and influence of Epicurus, see Zeller, *Stoics, Epicureans, and Skeptics*, London, 1892; Wallace, *Epicureanism*, London, 1880; and Guyan, *La Morale d'Epicure*, Paris, 1878. The name Epicurus appears in the Talmud as Apikoros. It is equivalent to "free-thinker" and is used in a way which shows that the writers of the Talmud had only the vaguest notions of his philosophy. *Cf. Jewish Encyc.* I, 665 *ff.*

The fact that the Babylonian influence reached some Greek philosophical thinkers has been made evident by the discovery that the mystic number of Plato's *Republic*, Book viii, is of Babylonian origin. This was first shown by Aurès, *Recueil de Travaux*, XV, 69–80, who, after examining the interpretations which Le Clerc in 1819, Vincent in 1839, Martin in 1857, and Tannery in 1870, had put upon Plato's language, finally adopted the explanation of Dupuis (1881) that the number was 21,600 and claimed that in the mathematical tablet of Senkereh this number represented 6 *shars*=30 US. = 1 kasbu. James Adam, in his *Republic of Plato*, Cambridge, 1902, Vol. II, p. 206 *ff.*, argued with great acuteness that the number contemplated by Plato was 12,960,000. The factors of this number Hilprecht (*Babylonian*

Expedition of the University of Pennsylvania, Series A, Vol. XX, Pt. 1) found on Babylonian exercise tablets in such a way as to show that it was regarded by the Babylonians as a mystic number. He holds this to be a confirmation of Adam's calculation and also of the Babylonian origin of the numbers. Even Georg Albert admits (*Die Platonische Zahl als Präzessionszahl*, Leipzig and Wien, 1907), that the Babylonian origin is possible, although he differs from Dupuis and Adam in the interpretation of the Greek, reiterating a view which he set forth in 1896 (*Die Platonische Zahl*) that the number intended is 2592, one of the factors of 12,960,000, and referred to the procession of the equinoxes.

Epicurus lived through the period of the conquests of Alexander the Great. He began teaching in Athens in the year 306 B.C., seventeen years after the death of Alexander, at a time when the channels through which Babylonian influences might pour into Greece were all open.

It is scarcely necessary to refute Dillon's statement that Qoheleth was influenced by Buddhism (see above, p. 27). Dillon supports his statement by no extended argument, and it seems clear that such parallels between Ecclesiastes and Buddhistic teaching as might be cited are in all probability due to independent, though parallel, developments of thought.

The fact is, as Edward Caird (*Lectures on the Evolution of Religion*; Vol. I, ch. vii, x, xiii, xiv) observed, that in various centres positive and theoretical religions have been developed out of primitive nature religions, and that wherever this has been the case, a similar course of evolution, independent though parallel, may be observed. The instances noted by Caird are Buddhism, Judaism, and Stoicism. That the primitive, and, to some extent, the prophetic conceptions of religion were to Israel's thinking minds proving inadequate, even before Qoheleth, the Book of Job attests. McNeile (*op. cit.*, p. 44 ff.) has already made good use of Caird's principle in showing that Qoheleth represents a stage in the development of Jewish religious thought parallel in some respects to Stoicism, though independent of it.

The principle may be applied with justice, though in a less extended way, to the likenesses between Ecclesiastes and Epicurus. Where primitive types of religious conception were beginning to be regarded as inadequate, it was natural for men to find a kind of satisfaction for a time in the effort to make the most out of the present life and its temporary pleasures. We have already seen how Babylonian thought passed through this phase, and Herodotus tells us (Bk. 2⁷⁸) that Egyptian thought passed through a similar phase, which gave birth to the custom of carrying a mummy around the table at a feast and exhorting each guest to make the most of his opportunity, for one day he would, like the mummy, be unable to participate in such joys. This point of view is also exhibited in native Egyptian poetry. See W. Max Müller's *Liebespoesie der alten Ägypter*, 30–35.

Qoheleth represents such a stage in Hebrew thought. He did not invent the conception of *Sheol*, which appears in his book, as a place of dismal half-consciousness. It is the old Semitic conception, set forth in the Babylonian poem of *Ishtar's Descent* (KB., VI), and in the OT. in Is. 14ᴶᶠ Ez. 32¹⁸⁻³¹, and is even reiterated by some late Psalmists (*cf.* Ps. 88¹⁰ 115¹⁷). Qoheleth's point of view is a natural evolution, therefore, from Israel's earlier thought —as natural as that which took place in Babylonia or in Egypt. The evolution of thought in Greece may as naturally have produced Epicurus. If either Qoheleth or Epicurus was in any way indebted to the Babylonian poet, it was because the development of thought in their respective countries made his conceptions of life welcome to many Hebrew and Greek minds.

The book of Ecclesiastes represents, then, an original development of Hebrew thought, thoroughly Semitic in its point of view, and quite independent of Greek influences.

> McNeile has pointed out (*Ecclesiastes*, pp. 45 *ff.*, 50 *ff.*) that more real affinity of thought exists between Qoheleth and Xenophanes of Colophon, or Qoheleth and Pyrrho and the Sceptics, than between Qoheleth and the Stoics. McNeile, however, rightly declares that no contact on the part of Qoheleth with either of these philosophies can be maintained. The Sceptics were in their way as dogmatic and as Greek as the Stoics or Epicureans (*cf.* Zeller, *op. cit.*, 514–563), while Qoheleth is thoroughly Semitic.

§7. THE INTEGRITY OF ECCLESIASTES.

It is clear from what has been said in §5 that the most diverse opinions upon this point exist among scholars. Cornill and Genung, on the one hand, maintaining vigorously the entire unity of the work as it stands (Cornill counting the work one of the greatest triumphs of Hebrew faith), while Siegfried and Haupt, at the other extreme, regard the book as the product of so many hands that its original features are entirely obscured. The truth will be found to lie somewhere between these two extremes, and somewhat nearer the former than the latter.

The title, ch. 1^1, "The words of Qoheleth, son of David, king in Jerusalem," may readily be granted without controversy to be the work of an editor. The analogy of the titles to the prophetic books makes this probable. To this same editor we probably owe the words "says Qoheleth" in 1^2 7^{27} and 12^8. The writer of the book usually speaks of himself in the first person (see 1^{12} $2^{1.\ 13.\ 18}$ $3^{12.\ 16}$ $4^{1.\ 4.\ 7}$ 5^{18} 6^1 $7^{15.\ 25.\ 26}$ $8^{10.\ 16}$ $9^{1.\ 11.\ 13}$ 10^5). The words "says Qoheleth" interrupt the rhythm in 1^2 and 12^8, while in 7^{27} they actually interrupt a discourse in the first person; we conclude, therefore, that they are probably editorial. Further, ch. $12^{9.\ 10}$, which speaks of Qoheleth in the third person and praises his work, is, as a number of recent interpreters have seen, doubtless the work of the editor also. Ch. $12^{11.\ 12}$, which praises the work of Israel's wise men in general, and utters a warning against reading other books (*i.e.*, probably books outside the OT. canon), is also from the hand of an editor or glossator. McNeile assigns it to the *Hokma* glossator, but it seems to me probable that the two are really one. I can see no reason for calling in the aid of another writer at this point. To these we must add the words, "End of discourse all has been heard," at the beginning of 12^{13}, which marked the conclusion of the book as the *Hokma* editor left it. (For reasons, see crit. note on 12^{13}).

If now we remove these editorial words and sentences, is the rest of the book a unity? Are there any utterances so contradictory that they could not have been uttered by the same mind? In answer we must examine the book. Through the first two chapters the thought flows on connectedly, as most interpreters have recognized, until we come to 2^{26}, when we suddenly come upon a sentiment which is in direct contradiction to most of the statements which have preceded it in the chapter, and which contains the orthodox Jewish doctrine of rewards and punishments. It is incon-

ceivable that a writer should say in the same chapter, that the wise
man and the fool have the same fate ($2^{15. 16}$) and that there is no
good but eating and drinking and enjoying one's self (2^{24}), and
also say that God punishes the sinner and rewards the good (2^{26}).
We accordingly are compelled to conclude that 2^{26} comes from the
hand of a *Chasid* or Jewish orthodox glossator, whose philosophy
of life was that of the Pharisees.

Did this glossator add any other passages to the book? If we
find any similar sentiments which interrupt and contradict their
context, we must conclude that he did. McNeile holds that ch.
3^{14b}, "God hath done it that men may fear before him," is such a
gloss, but in this he seems to me mistaken. That the mysterious
and inexplicable being whom Qoheleth considered God to be
should wish men to fear before him, is as consonant to the thought
of *Qoheleth*, as in a different sense to that of the *Chasid*. Sentiments similar to those of ch. 2^{26} are, however, found in 3^{17} $7^{18b.}$
$^{26b. 29}$ $8^{2b. 3a. 5. 6a. 11-13}$ 11^{9b} $12^{1a. 13}$ (from the words "fear God")
and ^{14}. All these breathe the same sentiments and either
interrupt or contradict the chief teachings of the book, and in
most cases do both. As the last of these glosses forms the conclusion of the book, coming after the concluding words of the editor,
we conclude that the *Chasid* glossator's was the last hand to anno-
tate Ecclesiastes as it stands in our canon. To the *Chasid* glosses
thus enumerated, McNeile would add 5^{1-7}, the passage on rash
vows. I see no reason, however, why the whole of this passage,
except the two allusions to dreams, may not belong to Qoheleth.
His views did not exclude the worship of God altogether, and they
would naturally lead him to denounce sham and insincerity in religion. The only real argument against the genuineness of this
section is that it interrupts Qoheleth's reflections on political affairs,
to which the preceding and following sections are devoted. No
ancient Jew, however (except possibly the Priestly Writers in the
Pentateuch), least of all Qoheleth, is sufficiently systematic in the
arrangement of his sections, so that this argument can really be of
weight where, as here, not a single verse but a whole section inter-
venes, and that section is not on the whole out of harmony with
Qoheleth's position. Vv. 3 and 7^a, however, interrupt Qoheleth's

thought, and are cast more in the form of the *mashal* proverbs. We conclude, therefore, that they were introduced by some writer who was especially interested in *wisdom* sayings cast in a poetic form.

We must next inquire whether there may not be other proverbial sayings in Ecclesiastes which so interrupt the argument of the book as to make it impossible that they should have been inserted by Qoheleth himself. A careful study of the work convinces us that there are, and that the following passages are such *wisdom* or *Hokma* glosses: 4^5 $5^{3.}$ ^{7a} $7^{1a.}$ $^{3.}$ $^{5.}$ $^{6-9.}$ $^{11.}$ $^{12.}$ ^{19} 8^1 $9^{17.}$ ^{18} $10^{1-3.}$ $^{8-14a.}$ $^{15.}$ $^{18.}$ ^{19}. To these passages McNeile would add 4^{9-12}, which Siegfried and Haupt also regard as glosses; but the verses, though proverbs, are so appropriate to the context that I cannot persuade myself that Qoheleth did not quote them. As we have seen above, the editor of the book was much interested in the work of the wise, and it is quite possible that the proverbial glosses just enumerated were introduced by him. There is no necessity, therefore, of supposing that more than two hands have made additions to Ecclesiastes since it left the hands of Qoheleth. One was an editor deeply interested in the Wisdom Literature, and the other who came after him, was deeply imbued with the spirit of the Pharisees. The first edited the book because it formed an important addition to the Wisdom Literature, and possibly, too, because he thought it a work of Solomon (see on 12^9). The second, finding such a work attributed, as he supposed, to Solomon, added his glosses, because he thought it wrong that the great name of Solomon should not support the orthodox doctrines of the time. The ·material, added by these glossators as catalogued above, is, however, but a small part of the material in the book.

§ 8. QOHELETH'S THOUGHT IN OUTLINE.

The book opens with an introduction or preface (ch. 1^{1-11}) in which Qoheleth sets forth his conviction that everything is vain. Life and the processes of nature are an endless and meaningless repetition. Men are unconscious of the repetition, because each generation is ignorant of the experiences of the generations which have gone before it.

As though to give a demonstration of the thesis of the preface Qoheleth, in the next section of the book (1^{12}-2^{26}), narrates his experiments, under the assumed character of King Solomon, in seeking satisfaction first in wisdom (1^{12-16}), then, in material and sensual things (2^{1-11}), next, in the virtues of folly (2^{12-17}), and lastly, he states (2^{18-26}) the conclusions to which his various experiments have led. These conclusions are that there is no permanent satisfaction in any kind of earthly activity. All labor is alike vain. There is nothing better than to eat and drink and gain such animal satisfaction as one can while life lasts. This is, it is true, vain, *i.e.*, fleeting, but it is the only ray of satisfaction in a world of vain toil and transient phenomena.

Qoheleth then proceeds (3^{1-15}) to exhibit man's helplessness in the grip of those laws which God has established. Human activities are limited to certain times and seasons in which man goes his little round doing only what other men have done before. His nature cries out for complete knowledge of the works of God, but God has doomed him to ignorance, so that the best he can do is to eat and drink and ignorantly get what little enjoyment he can within these limitations. The philosophy which is for the second time repeated here, bears a striking resemblance to that of the Gilgamesh fragment quoted above.

A section then follows (3^{16-22}) which is but loosely connected with the preceding, in which Qoheleth argues that the oppressions of human government and the injustices of human courts prove that men are like beasts, and the fact that both experience the same death, and return to the same dust, confirms this. Immortality is such a questionable thing, that another argument is found for the Semitic theory which the Babylonian poet had formulated long before Qoheleth, that the best one can do is to make the most of the present.

From the general reflections suggested by oppression and injustice, Qoheleth passes in the next section (4^{1-12}) to a closer examination of man's inhumanity to man, speaking first of the pathos of the oppression of the weak by the powerful, then, of the envy created by rivalry, and, lastly, of the lonely miser's inhumanity to himself. He contents himself here with a statement of facts; the conclusion to be drawn from them had been stated at the end of ch. 3. Ch. 4¹³⁻¹⁶ sets forth the vanity or transient nature of popularity as exhibited in the history of two young unnamed kings. The statement suggests that the acme of human glory is even more vain than other forms of human activity.

In ch. 5¹⁻⁷ Qoheleth offers us his most extended remarks upon religion. The two glosses (5³ and 7ᵃ) on dreams do not seriously interrupt the flow of his thought. He had in ch. 3 revealed his conception of God as a powerful being, who keeps man in ignorance (3¹¹ emended text), and who has circumscribed man in the inexorable meshes of fate, so that man may fear him. Now Qoheleth goes on to counsel obedience, reverence, and a faithful performance of one's covenants with God. His conception of God is dark, but such religion as he has is sincere. Qoheleth has no tolerance for shams, nor sympathy with the glib worshipper who in a moment of fright will covenant with God for anything, if only he may escape the impending danger, and then go his way and forget it when the danger is past. What in his view the real function of religion was, he does not tell us, but he does insist that such religious practices as one engages in should be reverent and sincere.

In ch. 5⁸⁻6⁹ Qoheleth returns again to the subject of oppression, which in every Oriental ‑country, as in every despotism, is so painful an element in life. He first observes that in a country ruled by a hierarchy of officers oppression is to be expected, though a king is on the whole an advantage, and then passes to the consideration of the various kinds of oppression which grow out of the love of money. In the course of this discussion he more than once (5¹⁸. ¹⁹ 6². ³) reiterates his theory, that the one ray of light on life is to eat and drink and gain what enjoyment one can, without wearing one's self out in useless labor. This is transient (vain, 6⁹), but there is nothing better.

These thoughts lead Qoheleth in ch. 6¹⁰⁻¹² to revert to the theme of ch. 3, the contrast between puny man and fate. In ch. 7¹⁻¹⁴ Qoheleth introduced a few proverbs which enforced his point of view. These the *Hokma* glossator has considerably amplified with proverbs which have no bearing on the question in hand.

Then, as though the indictment against the order of the world were not sufficiently strong, Qoheleth in the next section (7^{15}-10^3) enters upon a second arraignment of life. He sets forth, excluding interpolations, in 7^{15}-^{22} the uselessness of going to extremes, in 7^{23}-^{29} his judgment of women, in 8^{1}-^{9} he reflects once more upon despotism, in 8^{10}-^{15} he reiterates his conviction that the results of righteousness and godlessness are the same, in 8^{16}-9^1 he describes another fruitless experiment to fathom the world by wisdom, and in 9^2-^{6} the hopelessness of humanity's end; while in 9^7-^{16} he, in view of this argument, restates again more fully that Semitic philosophy of life, which he holds in common with the Babylonian poet, and at one point, as we have seen, almost quotes that poet's words. Ch. 9^{17}–10^3 are glosses added by the *Hokma* editor.

In the next section (10^4-^{20})—a section greatly interpolated by the *Hokma* editor—Qoheleth offers still further advice as to the proper conduct to be observed toward rulers.

Lastly, in the final section, ch. 11^1–12^8, Qoheleth utters his final counsels. He has probed life and the world relentlessly. He has stated his conclusions frankly, undeterred by any sentimental reasons. He has been compelled to find the older religious conceptions of his people inadequate, and the newer conceptions, which some about him were adopting, unproven. His outlook has forced him to pessimism, but, nevertheless, his concluding advice, in accordance with the Semitic philosophy, which more than once during his writing has come to the surface, is manly and healthy, if not inspiring. Enter into life heartily, be kindly, venture to sow and reap and fill the whole round of life's duties while you can. Let the young man, therefore, make the most of his youth, for the inevitable decay of bodily powers will come with advancing age, and the cheerlessness of Sheol will terminate all.

Such are Qoheleth's thoughts and such is his advice. His philosophy of life, though in a sense hopeless, is not immoral. He nowhere counsels debauchery or sensuality; he rather shows that in these there is no permanent enjoyment. Though a sceptic, he had not abandoned his belief in God. It is true that God is for him no longer a warm personality or a being intimately interested in human welfare. The ancestral faith of Israel in Yahweh has been outgrown; Qoheleth never uses the name. God is an inscrutable being. It is vain to seek to understand his works. All we can know is that he holds men in the iron vice of fate. Nevertheless Qoheleth preaches a gospel of healthy work and the full enjoyment of life's round of duties and opportunities. Let a man fulfil these while he bravely faces the real facts of life—this is the sum of Qoheleth's teaching.

It is a teaching which is to a Christian chilling and disappointing, but Qoheleth's negative work had, no doubt, a function to perform in clearing away outworn conceptions before a new, larger, truer, and more inspiring faith could have its birth.

His book probably owes its presence in the canon to the fact that he had impersonated Solomon in the early part of it. This was taken literally by the unimaginative. Orthodoxy afterward added, as we have seen, some sentences, to soften the teaching of the book for Pharisaical ears.

§ 9. WAS QOHELETH WRITTEN IN METRICAL FORM?

Two different scholars, Zapletal (*Die Metrik des Buches Kohelet*, Freiburg, Schweiz, 1904) and Haupt (*Koheleth*, Leipzig: his views were set forth in 1905 in English in his *Ecclesiastes*, Baltimore), propounded quite independently of each other the theory that the whole of the original work of Qoheleth was composed in metrical form. Both scholars have naturally proceeded to make this theory a guide in the textual criticism of the book, though the metrical criterion in the hands of Zapletal leads to far less radical results than in the hands of Haupt.

A candid study of the book leads, however, to the conclusion that, as applied to the whole book, this metrical theory is a mistake, however true it may be for parts of it. Clear, too, as some of the characteristics of Hebrew poetry are, our knowledge of Hebrew metre is still in too uncertain a state to enable any scholar to make it a basis for textual criticism with any hope of convincing any considerable number of his colleagues of the validity of his results. (See Cobb's *Criticism of Systems of Hebrew Metre*, 1905.) To bring any Hebrew text into conformity to the metrical rules of one of our modern schools requires the excision of many words and phrases. Such excision may, in a work clearly poetical, be often obviously right, though in many cases it seems probable that a Hebrew poet varied the length of his lines to the despair of modern students of metre. But to go through a book large parts of which are in prose and turn it into metrical form by cutting out much of its material seems unwarranted. Such methods are calculated to create doubts as to the validity of metrical criteria generally, and to cast unjust suspicion upon them even for real poetry.

The real form of Ecclesiastes was recognized as long ago as the middle of the eighteenth century. Bishop Lowth, in his *Lectures on the Sacred Poetry of the Hebrews*, Lect. xxiv, says: "The style of this book (Ecclesiastes) . . . possesses very little of poetical character, even in the composition and structure of the periods." He adds in a footnote: "It is the opinion of a very ingenious writer that the greater part of this book was written in prose, but that it contains many scraps of poetry, introduced as occasion served, and to this opinion I am inclined to assent." He refers to Desvœux, *Tent. Phil. and Crit. in Eccles.*, lib. ii, cap. i. (*Cf.* also J. D. Michaelis, *Poetischer Entwurf der Gedanken des Prediger-Buchs Solomon*, 1751). The correctness of this view was recognized by Ewald, who in his *Dichter des alten Bundes* translated parts of the book as poetry and the rest as prose. Driver has recently in his edition of the text of *Qoheleth* (in Kittel's *Biblia Hebraica*, 1905) arranged all the material metrically which will at all lend itself to metrical arrangement, but treats large portions of it as prose. Briggs holds the same opinion, although he regards the conception of the book as poetic fiction belonging with Job to the Wisdom Literature. Ewald's method is followed in the translation given below, where an attempt has been made to give in Hebrew parallelism all the parts which can justly be regarded as metrical. To suppose that the whole book was of necessity poetical in form because parts of it are, is to forget the analogy of the prophetical books, in which the degree of liberty which Hebrew writers might allow themselves in alternating between prose and poetry is amply illustrated. The thought of *Qoheleth*, as Genung has well said, is prosaic. It is a prose book; the writer, in spite of occasional parallelism, "has the prose temper and the prose work

to do." This is true, on the whole, in spite of the fine poetical
passage in ch. 12 with which the book originally closed.

§ 10. THE LINGUISTIC CHARACTERISTICS OF QOHELETH.

The Hebrew in which the book of Ecclesiastes is written exhibits
some of the latest developments of that language which appear in
the Old Testament.   The decadent character of the tongue, as
here employed, appears in the use of Aramaic and Persian words,
the employment of late words used elsewhere only in the Mishna;
in the use of late developments and mixtures of Hebrew forms, the
absence or infrequent use of characteristic constructions, such as
the *waw* consecutive, and the frequent employment of syntactical
constructions rare in the older books.

Proof of the statement just made may be offered as follows.   (This
list of linguistic peculiarities is by no means exhaustive):

A. *Aramaic words, forms and constructions.*—הֲבֵל as cstr. in 1²;
כְּבָר, 1¹⁰ 2¹⁶ 3¹⁵ 4² 6¹⁰ 9⁶˙ ⁷; עִנְיָן, 1¹³ 2²³˙ ²⁶ 3¹⁰ 4⁸ 5²˙ ¹³; תקן, 1¹⁵ 7¹³ 12⁹;
מְדִינָה, 2⁸ 5⁷; שַׁבַּח, 4²; עַל־יְמַח שֶׁ־, 5¹⁵; נְכָסִים, 5¹⁸ 6²; מַעֲנה, 5¹⁹; אִלּוּ, 6⁶; תַּקּוּף,
8⁸; מִשְׁלַחַת, 8⁸˙ ⁴; שִׁלְטוֹן, 8¹; פֶּשֶׁר, 8¹; חֶשְׁבּוֹן, 7²⁵˙ ²⁷ 9¹⁰; עַל־דִּבְרַת שֶׁ־, 7¹⁴; עַל־דִּבְרַת שֶׁ־,
6¹⁰; יְלָדוֹת, 11⁹˙ ¹⁰; מֵרַע, 10²⁰; בֶּן חוֹרִים, 10¹⁷; סכן, 10⁹; גוּמָץ, 10⁸; הֶרֶב, 9¹⁸; עֶבֶד, 9¹;
דרבנות, 12³; בטל, 12¹¹.

B. *Persian words.*—פַּרְדֵּס, 2⁵; פִּתְגַם, 8¹¹.

C. *Forms and words identical with those of the Mishna.*—אִי="woe,"
4¹⁰ 10¹⁶, *cf.* Mish. *Yebamoth,* 13⁷, and the references in Ja. 43b; אֲבִיּוֹנָה=
"caper-berry," 12⁵, *cf. Ma'aseroth,* 4⁶, etc., and Ja. 5b; זֹה=זֹאת, 2²˙ ²⁴˙
5¹⁶ 7²³ 9¹³, *cf.* זוֹ, *Erub.* 4⁶, *Yom.* 3³; זֶה־הוּא, where הוּא is a copula as in the
Mishnic abbreviated זֶהוּ, 1¹⁷, etc., *cf. Kel.* 5¹⁰, etc., also Dr. §201 (3);
Da. §106, rem. 2; the use of ה with nouns without the article, as זֶה כָּל,
8⁹ 9¹, like the Mishnic אִישׁ זֶה, and זֶה . . . . . זֶה="this" . . . "that," also
without the art., 3¹⁹ 6⁵ 7¹⁴˙ ¹⁸ 11⁶; אֵי="what" or "what then," 2³ 11⁶
cf. Peah, 7⁸, and Kö. §§ 70, 414m; צָדֵק="be guiltless" or "quit from,"
7¹⁸, *cf. Berakoth,* 2¹; מַרְאֵה="the power of seeing" or "enjoying," 6⁹ 11⁹,
cf. Yoma, 74b, BDB. 909b and Ja. 834b; מִי, 5⁹ and מִי שְׁאֵר, 9⁴="whoever," *cf. Sheb.* 9⁸˙ ⁹; שְׁ־ used instead of אֲשֶׁר as a relative 89 times.   It
occurs a few times in the older literature from the song of Deborah down
(see, on 1³); in Cant. and Eccl. it occurs side by side with אֲשֶׁר, marking
a transition period; in the Mishna it displaces אֲשֶׁר entirely.

D. *Late developments of Hebrew forms.*—Here may be noted the

omission of syncope in writing the article after prepositions, as כהחכם,
8¹; the fondness for abstracts in ון as יהרון, חשבון, שלטון, etc.; fondness
also for abstracts in וּת, as רעוּת, 1¹⁴, etc.; שכלוּת, 1¹⁷, סכלוּת, 2³, הוללוּת, 10¹³,
שפלוּת, 10¹⁸, ילדוּת, 11⁹; the confusion of stems לא״ and לה״, e.g., חוטא, 2²⁶,
8¹² 9². ¹⁸, see also Q.'s treatment of the forms of יצא, 7²⁶ 10⁵, יִשְׁבֶּא, 8¹,
and cf. Ges.ᴷ· §7500; the confusion of forms עע with forms ע״, as יחוֹשׁ
from חשׁשׁ, 2²⁵, ינאץ from נצצ, 12⁶, written with א like קאם from קם (in Hos.
10⁴); the pron. אנכי never appears, it is always אני; אֶסְפָה, 12¹¹, found
only 1 Chr. 26¹⁵· ¹⁷, Ne. 12²⁵, where it forms its plural differently.

E. *Late syntactical developments.*—*Waw* consecutive with the imperf.
occurs but three times, 1¹⁷ 4¹· ⁷. On the other hand, the participial construction is most frequent—1⁴⁻⁸ 2¹⁴· ¹⁹ 3²⁰· ²¹ 4⁵ 5⁷ 6¹² 8¹²· ¹⁴· ¹⁶ 9⁵ 10¹⁹,
etc. The part. is frequently accompanied by a personal pronoun as
its subject, as זוֹרֵחַ הוא, 1⁵. הם שבים, 1⁷. מוצא אני, 7²⁶, יודע אני, 8¹², cf.
the Mishna, *Nedarim,* 11⁷. These participial sentences are frequently
negatived with אין, as אֵינָם יודעים, 4¹⁷, אֵינֶנּוּ זֹבֵחַ, 9², אינך יודֵעַ, 11⁵, cf.
Mish., *Naz.,* 2⁴. A similar construction often occurs with verbal ad-
jectives, cf. אני עָמֵל, 2¹⁸, הוא עָמֵל, 2²², אֵינֶנּוּ חָסֵר, 6², אֵינֶנּוּ מָלֵא, 1⁷. אני is
often used pleonastically with the first person of the verb, as אמרתי אני,
2¹· ¹⁵, ראיתי אני, 2¹³· ²⁴ 5¹⁷; cf. also 1¹⁶ 2¹¹· ¹²· ¹³· ¹⁴· ¹⁸· ²⁰· ²⁴ 3¹⁷ 4¹· ⁷ 8¹⁵, etc.,
and Ges.ᴷ· 135b. בְּשֶׁ־="because," 2¹⁶ and כאשר="because," 7²· 8⁴,
as in NH., cf. Kö. §389e. עַד אשר לא="while not," 12¹· ⁵, like the
Mishnic עַד שלא, *Berakoth,* 3⁵; cf. Kö. §387 0.

F. *Hebrew used in Greek idiom.*—The one instance of this, יעשׂם=
"he passes them," *i.e.,* "days," 6¹², where the idiom of ποιεῖν χρόνον
is reproduced, has already been noted above, §6 (1).

§ 11. THE RELATION OF ECCLESIASTES TO BEN SIRA.

Wright (*Ecclesiastes,* pp. 41–46), Schechter (*The Wisdom of Ben
Sira,* by S. Schechter and C. Taylor, Cambridge, 1899), and
McNeile (*Ecclesiastes,* pp. 34–37) have proved that the book of
Ecclesiastes was known to Ben Sira and influenced him to such a
degree that the book of Ecclesiasticus clearly betrays its dependence upon Qoheleth's work. The evidence is so strong that
Nöldeke (*ZAW.* XX, 90 *ff.*) declares that contrary to his expecta-
tion he has been led to the same conclusion. Nöldeke and McNeile
agree that Ben Sira used *Qoheleth* in its completed form, and
this is clearly proved by the evidence. I quite agree with Nöldeke, *op. cit.,* 93, that DS. Margouliouth in his *Origin of the
"Original Hebrew"* of *Ecclesiasticus,* London, 1899, has failed to

show that the Hebrew of BS. is not original but dependent on the Greek.

The proof of the priority of Qoheleth is of three kinds: (1) Passages extant in the Hebrew text of Ecclesiasticus, which show dependence upon the Hebrew of Qoheleth; (2) Passages not yet recovered in the Hebrew, but the Greek of which is clearly a translation of Hebrew practically identical with that of Qoheleth, and (3) Passages in which Ben Sira has paraphrased the thought of Qoheleth, though clearly dependent upon it.

1. Passages of the first class are as follows:

BS. 39¹⁶ and ³³, מעשי אל כלם טובים	Qoh. 3¹¹: את הכל עשה יפה בעתו
BS. 5³: כי ייי מבקש נרדפים	Qoh. 3¹⁵: והאלהים יבקש את נרדף
BS. 40¹¹: כל מארץ אל ארץ ישיב	Qoh. 3²⁰·²¹: הכל היה מן העפר
ואשר ממרום אל מרום:	והכל שב אל העפר:
(𝕲 read this last clause, ἀπὸ	מי יודע רוח בני האדם העלה היא למעלה
ὑδάτων εἰς θάλασσαν)=אשר	ורוח הבהמה הירדת היא למטה לארץ:
ממים אל ים.	
BS. 32⁴ (35⁴): ובל עת מה תתחכם.	Qoh. 7¹⁶: ואל תתחכם יותר
BS. 6⁵: אנשי שלומך יהיו רבים	Qoh. 7²⁸: אדם אחד מאלף מצאתי
ובעל סורך אחד מאלף:	
BS. 13²⁴: לב אנוש ישנא פניו	Qoh. 8¹: חכמת אדם תאיר פניו
	ועז פניו ישֻנא:
אם לטוב ואם לרע:	Qoh. 12¹⁴: אם טוב ואם רע:
BS. 37¹²: אך אם איש מפחד תמיד	Qoh. 8⁵: שומר מצוה לא ידע דבר רע
אשר תרע שומר מצוה	
BS. 14¹¹·¹²: ואם יש לך היטיב לך	Qoh. 9¹⁰: כל אשר תמצא ידך לעשות
ולאל ירך הדשן:	בכחך עשה כי אין מעשה
זכור כי לא בשאול תענוג	וחשבון ודעת וחכמה בשאול
ולא מות יתמחמה:	אשר אתה הלך שמה:
וחוק לשאול לא הגר לך	
BS. 37²³: ויש חכם לעמו יחכם	Qoh. 12⁹: ויתר שהיה קהלת חכם
פרי דעתו בגויתם:	עוד למד דעת את העם
BS. 43²⁷: עוד כאלה לא נוסף	Qoh. 12¹³: סוף דבר הכל נשמע את
וקץ דבר הוא הכל	האלהים ירא ואת מצותיו
	שמור כי זה כל האדם:

If we were to accept Schechter's conjectural emendation of בני עת המון שמר (BS. 4²⁰) to בני עת וזמן שמר, we should then have a parallel to Qoh. 3¹: לכל עת וזמן. Nöldeke and McN. regard the conjecture as probable, but Peters and Lévi retain המון.

An unbiased examination of these coincidences makes upon me the same impression that it does upon Nöldeke and McN., *viz.:* that Ben

Sira knew the work of Qoheleth and used his words as a modern
writer might weave into his work the words of Browning or Tennyson
or any other well-known author. In at least one case (the ישׁנא of
Qoh. 8¹, employed by Ben Sira, 13²⁴) it is probable that Ben Sira, as
Nöldeke suggests, misunderstood Qoheleth. BS. 43²⁷ is also clearly
built on Qoh. 12¹³. As the parts of these two passages in *Qoheleth*,
which are referred to, are from the *Hokma* glossator, and one of them
forms his conclusion of the book, it is clear that *Qoheleth* had been
touched by the editor before Ben Sira used it.

2. The passages of the second class indicated above are as follows:

Qoh. 3¹⁴: עליו אין להוסיף וממנו אין לגרע
(where עליו refers to "all that God said").

Qoh. 8¹⁷: וראיתי את כל מעשׂה האלהים כי לא יוכל האדם
למצוא את המעשׂה אשׁר נעשׂה תחת השׁמשׁ

Cf. BS. 18⁶: οὐκ ἔστιν ἐλαττῶσαι οὐδὲ προσθεῖναι καὶ οὐκ ἔστιν ἐξιχνιάσαι
τὰ θαυμάσια τοῦ κυρίου.

Qoh. 5³: כאשׁר תדר נדר לאלהים אל תאחר לשׁלמו
Cf. BS. 18²²: μὴ ἐμποδισθῇς τοῦ ἀποδοῦναι εὐχὴν εὐκαίρως.

Qoh. 8¹²: כי גם יודע אני אשׁר יהיה טוב ליראי האלהים
(אשׁר ייראו מלפניו:)

Cf. BS. 1¹³: τῷ φοβυμένῳ τον κύριον εὖ ἔσται ἐπ' ἐσχάτων.

Qoh. 10⁸: חפר גומץ בו יפול
Cf. BS. 27²⁶: ὁ ὀρύσσων βόθρον εἰς αὐτὸν ἐμπεσεῖται.

(This may have been suggested to Ben Sira, however, by Pr. 26²⁷ᵃ,
as BS. 27²⁷ was apparently suggested by Pr. 26²⁷ᵇ.)

These parallels are as striking in their way as those given under class 1.
One of the quotations (8¹²) is from the hand of the *Chasid* glossator, but
it is probable that both the glossator and Ben Sira here quote an orthodox sentiment of the day, for there is reason to think that BS. used
Qoheleth before the *Chasid* expanded it. See below on 12¹³.

3. Instances in which Ben Sira has paraphrased the words of *Qoheleth*:

Qoh. 1⁴:

> "Generation comes and generation goes,
> But the world forever stands."

Cf. BS. 14¹⁸ (Heb.):

> "As leaves grow upon a green tree,
> Of which one withers and another springs up,
> So the generations of flesh and blood,
> One perishes and another ripens."

Qoh. 3⁷:

> "A time to keep silence,
> And a time to speak."

Cf. BS. 20⁵⁻⁶ (Heb.):

> "There is one who is silent for want of an answer,
>> And there is one who is silent because he sees the time."
> "A wise man is silent until the time,
>> But a fool does not observe the time."

Qoh. 4⁸ᵇ: "For whom do I toil and deprive myself of good?"

Cf. BS. 14⁴ (Heb.):

> "He who deprives his soul gathers for another,
>> And in his goods a stranger shall revel."

Qoh. 5²ᵇ (Heb.¹ᵇ): "Therefcre let thy words be few."

Cf. BS. 7¹⁴ᵇ (Heb.): "And repeat not a word in prayer."

Qoh. 5¹²ᵇ (Heb.¹¹ᵇ): "The satiety of the rich does not permit him to sleep."

Cf. BS. 34¹ (Heb.):

> "The wakefulness of the rich wastes his flesh,
>> The care of living dissipates slumber."

Qoh. 7⁸ᵇ: "Better is patience than pride."

Cf. BS. 5¹¹ᵇ (Heb.): "In patience of spirit return answer."

Qoh. 7¹⁴: "In the day of prosperity be joyful; and in the day of adversity, consider; even this God has made to correspond to that."

Cf. BS. 33¹⁴˙ ¹⁵ (𝔊): "Good is set against evil and life against death; so is the godly against the sinner. So look upon all the works of the Most High; there are two and two, one against another."

Also BS. 42²⁴:

> "All things are double one against another,
>> And he has made nothing imperfect."

Qoh. 9¹⁶: "Wisdom is better than might, but the wisdom of the poor man is despised and his words are not heard."

Cf. BS. 13²²c d (Heb.):

> "The poor man speaks and they say 'who is this?'
>> Though he be weighty also they give him no place."

Qoh. 11¹⁰:

> "Put away vexation from thy heart
>> And remove misery from thy flesh."

Cf. BS. 30²³ (Heb.):

> "Rejoice thy soul and make glad thy heart
>> And put vexation far from thee."

These three classes of parallels make it clear that the book of Ecclesiastes was known to Ben Sira, and that he regarded its teachings with favor. The *Chasid* glosses were probably added after his time. (See below on 12¹³.)

§ 12. THE ATTITUDE OF THE BOOK OF WISDOM TO ECCLESIASTES.

As Wright and McNeile have clearly proved, the author of the *Book of Wisdom*, like Ben Sira, knew the work of Qoheleth, but, unlike him, did not approve of it. In ch. 2^{1-9} he sets himself to correct various sayings of the ungodly, and palpably quotes as such several of the sayings of Qoheleth. The parallelism is as follows:

WISDOM.	QOHELETH.
2^1. For they (the ungodly, see 1^{16}) said within themselves, reasoning not rightly: Short and sorrowful is our life, and there is no healing at a man's end, and none was ever known who returned from Hades.	2^{23}. For all his days are pains, and his task is vexation, also at night his heart does not rest. $5^{1\ (17)}$. The (small) number of the days of his life.
2^2. For by mere chance are we born, and hereafter we shall be as though we had never been; because a smoke is the breath in our nostrils, and reason is a spark in the beating of our hearts.	3^{19}. For the fate of the sons of men and the fate of the beasts—one fate is theirs. As is the death of one, so is the death of the other, and all have one spirit. *Cf.* also Qoh. 9^{11}.
2^3. Which being quenched, the body shall be turned to ashes, and the spirit shall be dispersed as thin air.	12^7. And the dust shall return to the earth as it was, And the spirit shall return to God who gave it.
2^4. And our name shall be forgotten in time, and no one shall remember our works; and our life shall pass away like the track of a cloud, and shall be scattered as a mist chased by the beams of the sun and by its heat overcome.	1^{11}. There is no remembrance of former men. 2^{16}. For the wise like the fool has no remembrance forever. 9^5. Their memory is forgotten. 2^{11}. The whole was vanity and a desire of wind.
2^5. For our life is the passing of a shadow, and there is no retreating of our end, because it is sealed and none turneth it back.	6^{12}. The number of the days of his vain life, for he spends them like a shadow. 8^8. Nor is he ruler in the day of death.
2^6. Come then let us enjoy the good things that exist, and let us use the created things eagerly as in youth.	2^{24}. There is nothing better for a man than that he should eat and drink and enjoy himself.

WISDOM.	QOHELETH.
2[7]. Let us fill ourselves with costly wine and ointments, and let no flowers of spring pass us by.	9[7]. Drink thy wine with a glad heart.
2[8]. Let us crown ourselves with rosebuds before they be withered.	9[8]. At all times let thy garments be white, and let not oil be lacking for thy head.
2[9]. Let none of us be without a share in our wanton revelry, everywhere let us leave tokens of our mirth, for this is our portion and this is our lot.	3[22]. For that is his portion.
	5[18]. For that is his lot.
	9[8]. For it is thy lot in life.

As Qoheleth is the only Jewish writer known to us who champions such sentiments, there can be little doubt that this polemic is directed against him.   It is true that in the following verses the author of *Wisdom* denounces oppressions which Qoheleth nowhere countenances and couples them with these false doctrines; that does not, however, prove that his shafts are not aimed at Qoheleth, for it has in all ages been one of the methods of theological warfare to hold the opinions of heretics responsible for the most immoral practices.

§ 13.   DATE AND AUTHORSHIP.

It has been shown above (§5) that the Solomonic authorship of Ecclesiastes, denied by Luther in the sixteenth century, and by Grotius in the seventeenth, was in the nineteenth century demonstrated by scholarly interpreters to be impossible.   The fact that Solomon is not the author, but is introduced in a literary figure, has become such an axiom of the present-day interpretation of the book, that no extended argument is necessary to prove it.   No one at all familiar with the course of religious thought in Israel, as scientific historical study has accurately portrayed it, could for a moment ascribe the work to Solomon.   The language of the book also strongly reinforces the argument drawn from the thought.   It belongs to the latest stage of linguistic development represented in the Old Testament.   As shown above (§10) not only are older Hebrew forms and constructions changed or confused, but late developments kindred to those of the Mishna are present, Aramaic words and constructions are found, at least two Persian words are employed, while in one instance the influence of Greek usage can be traced. If we compare the language of Qoheleth with that of the earliest prophetic document of the Pentateuch (J.), we shall find that they stand at the two extremes of Hebrew linguistic development, the former representing the latest, and the latter the earliest. Under such circumstances the Solomonic authorship of Ecclesiastes is unthinkable.

It has also been shown above (§5) that recent interpreters are divided as to whether Qoheleth wrote in the Persian or the Greek period; though most of those writing in the last few years hold to the latter era. If our recognition of a Greek idiom in Ecclesiastes is valid, it points to a date posterior to the conquest of Alexander the Great, for we must agree with the almost unanimous opinion of recent interpreters that the author lived in Palestine. The absence from his work of any important Greek influence (see above, §6) is sufficient, to mention no other feature, to make a non-Palestinian residence on his part out of the question.

It has long been thought that in *Qoh.* 5^8 there is a reference to the Satrapial system which the Persians invented. If this be true, it does not prove that the work is not later than the Persian period, for, as is well known, practically the same system was continued by Alexander and his successors. We may take the conquest of Alexander, then, as a *terminus a quo* for the composition of our book. We should note, however, that some little period of contact with the Greeks should be allowed for before the writing of Ecclesiastes, in order to account for the use of a Greek idiom. We are thus brought down to the third century B.C.

A *terminus ad quem* for Ecclesiastes is, on the other hand, fixed for us by the book of Ecclesiasticus. As has been shown above (§11) *Qoheleth*, lacking the *Chasid* glosses, was known and used by Ben Sira—a fact which has been recognized by Tyler, Kuenen, Margouliouth, Nöldeke, A. B. Davidson, Wright, Peake, Cornill, and McNeile. The date of Ben Sira can be pretty accurately determined. His work was translated into Greek by his grandson, who in his prologue states that he translated it soon after he went to Egypt, and that he went thither in the thirty-eighth

year of Euergetes. As has long been recognized, this statement
can only apply to Ptolemy Euergetes II (Physcon), and is probably
reckoned from the time when he first assumed the regal dignity in
170 B.C., and not from his second assumption of it on the death of
his brother Philometor in 146 B.C., for his reign, terminating in 117
B.C., did not last thirty-eight years after that event. It could not
refer to Euergetes I (247–222 B.C.) as he reigned but twenty-five
years. We are thus brought to the year 132 (so most scholars,
e.g., Tyler, *Ecclesiastes*, 30; Wright, *Ecclesiastes* 35 *ff.*; Sanday,
Inspiration, 98; Toy, *Ecclesiasticus* in EB.; Kautzsch, *Apokryphen*,
I, 234–235) for the migration of the younger Ben Sira to
Egypt, soon after which he translated the work of his grandfather.
If we allow fifty years as the probable time which elapsed between
the composition of the book by the grandfather and its translation
by the grandson, we reach about 180–176 B.C. as the date of the
composition of Ecclesiasticus. It must have been written before
the Maccabæan revolt broke out in 168 B.C., for there is no allusion to Antiochus IV and his oppression of the Jews. This date
seems to be confirmed by the reference to the high priest, Simon
son of Onias in BS., ch. 50, for while there were two high priests of
that name (*cf.* Jos. *Ant.* xii, 2⁵ and 4¹⁰), the second of them, to
whom reference is probably made here, lived late enough so that
Ben Sira, if he witnessed the scene which he so vividly describes in
ch. 50¹¹ *ff.*, would have written about 180–175 B.C. The date of
Ecclesiasticus is thus in the opinion of most modern scholars pretty
definitely fixed.

As Ben Sira quotes Ecclesiastes after it had once been glossed
(see above §§7, 11), Qoheleth must have written at least twenty
years earlier. We are thus brought to about the year 200–195
B.C. as the *terminus ad quem* for our book. These indications
leave the whole of the third century B.C., or the very first years of
the second, open for it.

Can we define the date more closely within these limits? Our
answer to this will depend upon our interpretation of two passages, 4¹³⁻¹⁶ and 10¹⁶⁻¹⁷. The first of these passages reads:

¹³. Better is a youth poor and wise than a king old and foolish, who no
longer knows how to be admonished, ¹⁴. though from the house of the re-

bellious he came forth, although even in his kingdom he was born poor.

¹⁵. I saw all the living who walk under the sun with the (second) youth who shall stand in his stead.

¹⁶. There was no end to all the people—all whose leader he was; moreover those who came after could not delight in him; for this also is vanity and a desire after wind."

Many are the interpretations which this passage has received (see notes on 4¹³). One of the most attractive has recently been put forth by Haupt (*Ecclesiastes*), according to which the "old and foolish king" is Antiochus Epiphanes (175–164), and the "poor and wise youth" Alexander Balas (150–145 B.C.). This view I for a time adopted, but the external evidence just passed in review compelled me to abandon it. Like the theory of Winckler—that the contrast intended is between Antiochus Epiphanes and Demetrius I—it is rendered impossible by the clear proof that Qoheleth lived before Ben Sira.

If, with the date indicated by the external evidence in mind, we carry the book back to the verge of the third century, remembering that in that century Palestine was under the control of Egypt, we shall find that Hitzig was on the right track in his interpretation of the passage. The "old and foolish king" would be Ptolemy IV (Philopator), who died in 205 B.C., and to whom from the Jewish point of view the description very well applies, for according to 3 Mac. he greatly persecuted the Jews, both in Palestine and Egypt. The "poor and wise youth" would be Ptolemy V (Epiphanes), who was but five years old when he came to the throne. He is perhaps called "poor and wise" because of the Jewish sympathy with him and hopes from him. The "rebellious house" probably refers to his father's persecution of the Jews. The "second youth" (if the word "second" is genuine) would then be Antiochus III of Syria, who had succeeded to the throne of that country at an early age, and who, within seven years after the succession of Ptolemy V, was warmly welcomed as sovereign of Judæa (Jos. *Ant.* xii, 3³). These are the only reigns in the history of the period which at all correspond to Qoheleth's words, and it seems probable that he refers to these kings. This view receives confirmation from the second passage cited above, 10¹⁶, ¹⁷. It is as follows:

> Woe unto thee, O land, whose king is a child,
> And whose princes feast in the morning.
> Happy art thou, O land, whose king is well-born
> And whose princes feast at the proper time.

As Hitzig has seen, v. 16 probably refers to the years after the reign of Ptolemy V had begun, when Agathoclea and her brother were the favorites in power (Justin, XXX, 1), when revelry flourished, and when Antiochus III (the Great) at the height of his power was prosecuting those wars which, after inflicting much suffering upon them, robbed Egypt of her Palestinian dominions. Possibly, though it is by no means probable (see notes on $9^{14\,ff}$), the reference to the city delivered by a wise man from the siege of a powerful king (9^{14-16}) is a reference to some incident of the wars of Antiochus with Egypt. Probably "Happy art thou, O land, whose king is well-born and whose princes feast at the proper time," is Qoheleth's welcome of the strong rule of Antiochus III. Josephus tells us (*Ant.* xii, 3^3) that the Jews of their own accord went over to him, and welcomed him to Jerusalem, assisting him to take the citadel from the Egyptians. This passage apparently reflects the sentiments of that welcome. Qoheleth was, then, not completed before 198 B.C. Its use by Ben Sira, on the other hand, makes it impossible that it should have been written much later than that year.

On the whole, vague as these historical allusions are, they make it probable that Qoheleth did not finish his book until after the conquest of Antiochus III, about 198 B.C. Slight as the data are, they lead us with considerable confidence to place this work just at the end of the period which above we held open for it, if not to name the very year in which it was composed. This agrees with the judgment of Hitzig, Tyler, Cornill and Genung.

The last of the third and the beginning of the second century B.C. forms a fitting background for such a work as Ecclesiastes. The century which followed the death of Alexander was a trying century for the whole East, but especially so for Palestine. Possessed by the Ptolemies, but claimed by the Seleucidæ, Palestine found herself in the precarious position of an apple of discord. The gratitude which Seleucus I felt toward Ptolemy I for the aid rendered him in obtaining his empire (see Bevan, *House of Seleucus*, I), at first secured peace between Egypt and Syria. As the century advanced, however, the Seleucid claims were pressed and Palestine first had to pay taxes to both (Jos. *Ant*. xii, 4^1) and then, toward its close, became the unhappy bone of contention between her two powerful neighbors, suffering severely. Then, too, her internal organization must have been such as to bear heavily upon the poor. Ptolemy III had deputed Joseph, son of Tobias, to collect the taxes of the country (Jos. *Ant*. xii, 4^2), and Joseph had, in true Oriental fashion, grown rich by farming out the taxes to subordinates, and founded a powerful house. (The ruins of the palace of Joseph's son, Hyrcanus, may still be seen at Arak al-Emir, east of the Jordan.) Oppressed by the tax collectors, a prey to their rich and powerful neighbors, suffering increasingly as time went on from the ravages of war, oppressed during the later years of the century by the drunken favorites of a king who was a helpless child, what more fitting theatre than the Palestine of this time could be sought for a book like Ecclesiastes?

To our scanty knowledge of the history of this period, Qoheleth adds some valuable items. He tells us that both in the court and in the temple wickedness reigned (3^{16}). In both politics and religion men were striving for selfish and sordid ends, to which the claims of justice and righteousness were made to bend. The populace generally groaned and wept under the oppressions of the powerful (4^1) and had no redress. This oppression was aggravated by the hierarchy of officials who, rising one above another, culminated in a far-off king ($5^{8\ [7]}$). The land is controlled by an arbitrary despot, who often puts fools and slaves in office, degrading the rich and noble to subordinate places, but it is useless to oppose him (10^{5-7}). Should one be entrusted with an official position and incur the displeasure of his despotic master, it is better to be conciliatory and submissive than to abandon one's post and opportunity. The espionage of the despot is so complete that it is unsafe even to whisper one's discontent to one's self, lest it shall be borne to the ears of one who will regard it as treason (10^{20}). Moreover, the king is a child, and his nobles, who exercised the power in his name, devoted even the mornings to drunken feasting (10^{16}).

While the book of Ecclesiastes makes us well acquainted with
Qoheleth's thoughts and character, it throws little light upon his
circumstances and life.   Some gleams of light even here are, however, not altogether wanting.   We learn from 5¹ that Qoheleth
lived near the temple, and this fact is confirmed by 8¹⁰, in which
the connection between "the holy place" and the "city" makes it
clear that his home was Jerusalem.   Some infer from 11¹, taking
it to refer to corn-trade, that he lived in Alexandria.   Even if the
passage referred to trade, which is doubtful (see notes *ad loc.*),
it would not prove an Alexandrine residence.   He was a man of
wealth who could gratify every appetite for pleasure (2¹⁻⁸).   At the
time of writing Qoheleth was an old man, for he had begun keenly
to appreciate that breaking up of the physical powers and that loss
of enjoyment in the pleasures of youth which age inevitably brings
(11⁹–12⁷).   Further confirmation of this is found in the fact
that his many experiments to find the *summum bonum* in pleasure,
in wisdom, and even in folly, implies the lapse of years.   Apparently, too, he had lived long enough to find himself alone—without son or brother (4⁸).   His life had also been embittered by an
unhappy domestic alliance, for his declaration that he had found
more bitter than death "a woman who is snares and nets her heart"
(7²⁶), as well as his declaration that one man in a thousand might
be true, but in all these he had not found one woman (7²⁸), has the
ring of an expression of bitter experience.

Only this little can we clearly make out as to the private life of
Qoheleth.   Plumtre (*Ecclesiastes*, 35–52) draws an elaborate but
altogether fanciful picture of Qoheleth's life, while Winckler
(*Altorientalische Forschungen*, 2 Ser., 143–159) thinks that he was
either a king or a high priest.   He argues that had he not been, so
unorthodox a writing as his would not have been preserved.
Haupt (*Ecclesiastes*, 1 *ff.*) would interpret the word מלך (="king")
to mean the "head of a school," as in the Talmud (*Gitt.* 62a, *Ber.*
64a), and holds that Qoheleth was a Sudducæan physician, who
presided over such a school.   It is unthinkable that Qoheleth could
have been a king in the literal sense and write as he does about
government, and proof is altogether wanting that, at the time when
he wrote, schools such as Haupt contemplates had arisen.   It is

more probable that the word "king" is a part of his literary arti-
fice. It must be said also, that there is no proof that Qoheleth was
a physician. As already remarked (§5) the supposition rests upon
metaphors which are exceedingly indefinite, and which are open
to quite other than anatomical interpretations. In reality Qoheleth
betrays no more knowledge of either medicine or anatomy than any
other intelligent man. To call him a Sadducee is also to anticipate
history. He belonged undoubtedly to that wealthy sceptical
aristocracy out of which the Sadducees were developed, but we
cannot trace the Sadducees before the Maccabæan time. As
McNeile (*Ecclesiastes*, 10) suggests, Qoheleth may have been of the
high-priestly family, and himself a religious official, as this would
account for the care with which his unorthodox book was adapted
and preserved. Qoheleth, a pseudonym which probably designates the name of an office, points in the same direction. More
than this we cannot say.

COMMENTARY.

Title, I¹. THE WORDS OF QOHELETH, SON OF DAVID, KING IN JERUSALEM.

(This title was prefixed by the editor. *Cf. Introduction*, §7, and note on 12⁹.)

The term *king in Jerusalem*] is an appositive of *Qoheleth*, not of *David*. *Qoheleth* (𝕲, ʾΕκκλεσιαστής; ʾA, Κωλέθ) is a crux. It has been variously interpreted, but probably means "an official speaker in an assembly." See critical note below.—*Son of David*.] These words were intended to designate Solomon. They were added by the editor who, on account of a hasty inference from I¹² *ff.*, regarded Solomon as the author. As Solomon had the greatest reputation for wisdom, wealth, splendor, and voluptuousness, the author chose him as a character through which to set forth in literary fashion his observations on life and his convictions concerning it. This the prosaically minded editor mistook for authorship. For reasons why Solomon could not be he author, see *Introduction*, §13.

קֹהֶלֶת]. Tobiah ben Eleazar, in the eleventh century, explained it as "One who collects, assembles, and expounds, among rabbis" (קהלת שהיה מקהיל קהלות ודורש ברבים), *cf.* Feinberg's *Tobia ben Elieser's Commentar zu Koheleth*, Berlin, 1904.

In *Midrash Rabba* קֹהֶלֶת is explained as "Preacher," because it is said that Solomon delivered these discourses before the congregation (קהל). This meaning was defended by Luther and, among present-day scholars, by Wildeboer. Many take it to mean "Assembler" or "Collector," but opinions differ greatly as to what was collected. Ra. thought of *Qoheleth* as "Gatherer of wisdom," Grot. as a "Collector of experiences," Wang. as "Collector of the court," Dale as "Collector of aphorisms" which formed an address, and so "deliverer of an address"; Heng. and Gins., "An assembler of people into the presence of God." Jer. rendered it by "Concionator," "One who addresses an assembly,"

67

a meaning which is followed by Dat., De W., Kn., Heil., Del., Wr., Kö., Strack, McN. and Ha. This meaning comes in the end to be practically synonymous with "Preacher." To pass by many fanciful explanations, see Ginsburg's *Coheleth*, p. 4 *ff.*, Död. took it to mean "Assembly" or "Academy," and compared German and French royal academies. Hit. interprets it "Narrator," Pl. renders it "Debater," while Che. (1893) thought it might mean "The ideal teacher." Margouliouth, *Jewish Encyc.*, V, 32, takes it to mean "member of an assembly."

The 𝔊, 'Εκκλεσιαστής from 'Εκκλησία, "assembly," is an imitation of קֹהֶלֶת. It throws little light on the meaning, as we do not know the significance attached to it.

קֹהֶלֶת is found in the book as follows: ch. 1[1. 2. 12] 7[27] 12[8. 9. 10]. It has the article (הַקֹּהֶלֶת) in 12[8]. In 7[37] it is construed with a fem. verb, unless, as is probable, we are to read there אמר הקהלת. Probably, therefore, it is an appellative. The verb קהל, from which it comes, occurs in Hebrew only in Ni., "to be summoned" or "assembled" (*cf.* Ex. 32[1] Je. 26[9] Ez. 38[7] Est. 8[11] 9[2. 16. 18]), or Hi., "to collect" or "assemble" (*cf.* Ex. 35[1] Lev. 8[3] Nu. 20[8] Dt. 4[10] Ez. 38[13] Job 11[10], etc.).

The root קהל in Aram. is used in Ni. and Hi. in the same meanings as in Heb. (*cf.* Ja. 1322), Syr. = *qᵉhal* = "congregate," "collect"; Sab. קהל קהלת = "assembly," "congregation" (D. H. Müller, ZDMG., XXX, 685, and Hommel, *Chrest.*, 127). The root also survives in Saho, a south Hamitic language, in which *kahal* = "come together," "assemble" (Reinsch, *Saho Sprache*, 210). In Ar. *qahala* = "be dry," "shrivelled," "shrunk," the meaning of the root has developed in a different direction.

In form קֹהֶלֶת is a fem. segholate part. of the Kal. The use of the fem. here has received different explanations. 1. Ra., AE., Ew., Hit., Heng. and Kue. have explained the fem. on the ground that קֹהֶלֶת agrees with or stands for wisdom (חָכְמָה). 2. Ty. (*Ecclesiastes*, 57) suggests that it denotes "one who is an assembly," *i.e.*, it is a personification of the assemblies of men. The fact that קֹהֶלֶת is usually construed with a masc. verb, renders both these explanations improbable. 3. Wm. Wright, *Arab. Gram.* 3d ed., §233, rem. *c*, explains it on the analogy of Ar. formations as an intensive fem. formation, an opinion with which Wr. (*Ecclesiastes*, 279) agrees. 4. Del., Che., No., Strack, McN. and others explain קֹהֶלֶת as the designation of an office, on the ground that the fem. ending is so used in סֹפֶרֶת "scribe," Ezr. 2[55], and פֹּכֶרֶת הַצְּבָיִם "binder of the gazelles," Ezr. 2[57]. BDB. and Driver are undecided between 3 and 4.

This last (4) is probably the right understanding of the form; קֹהֶלֶת would mean, then, "an official speaker in an assembly." Another solution of the word should be noted. Re., *L'Ecclésiastes*, 13, suggests that it is a cryptogram, as *Rambam* is for Rabbi Moses Ben Maimon, or *Rashi* for Rabbi Solomon Isaac. This is not so probable.

AUTHOR'S INTRODUCTION, OR PREFACE.

Ch. 1²⁻¹¹. The thesis of this preface is that everything is vanity. Life and the processes of nature are an endless and meaningless repetition. Men do not perceive the repetition because each genera- tion is ignorant of the experiences of those which have gone before it.

> ². VANITY of vanities, (*says Qoheleth*)
>   Vanity of vanities,
>   All is vanity.
> ³. What gain has a man of his whole toil,
>   Which under the sun he toils?
> ⁴. Generation comes and generation goes,
>   But the world forever stands.
> ⁵. The sun rises and the sun sets,
>   Panting to his place he rises there.
> ⁶. Going to the south and circling to the north,
>   Circling, circling goes the wind,
>   And on its circuits the wind returns.
> ⁷. All the streams flow to the sea,
>   But the sea is not full ;
>   Unto the place whence the streams flow,
>   There they flow again.
> ⁸. All things are wearied,—
>   No one is able to utter it,—
>   The eye is not satisfied to see,
>   Nor the ear filled with hearing.

⁹. That which has been is what shall be, and that which has been done is what shall be done, and there is nothing new under the sun. ¹⁰. There is a thing of which one may say: see this is new! Already was it in the ages which were before us. ¹¹. There is no remembrance of former men, and also the men who shall be later shall have no re- membrance with those who shall be later (still).

Vv. **2–8**, as Ewald and Driver have recognized, are poetical in form.—**2.** *Vanity of vanities*]. "Vanity"—the word meant "breath," "vapor," and then "nothingness," "vanity." It is used of the past (Job 7¹⁶) and the worthless (Lam. 4¹⁷). It is a favorite word with Qoheleth. He employs it 40 times, while in all the rest of the OT. it is used but 33 times. As Vaih. and Re. observe, this is the theme of the book. It is repeated in 12⁸, the concluding words of the original writer. *Says Qoheleth*], these words were inserted by the editor. Qoheleth always speaks of himself in the first person, see *Introduction*, §7.—*All*], as has often been noted, does not refer to the universe, but to all the activities of life—"that which is done under the sun." This the latter context proves.—*Gain*], found in this book nine times (1^3 $2^{11.}$ ³ twice, 3^9 $5^{8.}$ ¹⁵ 7^{12} and 10^{10}) in the meaning of "surplusage," "advantage," "profit."—**3.** *Under the sun*]. This phrase is peculiar to Qoheleth among OT. writers. It is found in Ec. 25 times. It is used to denote all sublunary things, and is paralleled by the expressions *under heaven* (ch. 1^{13} 2^3 3^1) and *"upon the earth"* (ch. $8^{14.}$ ¹⁶ 11^2). These latter phrases are used by other writers, the former occurring in Ex. 17^{14} Dt. 7^{24} 9^{14} 2 K. 14^{27}, etc., the latter in Gn. 8^{17}, etc.

4. *The world forever stands*]. The thought which oppresses Qoheleth is that the earth, man's workshop, should continue, while man himself is so short-lived. Jer. correctly perceived that this is the meaning. A part of the thought of this vs. is paraphrased in BS. 14^{18}: "As leaves grow upon a green tree, of which one withers and another springs up, so are the generations of flesh and blood, one perishes and another ripens."

5. *The sun rises and the sun sets*]. From man Qoheleth passes to nature, noting first that the sun continually goes his wearisome round without accomplishing anything. Possibly as Gins. suggests, Qoheleth means to hint that the sun has a little advantage over man, for though the sun goes, he comes again, while man passes away to return no more.—*Panting*]. It is a question whether the writer means to say that the sun continually pants from weariness (Gins. and Cox), or whether he pants from eagerness to start upon his course again (Wr.). Wr. adduces in favor of the latter view the fact that the Hebrew word (שׁאף) is ordinarily used in the sense of panting for something (*cf.* Am. 2^7 8^4, Job 5^5, Ps. 56^2 57^4, etc.). It should be noted, however, that שׁאף also has the meaning of "panting" from exhaustion (*cf.* Is. 42^{14} Jer. 14^6 and perhaps, 2^{24}). As the latter meaning better fits the thought, it is doubtless the one intended by Qoheleth. His conception of the universe, as the 𝔗 and Ra. note, is that of a stationary flat earth resting on an abyss through which there is a subterranean passage by which the sun finds its way at night from the west to the east.

The word for "panting" in Heb. is used of the panting or snorting of animals. Cleric long ago perceived that Qoheleth was thinking of the chariot of the sun as drawn by panting steeds, as in Ovid, *Metam.* XV, 418 *ff.* and Virgil, *Georg.* I, 250. Kn. and Wr. object that such an idea is entirely un-Hebraic and consequently impossible. Ha. has, however, pointed out that 2 K. 23¹¹ shows that even before the exile the Israelites were familiar with it. The comparison of Ps. 19⁶ (Kn. and Heng.) is inapt. Qoheleth's mood is very different from that of the psalmist.

6. *Circling, circling goes the wind*]. The movements of the wind, as well as of the sun, present a similar series of endless, wearisome repetitions. *North* and *south* only are mentioned probably because east and west were mentioned in the preceding vs. (so Gins.). Pl.'s suggestion that they are alone mentioned because north and south winds are the prevailing currents of air in Palestine is erroneous. The Palestinian winds are mostly from the west, and are quite as likely to be from the east as from the north or south.

7. *All the streams*]. As a third example from nature, Qoheleth takes the fact that the streams all continually *flow into the sea* without filling it. Their ceaseless work accomplishes nothing.

8. *All things are wearied*]. The whole universe groans with man because of its useless and monotonous activity. The last two lines of the verse may be interpreted in two different ways. (1) With Gr., Pl., No. and Ha. it may be taken to mean that neither the *eye nor the ear* of man is able to take in all this weariness. This interpretation ignores, however, the literal meaning of the words, and gives them a sense derived from the context. (2) Wr. takes the words in their natural sense, understanding them to mean that the meaningless rounds of nature communicate themselves to the spirit of man, so that eye and ear enter upon endless courses of seeing and hearing that never satisfy. This last seems the more probable interpretation.

9. *What has been is that which shall be*]. This is a general statement of the fact that all things move in constant cycles. The fact has been illustrated in preceding verses by a few striking examples.—**10.** *Already was it*]. This anticipates and answers an ob-

jection which may be urged against the sweeping statement of v. 9.
—**11**. *There is no remembrance*]. This is a strong statement of the
transitoriness of fame. As Hit., Gins., Del. and Wr. have seen,
it is not a restatement of vs. 10—that things seem new because of
ignorance of history, but is a summing up of the whole prologue.
Q. asks at the beginning: "What advantage has a man of all his
labor?" Here he returns to say in substance that even the
most famous is soon forgotten. Pl. and Wr. note the parallelism
of the thought to utterances of Marcus Aurelius (*Lib.* ii, 17; iv,
34, 35), the burden of which is that posthumous fame is oblivion.
The vs. is quoted and opposed in Wisd. 2⁴· The phrase, *There is
no remembrance*, as Hit. observes, corresponds to "*what gain?*"
The thought has completed a cycle.

2. הֲבֵל הֲבָלִים is the gen. expressive of the superlative idea. *Cf.*
1 K. שְׁמֵי הַשָּׁמַיִם Ct. 1¹, שִׁיר הַשִּׁירִים Gn. 9²⁵, עֶבֶד עֲבָדִים Ex. 29³⁷, קֹדֶשׁ קָדָשִׁים
8²⁷. *Cf.* M. §81a and H. §9, 4a. The repetition of the phrase makes it
emphatic (*cf.* Da. §29, rem. 8, and Kö. §309m). Wr. notes that the
phrase is an acc. of exclamation (*cf.* Kö. §355q r). Q. means that everything is fruitless, ineffectual, unavailing. The use of הֲבֵל as constr.
instead of הֶבֶל is peculiar. Hit., followed by Zö., compares אֶבֶל in Ps.
35¹⁴, observing that owing to the kinship of ל and ב the chief vocal is
pressed forward. As Wr. notes, however, אֶבֶל is not a segholate. Ew.,
Del., Wr. and Wild. rightly regard it as an Aramaizing form.—מַה]
Kleinert renders "nothing" or "not," comparing Ar. *ma*. This is in-
correct. As Wr. observes, the negative idea grows out of the interroga-
tion.

3. וְיִתְרוֹן], from a root which appears as ותר in As., Ar., Sab. and Eth.,
but as יתר in Aram., Syr. and Heb. In north Sem. it means "to be
abundant," "remain over."—עמל], in the earlier language, means "sorrow," "suffering," "trouble" (*cf.* Gn. 41⁵¹ Nu. 23²¹ (both E.) and Job
3¹⁰ 4⁸, etc.). In the later lit. it means "toil," "labor" (*cf.* Ps. 107¹² Ec.
2¹¹· ²⁰ 4⁴· ⁶). As Sieg. notes, Q. employs it of toilsome labor. In Aram.
עמל also has the latter meaning (*cf.* Ja., *sub voce*). In Samaritan the
stem means "make," "do," as it does also in Ar. Perhaps עמל has
that force here.

שֶׁ]. This relative is kindred to the As. *ša* and Ph. אש. It is a demonstrative root quite distinct from אשר. The two existed side by side,
though שֶ־ is but little used in the earlier literary language. It does,
however, occur in various periods, *e.g.*, Ju. 5⁷, in what is, perhaps, the
oldest bit of Heb. in the OT., in Ju. 7¹² (J.) Ju. 6¹⁷ (JE.) and Ju. 8²⁶

(a late annotator). In Ct. and Ec. it occurs frequently side by side with
אִישׁר. Herzfeld, Del. and Wr. note that in Ec. ־שֶׁ occurs 68 times, and
אֲשֶׁר 89 times. In the Mishna it has quite displaced אֲשֶׁר. ־שֶׁ here does
not denote acc. of manner, but the object (Del., Wr.).—[תחת הַשֶּׁמֶשׁ]. Pl.
confidently, and Wild. hesitatingly, explain this phrase as a Græcism=
ὑφ᾽ ἡλίῳ. Kleinert and McN. hold that this is unnecessary; it may be
simply a peculiarity of this writer. It is interesting to note that it
occurs in two Phœn. inscriptions, those of Tabnith and Eshmunazer,
c. 250 B.C. (cf. G. A. Cooke, North Semitic Inscr., pp. 26, 30), in just
the way in which Q. uses it.

4. [כָּא . . . . . הֹלֵךְ]. These words are participles, denoting the continuity
of the action, cf. Da. §100 (f), Kö. §412. Q. frequently puts these words
in contrast (cf. ch. 5¹⁵ 6⁴ 8¹⁰). הלך="to die" is found in ch. 5¹⁵ Ps.
39¹⁴ Job 10²¹ 14²⁰. בוא="to be born" occurs ch. 5¹⁵ Ps. 71¹⁸.—[עוֹלָם]
denotes here, as often, simply a long, unknown period of time, BDB.
The misunderstanding of this by certain mediæval Jews occasioned the
comment of Maimonides quoted by Gins., Coheleth, 526, 527.—[עֹמָרֶת],
fem. part. of עמד, the part. again denoting duration. Umbreit, Vaih.
and Zö. bring into connection with the use of עמד here the fact that, in
common with others of the ancients, some Hebrews believed that the
earth rested upon pillars (cf. Ps. 75⁴ 104⁵ Job 9⁶ 38⁶), and hold that Q.'s
language shows that he shared that belief. This is, however, a mistake.
עמד is often used simply to signify continuance (cf. ch. 2⁹ Ps. 19¹⁰ Lv.
13⁵ Dn. 10¹⁷). It is thus that Q. uses it here. His form of statement
throws no light upon his belief or non-belief in the pillar-theory of the
earth's support. In the Talmud, Shabbath, 30b, it is said that vs. 4
was quoted by Gamaliel in a discussion with an unnamed disciple,
whom Bloch believes to have been the apostle Paul. Cf. Wright,
Ecclesiastes, 22 ff.

5. [בא]="set," cf. the As. irib šamši="sun setting," and sit šamši=
"sun rising." Ha., for metrical reasons, regards הַשֶּׁמֶשׁ after בא and הוא before שָׁם as glosses. Zap., for similar reasons, expunges the phrase הוא זוֹרֵחַ
שָׁם. The metrical form of the book, as a whole, is, however, too unsubstantial a theory on which to base textual criticism (see Introd. §9).—[שׁוֹאֵף] and
זוֹרֵחַ are participles denoting continuity of action.—[אל מקומו], according
to the accentuation, is separated from שׁוֹאֵף and connected with the first
part of the verse. Many interpreters endeavor to adhere to this punctu-
ation, but the results of the efforts are unsatisfactory. Del. has clearly
shown that this accentuation must be disregarded, and מְקוֹמוֹ taken with
שׁוֹאֵף. Many render the phrase "to his place where he rises," supposing
that אֲשֶׁר has been omitted before שָׁם. (So Kö. §380d). This seems
needlessly to obscure the thought. The force of the participles justifies the
rendering given above. The whole phrase is omitted in a small group
of MSS. (cf. Dr.). The ancient translators, with the exception of 'A

(who renders εἰσπνεῖ), ha,e missed the meaning. ᴳ renders ἕλκει, Σ
and Θ ἐπαναστρέφει, Jer. "revititur," ᴪ tā‘eb, "he returns," and the
ᵀ שׁחִיף "to crawl." Gr., despairing of finding in שׁוֹאף a satisfactory
meaning, emends the text to שׁב אף, rendering "returns to its place, again
it rises." This is, however, unnecessary.

6. The repetition of סׁובֵב] strengthens the idea of continuance expressed by the part. *Cf.* Da. §29, rem. 8. *Cf.* also Dt. 2²⁷ 14²² 16²⁰
28⁴³ and Ex. 23³⁰. In the last clause the same effect is accomplished by
combining הׁולֵךְ with סׁבָב. *Cf.* Kö. §361q. ᴳ, ᵀ, ᴪ and ᴴ wrongly take
the first clause with the preceding verse, as applying to the sun.
—צׁפון]="The hidden," and so "north," from צׁפן "to hide," *cf.* BD*B*.
and Ges.ᴮᵘ·—דָרׁום], from דׁרר="to flow," "give light" (*cf.* BD*B*.
204b and Kö., Vol. II, 1, §77), is regularly used for "south" in contrast
to צׁפון, *cf.* Ez. 40²⁴· ²⁷· ²⁸ 42¹⁸. It is a poetical and late word. *Cf.*
Job 37¹⁷.—עַל] is to be taken with the following verb (Del., Zö., Wr.).
Sieg. changes it to אֶל because Θ reads Ἐπί. Zap., p. 10, omits the first
clause of the vs. from הׁולֵךְ to צָׁפון for metrical reasons—a change which
the metrical theory seems too insecure to support.

7. As Kn., Del. and Wild. point out, שׁוּב with לְ and an inf. means
"to do a thing again," *cf.* Gn. 30³¹ Ho. 11⁹ Job 7⁷ Ezr. 9¹⁴. See Kö.
§399v. The idea is not that the streams return from the abyss by subterranean channels (ᵀ and Gins. and Cox), nor to the return of water in
vapor to fall as rain, as in Job 36²⁷· ²⁹ (Heng.). As Zö. and Pl. note, the
thought, as in Aristophanes, *Clouds,* 1248,

> (The sea though all the rivers flow to it,
> Increaseth not in volume,)

is confined to the fact that the flowing rivers accomplish nothing. The
participles, as in the preceding verses, denote the continuity of the
action.—נחל] is a more general term than נהר.—שׁב] is not = שׁמה
(Sieg.), but to be taken with שׁ="where," like שׁם.....אשֶׁר (Wr.).
מקׁום is in the const. state before the rel. sentence, שׁ פָקׁום being equivalent to פָקׁום אֲשֶׁר, *cf.* Gn. 39²⁰ Lv. 4²⁴ and Kö. §277v, so, Hit., Zö., Wr.
—מלׁא] in Jos. 3¹⁵ is="overflow," so, perhaps, here (Sieg.).

8. דׁברים] Kn., Heng., Heil., Ew. and Gins. take as equal to "words,"
and think the first clause means that speech is wearied in telling of the
ceaseless activities of nature. Most commentators—Wang., Vaih.,
Zö., Del., Pl., Wr., No., Gr., Wild., Sieg., Vl., Cox, McN., Gen. and
Ha.—rightly take it in the sense of "things." The meaning then is that
all things—the sun, the winds, the streams and all natural objects—are
weary with their ceaseless round of activities. This view is altogether
to be approved. Re.'s rendering: "Tout est difficile à expliquer,"
misses the point.—יָגֵעַ] as an adj. occurs but twice in the OT. outside
of this passage, Dt. 25¹⁸ 2 S. 17², and in both of these passages it has

the passive sense, "weary," not the active, "wearisome" (Dale): it accordingly means "weary" here.——לִדְבַּר], as Wr. observes, the object
to be supplied is כל.——מִשְּׁמֹעַ] Hit. and Zö. render: " so that I will not
longer hear." This, as Wr. notes, is unnecessary, for שבע is constructed
with מן of the thing satisfied, cf. ch. 6³, Ps. 104¹³ Job 19²². Kö. §399i
notes that מן might have stood before רְאִית instead of ל, cf. Is. 53¹¹.

9. מַה שֶׁ] is a late expression. 𝕲 and 𝔚 wrongly render it as an interrogative. It is used by Q. in the following passages: 3¹⁵ 6¹⁰ 7²⁴ 8⁷
10¹⁴, in all of which it signifies "that which," or "whatever." It is
parallel to Aram. מן דִי, cf. Kau., GBA. §22²; but מי אשר is used in a
similar way in earlier Heb., cf. Ex. 32³³.——היה] as Del. and Wr. note,
is used of the phenomena of nature, which occur without human inter-
vention (cf. 3¹⁵· ²² 6¹⁰· ¹² 8⁷ 10¹⁴ 11²), and עָשֹׂה of occurrences which result from human action (cf. 1¹³· ¹⁴ 2¹⁷ 4³ 9³· ⁶).——אין כל חדש] is a universal
negative in Heb., cf. Nu. 11⁶ Dt. 8⁹ Dn. 1⁴ and Kö. §352s-w. The
construction has passed into NT. idiom, cf. οὐ πᾶς, Mt. 24²² Lk. 1³⁷
21²⁷. Zap. and Ha. omit on metrical grounds the phrase ואין . . . . . השמש.
Although it is a striking coincidence that the two advocates of the metrical theory agree at this point, the fact does not overbalance the uncertainty of the metrical theory (see *Introd.* §9). The discarded phrase
materially strengthens the statement, and it is difficult to believe that
the original writer did not pen it.

10. יש], philologically equivalent to As. *išu*, is different from היה in that
it assumes existence as a fact. Its use is equivalent to saying: "There
really are things " (cf. Kö. §§325 i-m, 338 l-n).——דְּבָר], if the present
MT. stands="thing," cf. on v. 8. MT. is supported by 𝔚, Σ and the
Tal., 𝕲, 𝔏, 𝕶 and 𝔖 support the reading שׁידבר ויאמר, "there is one who
speaks and says." McN., p. 138, thinks this reading is older than
Aqiba, and that the present reading of MT. was introduced in Aqiba's
recension. The testimony of the Versions would support this view.
See the collected testimony, Euringer, *Masorahtext*, 35.——זֶה] follows
רָאָה in 7²⁷· ²⁹, in both of which cases it is connected with the following
word by a conjunctive accent. Here, on the other hand, there is a disjunctive *Tiphkha*. Wr. observes that the accent gives the clause the
force of "See this, new it is." McN. regards זֶה as=Mishnic זֶהוּ (cf.
Kelim, 5¹⁰), not as the obj. of רָאָה.——הוּא . . . . . זֶה is one of Q.'s favorite expressions, cf. 2²³ 4⁸ 6² and היא . . . . . זֶה in 5¹⁸.——כְּבָר] occurs in Biblical Hebrew only in Ec. (cf. ch. 1¹⁰ 2¹⁶ 3¹⁵ 4² 6¹⁰ 9⁶· ⁷), though common in J.Ar.
It is connected with the Ar. *kabara* and Eth. *kabra*, "to be great." Its
meaning seems to be "already," *B*DB. Ja. assigns it also the meaning
"long ago," but none of the passages from the Mishna, which he quotes,
substantiates this meaning. The word constitutes one of the Aramaisms
of our book.——לעלמים אשר היה], the verb in the phrase, should strictly be היו.
as five MSS. actually read (cf. Ken.), but Heb. is not always careful about

the agreement of subj. and pred., *cf.* ch. 10¹⁵ Je. 48¹⁵ Zc. 11⁵ Dn. 9²⁴. Some regard עלמים as a pl. of eminence (Kö. §260k), and such plurals regularly take a sing. vb. (*cf.* Da. §116, rem. 4).—מֶלְפָּנֵינוּ] is a strengthened form of לְפָנֵינוּ, *cf.* Ju. 1¹⁰.—**11.** זִכְרוֹן] is usually regarded as cstr. before the prep. לְ; so, Kn., Heil., Zö., Ew. and Kö. §336z. Del. observes that such refinements of syntax are not to be expected in our writer, and that זִכְרוֹן is to be taken as a variant spelling of זְכָרוֹן. He compares יִהְרוֹן and כִּשְׁרוֹן, but adduces no example where זִכְרוֹן is an abs. Wr. repeats Del., adding that זִכְרוֹן may be regarded as a form more common in later Heb., but still adduces no example. Sieg. agrees with them. There is in reality no parallel, so far as I know, which substantiates this view. In the OT., wherever זִכְרוֹן occurs, except here and in ch. 2¹⁶, it is in the cstr. state (*cf.* Lv. 23²⁴ Is. 57⁸). It is better here to regard the word as cstr. before לְ, especially since such construction finds parallels in the Mishna (*cf.* יוֹשֵׁבֵי לָפָבֵי, הוֹלְכֵי לָבֵית *Aboth*, 5¹⁴, *ibid.*, 5¹⁵, *cf.* also 5¹¹ and Kö. §336z).—רִאשֹׁנִים] and אֲחֲרֹנִים] were formerly incorrectly understood to refer to things, but modern writers, except Gr. and Ha., take it rightly to refer to persons. The masc. forms refer to persons (*cf.* Gn. 33² Dt. 19¹⁴ Job 18²⁰), and the fem. forms to things (*cf.* Is. 42⁹ 43⁹˙ ¹⁸ 46⁹).—קדמנים and קדמניות are similarly used, the former of persons, the latter adverbially (*cf.* 1 S. 24¹³ Is. 43¹⁸).

1¹²–2²⁶ QOHELETH'S EXPERIMENTS IN THE CHARACTER OF THE SON OF DAVID.

Qoheleth represents himself in the character of Solomon as seeking wisdom more than anyone else, but finding in it no permanent satisfaction (1¹²⁻¹⁸); then, as seeking joy in material and sensual things, with the same result (2¹⁻¹¹); next, as trying the virtues of folly and finding them no better (2¹²⁻¹⁷); and lastly, he states the conclusion to which his various experiments have led him (2¹⁸⁻²⁶).

¹². I Qoheleth was king over Israel in Jerusalem. ¹³. And I gave my heart to search and to explore with wisdom concerning all that is done under the heavens—it is a bad business God has given the children of men in which to toil. ¹⁴. I saw all the works which are done under the sun and behold the whole is vanity and desire of wind.

¹⁵. The crooked cannot be straightened,
And the wanting cannot be numbered.

¹⁶. And I spake with my heart, saying: Behold I have greatly increased wisdom above all who were before me over Jerusalem, and my heart has abundantly beheld wisdom and knowledge. ¹⁷. And I gave my heart to know wisdom and knowledge, madness and folly, I know that

this also is desire of wind.   ¹⁸· For in much wisdom is much vexation, and he who increases knowledge increases pain.

2¹· I said in my heart: "Come now, I will test thee with joy, so look upon good," and behold also it was vanity.   ²· Of laughter I said it is mad, and of joy, what does this accomplish?   ³· I searched out in my heart how to stimulate my flesh with wine, while my heart was acting with wisdom, and to lay hold on folly until I should see what good there is for the children of men to practise under the heavens the few days of their life.   ⁴· I undertook great works; I built me houses, I planted me vineyards.   ⁵· I made me gardens and parks and planted in them every kind of fruit tree.   ⁶· I made me pools of water in order to water a plantation springing up with trees.   ⁷· I bought bondmen and bondmaids and had slaves born in my house; also I had many possessions of cattle and sheep—more than all who were before me in Jerusalem.   ⁸· I collected for myself silver and gold, the treasures of kings and provinces; I provided me male and female musicians and the luxuries of the sons of men—all sorts of concubines (?).   ⁹· And I became continually more wealthy above all who were before me in Jerusalem; also my wisdom remained with me.   ¹⁰· And nothing which my eyes asked did I withhold from them; I did not deny my heart any joy, for my heart rejoiced in all my toil, and this was my portion of all my toil.   ¹¹· And I turned (to look) at all my works which my hands had wrought and at the toil which I had toiled to accomplish and behold the whole was vanity and desire of wind and there is no gain under the sun.   ¹²· And I turned to observe wisdom and madness and folly, for what (can) the man (do) that comes after the king?   That which he (the king) hath done.   ¹³· And I saw that wisdom has an advantage over folly like the advantage of light over darkness.   ¹⁴· As for the wise man his eyes are in his head, but the fool walks in darkness.   But I know also that the same event will happen to both of them.   ¹⁵· And I said in my heart according to the fate of the fool thus will it happen to me, so why have I then been wise overmuch?   So I said in my heart: this also is vanity.   ¹⁶· For the wise. like the fool, has no remembrance forever, inasmuch as in days to come both will have been already forgotten.   And how does the wise die like the fool!   ¹⁷· And I hated life, for evil unto me was the work which is done under the sun, for all is vanity and desire of wind.   ¹⁸· And I hated all my toil which I toiled under the sun because I shall leave it to the man who shall come after me.   ¹⁹· And who knows whether he will be a wise man or a fool?   And he shall rule over all my toil on which I have toiled and exercised wisdom under the sun.   This also is vanity.   ²⁰· And I turned about to give my heart up to despair concerning all the toil which I had toiled under the sun.   ²¹· For there is a man whose toil is with wisdom and intelligence and success, and to a man who has not toiled for it he will leave his portion.   This also is vanity and a great evil. 22. For what shall be to a man for all his toil and the striving of his heart in which he toils under the sun. 23. For all his days are pains, and his task vexation, also at night his heart does not rest, moreover this is vanity. 24. For there is nothing better for a man than that he should eat and drink and enjoy himself in his toil. Also this I saw that it is from the hand of God. 25. For who can eat and who can enjoy apart from him? 26. FOR TO A MAN WHO IS GOOD BEFORE HIM HE GIVES WISDOM AND KNOWLEDGE AND JOY, BUT TO THE SINNER HE GIVES AS A TASK TO GATHER AND AMASS TO GIVE TO ONE WHO IS GOOD BEFORE GOD. Also this is vanity and a desire of wind.

12. *Was king over Israel in Jerusalem*]. The author indicates that he proposes to speak in the character of Solomon. It is his aim to offer proof of the general position taken in the prologue by adducing the concrete experiences of Solomon. Solomon had had wealth, wisdom and opportunities for sensual enjoyment. He had drawn upon every source of "profit." To adduce these concrete experiences would be the most powerful literary form in which to couch his argument, so in this verse he assumes that mask. He mentions the fact of kingship as a claim to especial opportunities for experience in these matters, since "the wisdom of a learned man cometh by opportunity" (BS. 38²⁴). The words: *"over Israel in Jerusalem,"* exclude any king of the northern kingdom and sufficiently indicate Solomon.—**13.** *Gave my heart*]. This is not an uncommon idiom for turning the attention (*cf.* ch. 1¹⁷ 7²¹ 8⁹·¹⁰ Dn. 10¹² 1 Ch. 22¹⁹). It is parallel to *"set one's heart* (or mind)" (Job 7¹⁷ Ps. 48¹³ 62¹⁰ 2 Ch. 12¹⁴ 30¹⁹). It is used mainly in late Biblical Heb. *"Search"* and *"explore"* are synonyms. They do not refer to higher and lower forms of investigation (Zö.), but to different methods. "Search" means to investigate the roots of a matter, and "explore" to investigate a subject on all sides (Del., Wr.).—*Is Done*]. This is, as in v. 9, employed of human activities.

14. *Works*] refers also to human actions.—*Desire of Wind*], *i.e.*, an unsatisfying desire. The word for *desire* has occasioned much discussion. The peculiar phrase occurs in Biblical Heb. only in this book, where it occurs seven times altogether (1¹⁴ 2¹¹· ¹⁷· ²⁶ 4⁴· ⁶ 6⁹). See critical note.—**15.** *The crooked cannot be straightened*].—Re., Pl., Wr. and Gen. are probably right in re-

garding this as an aphorism quoted by Qoheleth because appli-
cable to his theme.—*The wanting cannot be numbered*], i.e., an
untold number of things are lacking.

16.·*All who were before me over Jerusalem*], it is difficult for the
writer to maintain the mask which he has assumed, and as Del.,
Wr., Wild. and McN. have noted, he falls into an anachronism
here in this phrase, since Solomon had but one predecessor, David.
It is hardly possible with Heng., Zö., No. and Pl., to think of Jeb-
usite kings, or Melchisedek (Gn. 14¹⁸), and Adonizedek (Jos. 10³,
cf. also, 2 S 5.⁷), or Ethan, Heman, and Calcol (1 K. 4³¹). It is
more likely the phrase of one who was familiar with some set formula, like the Assyrian "the kings my predecessors," which he supposed it appropriate for kings to use. After letting the mask slip
once more in 2⁷·⁹, he finally throws it aside altogether in 2¹².—**17.**
Madness and folly], "*Contrariis contraria intelliguntur.*" Qoheleth determined to know not only wisdom but the opposite.—**18.** *In
much wisdom is much vexation*]. The burden of the verse is *blessed
be ignorance!* It reminds one of the point of view of J. in Gn. 3,
where toil and pain in child-bearing are attributed to knowledge.

2¹. *I will test thee with joy*]. Having proved the futility of wisdom (1¹²⁻¹⁸), Qoheleth now tries material pleasures (2¹⁻¹¹). In this
introductory verse he expresses his resolution. The context shows
that *joy* is used of the pleasure derived from the possession of
wealth and the excitements of sensual pleasure.—**2.** *Of laughter*],
unrestrained merriment is represented by laughter and pleasure
in general by "joy." To the beholder both often seem folly or
delirium. Scholars differ as to whether we should translate "of"
or, "to." Gins., Ew. and Wild. advocate the latter view and render as though the sentence were a direct address. Heil., Vaih.,
Del., Sieg., and most recent interpreters take the former view,
which the above rendering follows. Parallel examples are found
in Ps. 3² 22³¹ 41⁵. Kn. remarks that *laughter* means "lusty rejoicing," *cf.* 7⁶ 10¹⁹.—**3.** *Searched*], as Del. notes, this is, as in
Nu. 10³³, equivalent to "explore." Combined with "heart" it
denotes discovery by mental processes (so Wr.).—*Stimulate*],
literally to "draw" (*cf.* Dt. 21³ 1 K. 22³⁴ 2 Ch. 18³³ Job 24²²),
but here used figuratively, either in the sense of "stimulate,"

"give pleasure to," or "refresh." It resembles Talmudic usage as Del., No. and Wild. have observed.—*My heart was acting with*]. This is, as several interpreters have noted, in the nature of a parenthesis.—**4.** *I built houses, I planted vineyards*]. From the excitements of wine Qoheleth turns to the more healthy pleasures of a country gentleman's enterprises. As he is speaking in the character of Solomon, probably he had in mind Solomon's buildings (*cf.* 1 K. 7 9[1, 16] 10[18ff]). Near these buildings there were vineyards (*cf.* Je. 52[7] Ct. 6[2] 8[11]). *Works*] is used by metonomy for the gains of work, wealth, riches, possessions (*cf.* 1 S. 25[2]).

5. *Gardens and Parks*]. To the vineyards, gardens and parks were added. The former were perhaps devoted to practical vegetables (*cf.* Dt. 11[10]), and the latter to trees, though in older Hebrew "garden" stood for both. Frequent allusion is made in the OT. to the "King's gardens" (Je. 39[4] 52[7] 2 K. 25[4] and Ne. 3[15]). Such enclosures, constructed by the wealthy, contained refreshing streams, cool shade and all manner of fruit trees (*cf.* Jos. *Antiq.* viii, 7[3] and *Qur'an,* 13[35] and 55[46ff]). Sometimes they also contained wild animals (Xen. *Anab.* i, 2[7]). How in the hot and thirsty east such scenes attracted the imagination may be seen in the exaggerated description in *Qur'an,* 47[16ff].—**6.** *Pools of water*]. In Palestine, where the rainfall of the winter has to be stored for the long drought of summer, rock-cut reservoirs or cisterns are of such importance that their structure was a worthy boast for a king (*cf.* Mesha of Moab, *Moabite Stone,* ll. 9 and 23–25). Ne. 2[14] 3[15], as well as the Siloam inscription and Jos., BJ., v. 4[2], testify to the existence of an important reservoir near Jerusalem, while Ct. 7[5] alludes to one in Heshbon and 2 S. 4[12] to one in Hebron. There may be seen to-day near ancient Etam three such reservoirs, which are attributed by tradition to Solomon. The importance of such reservoirs to gardens is alluded to in Is. 1[30] and 58[11].

7. *Bondmen and bondmaids*]. Slaves formed a large percentage of the population in all the civilized countries of antiquity. How frequently they were bought and sold may be seen by consulting any body of Babylonian contracts such as *Keilinschriftliche Bibliothek,* Vol. IV. The purchase of new slaves was probably an experience in the life of every wealthy man. About 750 B.C., when the "Book of the Covenant" was written, a slave was valued at 30 shekels (Ex. 21³²), while after the exile they were valued at 50 shekels (Lv. 27³). For Solomon's slaves, see 1 K. 9²⁰· ²¹ and 10⁵. Slaves are associated with flocks and herds as evidences of wealth (cf. Gn. 12¹⁶ 30⁴³).—*All who were before me*], the author permits his Solomonic mask to slip, for this implies that he had had many predecessors in Jerusalem.—**8.** *Treasures of kings*]. To the delights of rural possessions, Qoheleth added the treasures of a monarch who controls the taxes of large provinces, and the luxuries of sensual gratification. He is still posing as the "Son of David," and these details were no doubt suggested by 1 K. 4⁷ 9²⁸ 10¹⁴ 7¹⁵· ²⁷ 11¹⁻³.—**9.** *Continually more wealthy*], in 1¹⁶ Qoheleth claims to have surpassed others in wisdom, so here he claims to have surpassed them in wealth. In the last clause of the vs. there is probably a reference to vs. 3. He means that in spite of his folly in the pursuit of wealth and sensual delights his wisdom remained with him. It suggests that this clause about wisdom has also a forward look, and refers in part to the next verse.—**10.** *Not deny my heart any joy*]. Still drawing on the accounts of Solomon's splendor for his illustration, Qoheleth represents himself as able to gratify every desire. He denied himself no material possession or pleasure, and, like the man in the parable of Jesus (Lk. 16²⁵), he obtained enjoyment—a real good—for a time. This was his advantage, or gain from his toil. The passage was suggested by the statements of Solomon's wealth in 1 K. 4²⁶ᶠᶠ (Heb. 5⁶ᶠᶠ), and 10⁵ᶠᶠ. The eyes are used by metonomy for desire which is not sensual, cf. 1 K. 20⁶ Ps. 145¹⁵ Ec. 1⁸ 4⁸ and Pr. 27²⁰. Similarly we have in 1 Jn. 2¹⁶ "lust" (literally, "desire") of the eyes, which, though closely associated with "lust (*i.e.*, desire) of the flesh," is not identical with it.—*Withhold*], for the meaning cf. Gn. 27³⁶ Nu. 11¹⁷· ²⁵, where the word is rendered "take away," "take of."—*Portion*] is here equivalent to gain or reward.—**11.** *And I turned*]. This is as Del. and others have noted a pregnant construction, meaning "I turned to look," cf. Job 6²⁸. It implies that Qoheleth turned from the absorption of his active material labors and his sensual pleasures to consider the meaning of them all, and finds that, like the

delights of wisdom, the delights of possession are but vanity.
From v. 3b to this point a cycle is completed—an experiment has
been carried through and a result reached.

12. Qoheleth is now led to make a comparison between wisdom
and folly, to discover, if possible, whether wisdom had any real
advantage. The last clause of the verse is difficult of interpretation because the text is corrupt. It is rendered above from an
emended text. For reasons and the opinions of interpreters, see
critical note.—**13.** Sieg. assigns this verse and 14a to his Q³, or
Hokma annotator, on the ground that it contradicts Q.'s thought,
but the objection does not seem well taken. As Pl. suggests Qoheleth might believe that all is vanity, and yet hold that it is better
to face the reality intelligently than to be carried into the vortex of
oblivion while absorbed in senseless folly. A line from the *Iliad*
(17^{647}) is apposite: "And if our fate be death, give light, and let us
die." It is the attitude of a strong, though agnostic mind. The
comparison of wisdom to light is kindred to the use of light in Is.
51^{11} Ps. 36^9 43^3 119^{105} Pr. 6^{23}. For "darkness" in the sense of
"folly," *cf*. Job 37^{19}. *Cf*. also Job 12^{25}.

14. *His eyes are in his head*]. The wise man has this advantage,
he can see. The expression, as Gins. notes, is equivalent to "his
eyes are open." The fool goes on in unconscious darkness.
Nevertheless the same death overtakes both. The wise ought to
have some advantage, but experience shows that he does not.
The fact that death relentlessly claims both wise and foolish, oppressed others. *Cf*. Ps. 49^{10} Job 21^{26} and Horace's

> Sed omnes una manet nox
> Et calcanda semel via leti.—*Od*. I, 28^{15ff}.

15. *According to the fate of the fool*.] The fact that death buries
the wise and the foolish in the same oblivion, makes Qoheleth pro-
nounce great wisdom vanity, in spite of the fact that he has just
seen in wisdom the advantage of reality. *I said in my heart*], see
on 1^{16}. On *Vanity*, see on 1^2.

16. *The wise die like the fool*]. Wild. has noted that Qoheleth
contradicts here Pr. 10^7 and Ps. 112^6. This vs. is quoted and opposed in *Wisdom* 1^{4a}.—*Has no remembrance forever*]. *Cf*. on 1^{11}.

The discovery that at death both are alike strikes Qoheleth as a painful surprise. It is not what one would expect.—**17.** *And I hated life*]. This expresses a strong revulsion of feeling from something, *cf.* 2 S. 13¹⁵ Is. 1¹⁴ Am. 5²¹ Mal. 1³. The fact that the wise are swallowed up by the same oblivion as the fool caused this revulsion of feeling. As Plumtre remarks, the only logical outcome of such pessimism is suicide, but from Qoheleth to Hartmann it has never produced suicide. A pessimist who is able to vent his feelings in literary expression continues to enjoy life.—*Evil unto me was the work*], *i.e.*, it was evil in my eyes.—*Vanity and desire of wind*], see on 1¹⁴.

18. *I hated all my toil . . . because I shall leave it*]. Qoheleth not only loathed life, but also his toil. This latter revulsion was produced by the thought that he must leave all the results of his labor to some one else. Probably the reference is to such works as were described in vv. 4, 10, 11. As Plumtre points out others have been oppressed by the same thought. Mazarin walked through his palace and said to himself: *Il faut quitter tout cela,* while Frederic William IV of Prussia, looking at his garden at Potsdam, said to his friend Bunsen: *Das auch, das soll ich lassen.*— *And I hated*] is the repetition of a formula. Qoheleth is fond of such repetition.—**19.** *Who knows whether he shall be a wise man or a fool?*] One must not only leave his possessions, but he does not know into whose hands they will fall after he is gone, or whether his own wise policies concerning them will be pursued or not. This added to Qoheleth's bitterness. The thought is similar to that of Ps. 39⁶ and Lk. 12²⁰. The Targ. takes this and the preceding vs. to refer to Rehoboam, but Qoheleth's statement is entirely general. As No. and Sieg. have noted, Rehoboam was forty-one years old when Solomon died (1 K. 14²¹), and Solomon must have known whether he was a fool or not.—**20.** *Give my heart up to despair*]. The facts stated in the preceding verses dried up the springs of Qoheleth's impulse to active labor.—**21.** *To a man who has not toiled he will leave his portion*]. Qoheleth broods over a fact and views it from different aspects. This vs. is not a repetition of vs. 19; the thought which tortures him here is not that his heir may be a fool, but the mere idea that that upon which one

toils with so much care should go into the possession of one who
has never worked for it at all.—**22.** *What shall be to a man*], as Gins.
suggests, this corresponds to "what advantage to a man," of
ch. 1³. The thought has nearly completed a great cycle, and
Qoheleth now comes back to sum up his reasons for pessimism.
—**23.** *All his days are pains*]. This verse echoes the experience of those who follow pursuits which cannot satisfy the heart.
They obtain no real pleasure even in the performance of their
chosen occupations. One phrase of it—"his days are pain"—is
in substance quoted and opposed in Wisd. 2¹.—**24, 25.** *There is
nothing better for a man*]. The rendering of these verses given
above rests on an emended text, the authority for which is given
in the critical notes below. Qoheleth here states the conclusions
to which his various investigations had led. The best thing for
man is to get the most physical pleasure he can out of life. This
is not stated from the Epicurean standpoint, but from the point
of view of Hebrew monotheism. Qoheleth, as a Hebrew, believes
that this would not be the order of life, if God had not so ordained
it. The sentiment of this verse is quoted and denied in Wisd. 2⁶.

26ᵃ. *To a man who is good He gives wisdom*]. Recent interpreters have, with some differences in detail, regarded the verse as a
gloss; so Wild., Sieg., McN., and Ha.   Sieg. and McN. divide it
into two glosses, regarding: "*This also is vanity and a desire of
wind*," as a touch of a late hand.   That the verse with the exception of the last clause is the work of a *Chasid* glossator, must be
granted. It contradicts Q.'s fundamental philosophy. The
doctrine that all the good things of life come to the morally good,
finds expression in many parts of the OT., and the thought that
the good finally receive the fruits of the toil of the wicked is also
not lacking (*cf.* Job 27¹⁷ Pr. 13²² 28⁸). Such a cheerful view of
the moral order of the universe is, however, totally opposed to
Q.'s whole thought, and justifies us in seeing here the work of
another hand. I cannot agree with Sieg. and McN., though, in
seeing the hand of an annotator in the last clause. If it originally
followed vs. 25, it expressed, as pointed out above, an intelligible
thought, and one thoroughly consonant with Q.'s point of view.

26ᵇ. *Desire of wind*] originally followed vs. 25. Q.'s declaration

was, that there is nothing better for a man than to eat and drink
and enjoy life, that God had ordained that this is man's destiny,
but that there is no real satisfaction even in this—this also being
vanity and a desire of wind. This is a note of profound pessimism.

1¹². הייתי]. The tense has occasioned a curious amount of discussion
among commentators. It is in fact a perfect denoting a state, whether
mental or physical (*cf.* Dr. §11, Da. §40, Kö. §124 and Ex. 2²² Gn.
42¹¹ Ps. 15⁶). The Talmud (*Gittin*, 68b), *Midrash Yalkut*, AE., and Ra.,
thinking in accordance with later Hebrew that it could be used only of
past events, adopted the legend that in his old age Solomon was deposed
by Asmodæus, king of the demons, and then wrote, "I *was* king."
Gins. agrees that the writer was no longer king. Gr., who believes that
Herod the Great was referred to, falls back on the theory that היה means
here "became," not "was." Bullock quotes Louis XIV, who toward
the end of his life used to say: "*Quand j'étois roi*," and supposes that
Solomon, like Louis, had become weary of kingship. Of course Q. is
using the character as a mask, but the indefiniteness of the tense in
Heb. suits his purpose well, as it would be right if Solomon were really
writing. מלך על ישראל], the more usual expression is מלך ישראל (*cf.* 1 S.
26²⁰ 1 K. 15⁹ Ho. 1¹ 10¹⁵ Am. 1¹ 7¹⁰, etc.), but מלך על ישראל also occurs
(2 S. 19²³ 1 K. 4¹ 11³⁷). Ha.'s statement that מלך may mean "head of
a school," while substantiated by *Gittin*, 62a, and *Berakoth*, 64a, does not
fit the mask which Q. was wearing throughout the passage.

13. תור] has been claimed as a Græcism=σκέπτεσθαι, a Gr. philosophical term, but it is good Heb., being used of the spies in Nu. 13². ¹⁶. ¹⁷
(*cf.* McN., p. 40). ענין]="business," "occupation," occurs in OT.
only in Ec. (*cf.* 2²³. ²⁶ 3¹⁰ 4⁸ 5². ¹³). It is an Aramaic loan word, occurring in the Targ. on Ps. 19⁶ 41² Ct. 1¹. Ha. curiously regards this vs.
as a gloss, even though, according to his own rendering, it conforms to a
metrical standard.—14. שנעשׂו]. In the Mishna the usage of עשׂה is similar,
cf. Berakoth, 2⁶, *Baba Batra*, 10⁸.—רעיּת], a very ancient rendering derived from רעע=רצק "to break," makes it mean "breaking," "affliction,"
or "vexation of spirit." Thus, 𝔖, 𝔗, 𝔚, Ra., and AV. Another old
interpretation derived it from רעה to feed. So 'A, Θ, Σ, AE., Mich.,
Ros., Pl., Re. and RV.ᵐ. Others, as No. and Wild., take it from
רעה "to be behind" (*cf.* Gn. 32¹⁹. ²⁰). Most recent interpreters derive
it from רעה "to wish," "desire," "strive for," so 𝔊, Kn., Hit., Eur.,
Heil., Wang., Vaih., Gins., Ty., Zö., Gr., Del., Wr., Vl., Sieg., McN., Ha.,
RV., BDB., Ges.ᴮᵘ· These scholars differ, however, as to whether
it is or is not an Aramaism, and some, as McN., who so render it, derive
it from the stem רעה "to feed." Ges.ᴮᵘ· calls it an Aramaism, and it is
true that it occurs in the Aram. portion of Ezr. (5¹⁷ 7¹⁸). It occurs

twice, however, in the form רעת in Ph. inscriptions where there is no reason to suspect Aram. influence, one coming from the Piræus and the other from N. Africa (cf. G. A. Cooke, *No. Sem. Ins.*, 97; 150). Probably the root is רעה, which occurs in Ps. 37³ Pr. 15¹⁴ Hos. 12².—**15.** מְעֻוָּת], Pu. part. from עות used only in Pi. and Pu., "to be perverse, crooked." The figurative uses in Ps. 119⁷⁸ and Lam. 3³⁶˙ ⁵⁹ are no objection to this general meaning (cf. ch. 7¹³ 12³ Job 8³ 19⁶ 34¹² Am. 8⁵ Ps. 146⁹). Gins.'s inference from this latter passage that the word means "depressed" is unfounded. Bick. (10, 47) erases the second יוכל], but such repetitions are characteristic of Q. (cf. 4² 6³ 8¹²). לִתְקֹן] is rendered as a passive by several of the versions (𝕲 ἐπικοσμηθῆναι, J. C. *adornari*, 𝕾ᴴ *lemeṣṭabātu*, 𝕿 לאתקנא, 𝖀 *corriguntur*, Ar. *yuzayyana*). This leads Del. to observe that we should have the intrans. לְתְקֹן instead of the trans. לִתְקֹן; Gr. says לתקן must be a passive= לְהִתָּקֵן. Sieg., McN. and Dr. would emend to Ni. לְהִתְקֵן· A passive sense is necessary to correspond with לִהְמָנוֹת. The root occurs in BH. only in Qoh. (cf. 1¹⁵ 7¹³ 12⁹). It is found in Aram. (cf. Dn. 4³³ and Targ. to Jer. 7³ 18¹¹ and frequently elsewhere and in Tal. (see references in Ja.), and must be regarded as an Aramaism. Cf. As. *takana*.—חסרון] is, as Wr. observes, a α.λ. in BH. חֹסֶר occurs, however, in Dt. 28⁴⁸˙ ⁵⁷, in the sense of "want," "destitution." מַחְסוֹר from the same root, is the word usually employed (cf. Pr. 6¹¹). חִסָּרוֹן is often employed in Mish. and Tal. for "deficit" in money matters, see *BDB*. and Ja., *ad loc.*—לִהְמָנוֹת] from מָנָה. "to count," "number," occurs often in BH. Cf. As. *manū*, Ar. *manā*. Ew., who is followed by No., Wild. and Dr., suggested that הִמָּנוֹת is corrupted from הִמָּלוֹת, from הִמָּלֵא, "to be filled up," or "supplied." —**16.** דברתי אני], אני, as Gins. and Wr. have perceived, is not emphatic, but pleonastic, see ch. 2¹˙ ¹¹˙ ¹⁴˙ ¹⁵˙ ¹⁸˙ ²⁰˙ ²⁴, also Kö. §18, and Da. §107, rem. 1. —דברתי עם לב—]="commune with myself." Generally another preposition is employed as בלב, ch. 2¹˙ ¹⁵ Ps. 14¹ 15²; or אֶל לב, Gn. 24⁴⁵, or עַל לב. 1 S. 1¹³. Probably עם is employed to personify the heart, cf. דבֶּר יהוה עִמָּכֶם. Dt. 5⁴.—הגדלתי והוספתי]. Gr. thinks, from the form גְדַלְתִּי 2⁹, that the ה is a dittograph from the preceding הנה. The two perfects are coördinated when in reality one modifies the other, as Gins., Wr. and McN. have seen (cf. 2⁹, 8³). The combination means "I greatly multiplied" (cf. Da. §83, Dr. §157).—עַל כל], the prep., as Sieg., Vl. and Kö. (§308d) note, is equivalent to a comparative "more than" (cf. Gn. 48²² 49²⁶ Ps. 16² 89⁹ 137⁶ and also ὑπὲρ πολλοὺς, Gal. 1¹⁴).—היה] is sing., although אֲשֶׁר refers to pl. subject, perhaps as Gins. suggests because the plural is taken distributively in the writer's thought. Cf. Da. §116, rem. 1.—עַל ירושלם]. 140 MSS. read בירושלם (cf. Dr.). הַרְבֵּה, as Kn., Heil., Gins., Wr. and Wild. note, is a Hiph. inf. used adverbially (cf. H. §28, 2b, rem. g). It is a favorite word with our author (cf. 2⁷ 5⁶˙ ¹¹˙ ¹⁶˙ ¹⁹.

7¹⁶· ¹⁷ 9¹⁸ 12⁹).—ראה חכמה], as Sieg. observes, is a phrase peculiar to Qoh., *cf.* 2¹² 9¹³ and ראה דבר יהוה, Je. 2³¹. Pl. observes that הכמה and דעת correspond respectively to ethical and speculative knowledge.—**17.** McN. (pp. 57, 156) suspects לדעת.....ואתנה to be a corruption introduced into the text from 𝕲. It is omitted in a number of MSS. of 𝕲, but that seems a slender basis on which to discard it. Its omission, as he admits, may have been accidental.—וָאֶתְּנָה] is one of the three instances of *waw* consecutive with imper., which occur in this book. The others are ch. 4¹· ⁷ (*cf.* Dr. §133). Del. notes that the ending ה‏ָ, as in Gn. 32⁶ 41¹¹, expresses the writer's purpose (*cf.* Kö. §200b). Zap. and Ha. omit ורעת הללות ושכלות on metrical grounds. Gins. omits הללות ושכלות, believing that they crept in through a transcriber's carelessness, because in the next vs. only הכמה ורעת are mentioned. Gr. emends הללות to משלות, "proverbs," on the ground that 𝕾 and Targ. so render it. (It might be added that 𝕲 and 𝕶 also so translate.) He then takes שׂכלות= "intelligence," comparing Pr. 1⁶ Ps. 78² and BS. 3²⁹ 39². The omissions of Zap., Ha. and Gins. are not justified by the reasons urged, while Gr.'s emendation is unnecessary. All the versions, as Eur. has pointed out, go back to MT. Most recent interpreters have rightly taken שׂכלות to be a variant spelling of סכלות="folly," which occurs in 2³· ¹²· ¹³ 7²⁵ 10¹· ¹³ (so Dat., Kn., Del., Wr., Wild., Vl., McN. BDB. Ges.ᴮᵘ·)—a variant which is parallelled by משמרות for the usual מסמרות in ch.12¹¹. This spelling antedated the versions and was misunderstood by them, though many MSS. actually have סכְלוּה (*cf.* Ken.).—וֹרעת]. Del. and Vl. regard דעת as an inf. for לדעת, ל being omitted because expressed with the preceding inf., and so the Massorets took it, but as Gins. and McN. note, it should with 𝕲 and 𝕿 be taken as a noun and pointed וָרַעַת. "Wisdom and knowledge" balance "madness and folly."—הללות]. Probably to be read הללוּת (*cf.* ch. 10¹³, also BDB. and Kö. §262d), is from הלל, Ar. *halla*, to "shout," "rage" (so Del. and BDB.), is peculiar in BH. to Q.'s vocabulary (*cf.* 2¹² 7²⁵ 9³ 10¹³)="folly." Probably as 10¹³, and the fact that in 2¹² and 7²⁵ 𝕲 renders it in the sing., shows the ending is ית, an abstract, and not ות, a plural of intensity (Vl.). Ty. and Sieg. contend that it is a Græcism=μανία, but such an assumption seems unwarranted.— שֶׁנַם is not necessarily a late expression. *Cf.* כְּשֶׁנַם in J., Gn. 6³.—הוא [זה הוא], is used frequently in Q. as a copula. In Mishna it is frequently abbreviated to זהו (*cf.* Dr. §201 (3), and Da. §106, rem. 2).—רעיון] is a variant formation to רעות (*cf.* v. 14), with the same meaning. *Cf.* דִּמְיוֹן and דְּמוּת from the stem דמה.—**18.** כעס]. 𝕲, 𝕶, 𝕾ᴴ, 𝕬, read דעת=γνῶσις, instead. This fact has caused some discussion among scholars, but probably all of the three latter versions are dependent upon 𝕲, and its reading as Eur. suggests was a *lapsus calami*.—כעס="vexation," a word in Heb. found from the D. literature onward. It also occurs frequently in the Mishna (*cf.* Ja.). It occurs

several times in Q. (*cf.* 2²³ 7⁹ 11¹⁰). In the book of Job it is spelled
כעש (see Job 5² 6² 10¹⁷ 17⁷).— יוסיף] Hit., Wr., No., Vl. and Kö. §3440
take it as a part. Some regard it as a pure Kal., misspelled for יֻסָף.
others as a Hiph., "returning to a Kal." Del., however, regards it as
a regular imperf. The latter is the preferable view. The sentence is
similar to Prov. 12¹⁷ 18²².

2¹. אמרתי אני]. The אני is pleonastic, as was the אני of 1¹⁶. Heng.
claims that it is emphatic, but most scholars take the opposite view
(*cf.* Gins., Zö., and Da. §107, rem. 1).— בלבי] is a variant of the expression
עם לבי, 1¹⁶. For parallel usage see the citations made there. The rest
of the vs. shows that Q. was not saying *in* his heart, but talking *to* his
heart, for he addresses to it an exhortation. (See *BDB*.)—אנסכה] has occasioned much discussion. The Targ. and Mid., which Bick. follows,
evidently read אֲנַסֶּנֶה = "I will test it;" 𝔐 made it a Ni. of נסך, "to pour
out." AE. took it from נסך and supposed that "wine" was to be supplied as an object. Most modern interpreters follow 𝔊 and take it
from נסה = "to test," regarding the כָה as a strengthened form of ךָ,
Wr. observes that the verb is used with ב of instrumentality (*cf.* ch. 7²³
1 K. 10¹). Wr. also observes with justice that the longer כה is used (1)
to make the suffix more distinct in words ending in ךָ as אֶקְּכָה (2 S. 2²²);
(2) to lengthen in writing shorter words, as באכה (Gn. 10¹⁹); and (3)
less frequently in longer words, as here, where the usage perhaps marks
a later date.—ראה ב] the Hebrews used words which describe the action
of the primary senses in a figurative way. ראה means in such uses "to
experience," and is applied to the whole gamut of experiences from
life (היים, ch. 9⁹) to *death* (מות, Ps. 89⁴⁹). For some of these see ch. 2²⁴
3¹³ 5¹⁷ 8¹⁶ 9⁹ Ps. 16¹⁰ 85⁸ 89⁴⁹ Job 9²⁵ Is. 44¹⁶ La. 3¹. Ἰδεῖν and its
synonyms are similarly used in the NT. (*cf.* Lk. 2²⁶ Jn. 3³⁶ 8⁵¹). Frequently, as here, ב follows ראה (*cf.* Gn. 21¹⁶ 44³⁴ Je. 29³² Job 3⁹). An
examination of these passages will confirm the justice of the observation of Kn. and Wr. that those who hold that ראה ב׳ denotes enjoyment, are
quite mistaken. It is used for any experience, pleasurable or otherwise.—
2. מְהוֹלָל] is a Poal part. = "mad," *cf.* Ps. 102⁹. The Hithpoal means
"to act like a madman," *cf.* 1 S. 21¹⁴ Je. 25¹⁶ 46⁹ 50³⁸ 51⁷⁷ Na. 2⁵.
The versions, except 𝔏, render incorrectly.—זה is a fem., a shorter way
of writing זאת; so Heil., Zö., Del., Wr., No. and Kö. §§44, 45β. It is
also found in 5¹⁵ 7²³ 9¹³. As Del. noted, the use of זה in Q. resembles
that of the Mishna (*cf.* also *Introduction*, §10). This form occurs,
however, in earlier Heb., *cf.* 2 K. 6¹⁹, and Ez. 40⁴⁵. The form of the
question is identical with that in Gn. 3¹³.—עֹשָׂה] is fem. part. Kal agree-
ing with זה, which represents שמחה. Hit. supposed that some word like
פרי should be supplied after it, but it seems to be used as in Dn. 8²⁴
in the meaning of "accomplish a purpose." Kn. compared it with
Ju. 13¹⁵ and Ez. 28⁴, where definite objects follow it.—**3.** מָשַׁךְ]. In

favor of taking this to mean "refresh," Del. recalls *Khagiga*, 14a:
בעלי אגרא מושכין לבו של אדם כמים. The reading of 𝔊, κατεσκεψάμην εἰ ἡ
καρδία μου ἑλκύσει, may, as McN. has noted, indicate that the original
Heb. read והרתי אני בלבי משוך, the אני becoming corrupted to אם. 𝔊's
reading may, however, be a corruption of 'A, Σ and Θ's ἐν τῇ καρδίᾳ, etc.
The unanimity of reading in MSS. of 𝔊 is in favor of the former view.—
כיין [𝔊 and Θ read כיין. Ha., for metrical reasons, regards it as a gloss.
ולבי נהג בחכמה [is, for the same reason, rejected by him as a gloss.—נהג]
ordinarily means "lead" or "drive," as in 1 S. 30²⁰ Is. 11⁶ Ps. 80² La. 3² Ct.
8², but here, as McN. has pointed out, the meaning is much more nearly
akin to the Mishna (*cf. Aboda Zara*, 3⁴). It means (*BDB.*) "behaving
itself," to "be practised in" (Ja.), or "act." וילאחז] like למשוך is an indirect object of הור.—סכלוה] describes a course which seems reasonable,
but which turns out to be unwise (*cf.* Gn. 31²⁸ 1 S. 13¹³ 2 S. 24¹⁰ Is.
44²⁵), not absolute folly. The root, spelled with a *z*, occurs in this sense
in the code of Hammurabi (*cf. Zikilta*, Code XXIII, 39). In late Heb.
the Hith. means "be confused" (*cf.* Ja. 991ª). Q. determined to explore the courses of life which men counted foolish, to see whether there
might not be some good there.—אי זה] here means "what" (Kö. §§ 70
and 414m). It introduces an indirect question.—מספר] is an acc. of time
(Kö. §331a). It denotes what one can number and so comes to mean
"few" (*cf.* Gn. 34³⁰ Dt. 4²⁷ Is. 10¹⁹ Ps. 105¹² Job 16²²).—יָמֵי אֲשֶׁר
is in one MS. pointed אֲרֽוּ אֲשֶׁר, *cf.* Baer, מגלות, p. 61.—טוב], Θ renders
τὸ σύμφορον. Ty. notes that "good" was the great object of the search
of both Stoicism and Epicureanism, and finds in this expression evidence of Greek influence upon Q. But see *Introduction*, §6 (2).—
השמים [𝔊, 𝔙 and 𝔖 read השמש.—4. בָּתִּים] *battîm*, not *bottîm*. It is frequently
pointed with Metheg, as Baer and Dr. point it in this passage, to insure
the pronunciation. *Cf.* Ges.ᴷ §16, 2 *f.*—5. גן] is derived from the גנן,
stem גנן, "to protect" (*cf.* Is. 31⁵).—פרדס] occurs but twice outside Qoh.
in BH., Ct. 4¹³, where we have the sing. פַּרְדֵּס and Ne. 2⁸, where we have
הַפַּרְדֵּס. It is Persian and occurs, my colleague, Professor Collitz, in-
forms me, in the Avesta (*Vendidad*, 3, 18 (58), and 5, 49 (145), as *pairi-
dieza*, composed of *pairi*=Gr. περὶ, and *dieza*=Gr. τοῖχος, "wall."
In Pers. it means, according to Bartholomæ (*Altiranisches Wörterbuch*, col. 865), "Umwallung," or "circumvallation," according to
Darmsteter, "enclosure." It came into Gr. as παράδεισος and into Heb.
as פַּרְדֵּס. It also found its way into Semitic Babylonian (*cf.* Strass-
maier's *Cyrus*, No. 212, 3), into Aramaic, Arabic and Armenian. In
the Mishna (*Arakin*, 3²), the pl. is פרדסות instead of פרדסים as here.—
6. בְּרֵכוֹת] is constr. of בְּרֵכָה, which in BH. is frequently used for "pool"
or "reservoir." It also occurs in the Siloam inscr., l. 5. בְּרֵכוֹת is different
in form from בְּרָכוֹת, the constr. of בְּרָכָה, "blessing." Graetz, recalling
the facts that Solomon and Herod were the two great builders among

Israel's kings, and that Herod built reservoirs, uses this allusion as an argument for the Herodian date of the book.—מים] is omitted by Ha. on account of the metrical exigency. בְּרֵכָה is, it is true, usually not followed by מים in BH., but Nah. 2⁹ presents a parallel in favor of the present reading.—מהם] is used after בְּרֵכוֹת for מהן. There is considerable inaccuracy in BH. as to the agreement in gender in such cases. *Cf.* Ges.ᴷ· § 145u. See also below on 2¹⁰.—עצים] is acc. after the intrans. צוֹמֵחַ. *Cf.* Ges.ᴷ· §117y.—**7.** קנה], "to gain possession of," was used with בכסף for "buying" (*e.g.*, Am. 8⁶ Is. 43²⁴), and then came to mean "buy" when used without כסף (*cf.* Gn. 39¹ 47²³ Ex. 21¹ 2 S. 12³, etc.).—בני בית] are slaves born of slaves already in the master's possession (*cf.* Gn. 15²). The usual expression for this is ילידי בית See Gn. 14¹⁴ 17¹². ¹³. ²³. ²⁷ and Je. 2¹⁴.—בני בית היה] is a phrase with a pl. sub. and a sing. pred. Ty. thought the expression a collective, but Ges.ᴷ· (§145u) and Kö. (§349g) explain it better as a case where the sing. dependent gen. has attracted the verb to its number. One MS. has corrected to חיו (*cf.* Dr.).—מְקְנֶה] was read as a const. מִקְנָה by 𝕲, Θ, 𝕃 and 𝕊. On the pointing מקנה, see Baer, *Mg.*, p. 61. Buxtorf and Dr., in their editions, point is as a constr., and Wild. so regards it. The analogy of Gn. 26¹⁴ and 2 Ch. 32²⁹ favors this view. No., Wr., Vl. and Kö. (§330) explain מְקְנֶה as absol. and בקר and צאן as appositives of nearer definition. *Cf.* Ges.ᴷ· §127h.—הַרְבֵּה] is in one source pointed הַרְבֵּה. See Baer, *Mg.*, p. 61.—שֶׁהִיוּ] is read שֶׁהָיָה by 87 MSS. *Cf.* Dr. בירושלם . . . . . מכל] Bick. and Zap. omit for metrical reasons. Ha. goes still further, arbitrarily reducing the original verse to 7a. The reference to cattle and predecessors was in his view a gloss which reached its present form by the addition of two glosses.—**8.** כנסתי]. Kn.'s contention that כנס means "collect" only in late Heb. will hardly stand. Even its meaning in Is. 28²⁰ may be explained as a derivative of this meaning, as also the derived noun in Lv. 16⁴. The root is found in all the Semitic languages. In Heb., Aram., Syr. and Eth. it means to "collect," "assemble," etc., while the meanings in Ar. ("to lie down in a lair") and As. ("submit") probably go back to this primitive meaning. 𝕲ᴮᴬ reads καὶ γε χρύσιον. McN. suggests that the original text may have been סְגֻלָּה.—גם זהב] denotes a "treasure," or "precious treasure" (*cf.* Ex. 19⁵ Mal. 3¹⁷). In the Targ. it denotes "investments," "heirlooms," "treasures" (*cf.* Ja.). In As. its pl. *sugullāti* means "herds." Hit. compares the Ar. *shaghl*, "work," holding that סֻגְלָה means that which is worked upon, and so "valuable," "precious." It is doubtful, however, whether *Ghain* is an equivalent of ג.—המדינות], the article here is peculiar in view of the fact that מלכים is undefined. Gr. thought that some word had fallen out of the text adducing מְשַׁמְּעֵי מְדִינָה (Dn. 11²⁴) as a suggestive parallel, but as Ty. long ago noted, ch. 7²⁵ affords an example of the introduction of an article in a somewhat similar way, and makes it probable that מדינות is gen. after סגלת in spite of the article. מדינה itself, although it occurs once as early as 1 K. 20¹⁴, is an Aram. word, from דין. Its primary meaning is "place of judgment," but it is used in the sense of "province" (cf. BDB. Est. 1¹·³·²² 3¹²·¹⁴ La. 1¹· Ne. 1³ 11³ Dn. 8² 11²⁴, etc.). Bick. (p. 10) rejects the words וסגלת . . . . . חמדינות as a gloss, because the exigencies of his metrical theory demand it.—תענוגות] occurs in Mi. 2⁹ Pr. 19¹⁰ and BS. 41¹ in the sense of "pleasures," "luxuries." With this the Talmudic usage corresponds, cf. BDB., Ja., sub voce.—שרה ושרות] the sing. of a word followed by its pl. or masc. followed by fem. is used to denote totality, cf. Ges.ᴷ· §122v and Kö. §91. As to the meaning of these words the greatest diversity of opinion has prevailed. 𝕲 and 𝚯 read οἰνοχόον καὶ οἰνοχόας, "male and female cupbearers"—(i.e., שׂרה ושׂרות, cf. sub. voce) a reading supported by 𝕷, 𝕾 and 𝕶. 'A. read κυλίκιον καὶ κυλίκια, "a cup and cups." Similarly 𝟅 rendered "scyphos et urceos in ministerio ad vina fundenda." According to Jer., Σ read "mensarum species et appositiones." 𝕿 rendered מרובין דשרין מיא חמימי דשרין מיא פשורי ומרובין, i.e., "tubes (siphons?) which pour forth cold water and tubes which pour forth hot water." The ancients accordingly understood the word to refer to the pleasures of the table in some way. Among modern interpreters Dat. supports this view. According to Gins., Ibn Melech interpreted the words to mean כְּלֵי זֶמֶר, in which he was followed by Luther and AV. in: "musical instruments and that of all sorts." Dale, among recent interpreters, still holds to this. Ew. and Zö. derive the root from a word meaning "mass," "heap," and render "a heap and heaps." Heng. and Re. connect it with Ar. root shadda, robur, vehementia, and render "plenty of all sorts." Ra., whom Gr. follows, makes it refer to sedan-chairs. Most modern scholars take the words to refer to a harem and as completing the meaning תענוגות, which is thought to refer to sexual pleasures (so Död., Mic., Kn., Hit., Heil., Vaih., Wang., Ty., Gins., No., Vl., Wr., Pl. Eur., Wild., Sieg., McN., Gen., Marsh. and Ha.), though they differ as to the root from which it should be derived. Some connect it with sadda, "to hide," supposing it to be an appropriate reference to oriental women. Others, as Hit., derive it from sanada, "to lean upon"; so they suppose it to mean "bed," and hence "concubine." Others (e.g., Olshausen) derive it from sîd (Heb. שׂיר, "demon," As. šidu, "bull-deity")), which in Ar. not only means "demon" (Spanish Cid), but also "lord," and sayyidat, "lady" (modern Ar. sitti). (In Talmud Babli, Gittin, 78a, it is said that in Palestine the word was understood to mean chests, or sedan-chairs, but in Babylon, demons, both male and female.) Ros. and Marsh. connect it with שׂר, "the breast," and so reached the meaning "female," while Wr. and others derive it with more probability from שׂדר, As. šadādu, "to love." Dr. (Kittel's Bib. Heb., p. 1137n) supposes the original reading to have

been שָׂרָה וְשָׂרוֹת, "a princess and princesses," a view which BDB.
also shares. Though the etymology is obscure, the connection demands
the meaning "mistress" or "concubine." In picturing the life of one
who, like Solomon, tasted all pleasures to the full, the luxuries of the
harem would surely not be omitted. Zap. and Ha. omit שרה ושרות on
metrical grounds, without sufficient reason.—9. וֹגרלתי והוספתי], see
comment on 1¹⁶ and *cf.* Kö. §§ 370f and 371b, d, and Ges.ᴷ §120d.
Sieg. emends the text to וגרלתי והוספתי מעשי, supposing that הספתי
must have an object, but as Del. had observed its object is an implied
גְרֻלָּה understood from גרלתי.—גרל] is used of one who increases in
wealth, *cf.* Gn. 24³⁵ 26¹³ 1 K. 10²³ and Job 1³. On אף]="also," *cf.*
Kö. §371d. עמד] has the meaning "remain," see Is. 47¹² Je. 48¹¹
Ps. 102²⁷. Most modern exegetes so render it here. Herz, Ew., Elst.
and Gins. follow an explanation of Ra.'s which takes the word in the
sense of "assist." This is not so probable.—10. שאלו] Σ happily renders
ἐπιθύμησαν. *Cf.* for similar meaning Dt. 14²⁶.—מהם] occurs instead of
מהן. As Del. noted this has resulted from the transfer of the inaccuracies
of the common spoken language to literature, *cf.* Gn. 26¹⁵ 31⁹ 32¹⁶
Job 1¹⁴ Ges.ᴷ §135⁰ and Kö. §14. Cases of faulty agreement not
strictly parallel to this also occur in Zc. 4¹⁰ and Ct. 4⁹.—מנע] frequently
takes the acc. of the thing and the gen. (מן) of the person, but that construction is reversed here as in Gn. 30² and Nu. 24¹¹.—שמח] is rarely used
with מן; when it is, מן denotes the source of the joy, *cf.* Pr. 5¹⁸ 2 Ch. 20²⁷.
Gr. believed that the original reading was ישמח, the י being omitted
because of the י of לבי. 𝕲ᴮ ¹⁵⁵. ²⁵³. ²⁵⁴ and ²⁹⁶ reads εὐφούνης μου=
"my mirth" for שמח. The μου is probably a corruption, introduced
because it occurs so many times in the passage.—חלק], *cf.* on 3²². Ha.
omits כי לבי שמח מכל עמלי and כל before the last עמלי on account of the
supposed exigencies of his metrical arrangement.—11. פנה] is usually
followed by אל, but here and in Job 6²⁸ by ב. In Is. 8²¹ פנה למעלה is used
for "look upward." Hit. urges that the analogy of vs. 12 would lead us
to supply לראות after פנה here.—אני], the pleonastic use of this pron.
after verbs is peculiar to Qoh. *Cf.* Da. §107, rem. 1. On the phrases
מעשי שעשי ידי and עמל שעמלתי, *cf.* Kö. §329d. On the inf. לעשות,
cf. Gn. 2³ Jo. 2²⁰ and Kö. §402a. Ha. omits ידי ..... בכל and
ורעות רוח for his metrical arrangement.

12. מֶה הָאָרָם]. 𝕲 has τίς ἄνθρωπος=מי ארם; McN. thinks this was
the reading before Aqiba, and to which Gr. would emend the text.
Most of the Vrss. favor מה, which makes better sense.—המלך]. βουλή
in 𝕲 and Σ is a rendering of the Aram. מָלַך for מֶלֶך. *cf.* Dn. 4²⁴. The
clause has been variously understood and rendered. Ty. and Pl. regard the expression as proverbial, which Ty. thinks would account for
the elliptical omission of יעשה after הארם. Hit. and Heng. take the question to refer to the king's successor, and Hit. emends עָשׂוּהוּ to the inf.

עָשׂוּהוּ. In substance the question on this view becomes "What can the king's successor do? That which he (the king) already is doing." Del., Wr., and Ha. render: "What shall the man do who comes after the king whom they long ago made?" believing on the basis of I Ch. 29²² that Israelites could believe that Solomon had been made king by the people. This rendering seems harsh and unnatural. Sieg. transposes the two halves of the vs., so as to connect the question: "What can the man do," etc., with the statement of vs. 11 that all is vanity. כְּבָר] is omitted by 𝕲, 𝕾ᴴ, 𝕾, Θ and 𝕳, and should probably be dropped from the text. 𝕿 and *Biresh. Rab.* are the only ancient authorities which support MT. Dr. notes that for עָשׂוּהוּ, 68 MSS., 𝕲ᴮ, 𝕾 and 𝕳 read עָשָׂהוּ. The text adopted in the above rendering is, therefore, מה האדם יעשׂה שׁיבוא אהרי המלך את אשׁר עשׂהו. Ha. omits האדם and המלך ..... עָשׂוּהוּ for metrical reasons.—13. פִּיתָרוֹן] of Walton's Pol. and of Hahn is pointed פִּיתָרוֹן by Baer and Dr. For the reasons, see Baer, *Megilloth*, p. 61, and for analogies, Je. 25³⁶ Ps. 45¹³ and Pr. 30¹⁷. See also Ges.ᴷ §24e. Zap. and Ha., in view of their conceptions of the metre, reject החשׁך ..... כיתרין as a gloss—a view which we cannot share.— מן] on מן in comparisons, see Ges.ᴷ §133b.—14. נס]. That Sieg. regards 14a as a gloss has been treated under vs. 13.— גם]. Kn., Gins. and Zö. take this in an adversative sense, but as Del., Wr., and Vl. note, if it were adversative, it should come at the beginning of the sentence. The real adv. particle here is וֹ.—אחר] is used, as several times in Qoh., in the sense of "the same," *cf.* 3¹⁹· ²⁰ 6⁶ 9². ³ 12¹¹.—מקרה] from קרה, "to happen," "befall" (*cf.* Gn. 44²⁹), means "chance" or "accident," as in I S. 20²⁶ Ru. 2³, and then passes to the meaning of "fate," *B*DB. (I S. 6⁹ Qoh. 2¹⁴· ¹⁵ 3¹⁹ 9². ³). Vv. 15–17 show that it refers to death or oblivion. Sieg. considers it a Græcism, but, as McN. notes, its use in I S. 6⁹ proves that it has good Hebrew precedent.—הַכֹּל], literally, "the whole," but used of two things, it is equivalent to "both," *cf.* ch. 3¹⁹· ²⁰ 6⁶ 7¹⁵ 9¹· ² 10¹⁹.

15. כְּמִקְרֶה]. Baer points this as though in *st. abs.*, claiming (p. 61) that the authority of the Massora for this is quite clear. But most modern editors, including *B*DB., Dr., point as constr. מִקְרֶה—נם אני], this is an emphatic expression. The emphasis is obtained by the anticipation of the suffix in אני, *cf.* Gn. 24²⁷ Ez. 33¹⁷ 2 Ch. 28¹⁰, and for a kindred use, Nu. 14³² and 1 K. 21¹⁹; also Ges.ᴷ §135e and Kö. §19.—אָז וְהֵר], the phrase has occasioned much difficulty both in ancient and modern times. אז is omitted by 𝕲ᴮᶜᴺ* (and several cursives). 𝕾, 𝕳 and 𝕶, followed by Gr., omit it as without meaning. 𝕲ᴬᴺ°·ᶜⱽ supports MT., and most modern scholars adhere to MT., although Kn. changed it to אַך. They differ, however, in their interpretations of it. Zö. and No. take it to refer to the moment of death; *then* wisdom will avail nothing. Del. says it may be either a temporal or a logical "then." Wild. takes it in the

logical sense, while Gins. regards it as introducing the apodosis. Kö.
§373 1 takes it temporally, citing as parallels Ju. 5⁸ 1 K. 9¹¹ Mi. 3⁴
Ps. 40⁸ 56¹⁰ Ct. 8¹¹. Our passage seems to differ from these, and I in-
cline to agree with Gins. and Wild., and take it as a logical "then," introducing a conclusion.—וְיֹתֵר] has also been variously treated. BDB.,
and most recent interpreters, take it as an adverb as in 7¹⁶ 12⁹. This
is probably right, though Dale would correct to יֶתֶר, and Winckler (AOF.
IV, 351), who is followed by Sieg. and Dr., would correct to אָז הֲרָתִי,
comparing vs. 3.—לָמָּה]. Del. and Wr. point out that למה in a question asks
after the object or design, while מַדּוּעַ asks for the reason of the object.
Ha., for metrical reasons, omits גם אני and בלבי as glosses.—16. זָכְרוֹן]
for the form, see on 1¹¹. אֵיךְ]. Winckler (AOF., IV, 351) corrects to
אַךְ, but as McN. has said, it is unnecessary. A better sense is obtained
as the text stands.—עָם], lit. "with," is used in comparisons; so, Hit.,
Heil., Gr., Del., Wr., Gins., No., Vl. Compare ch. 7¹¹ Job 9²⁶ 37¹⁸
Ps. 88⁵, also BDB. 768a, and Kö. §375 1.—בְּשֶׁכְּבַר is a compound expression.—בְּשֶׁ] is equivalent to בַּאֲשֶׁר, "inasmuch" or "because," BDB.,
cf. Gn. 39⁹· ²³ and Kö. §389e.—בְּשֶׁ is compounded as in post-Bib.
Heb. (cf. above Introd. §10E). כבר] means "already," see on 1¹⁰.
As McN. remarks, Q. puts himself at the point of view of future days and
looks backward.—הימים הבאים] is acc. of time, cf. Ges.ᴷ· §118i, and Je.
28¹⁶.—הַכֹּל] refers here to persons, as in Ps. 14³. For the meaning
"both," see on 2¹⁴.—נשכח] may in form be either the perf. or a part.
Gins. takes it as a part., but it is better to regard it as a perf. used to
express the future perfect, cf. Da. §41(c).—אֵיךְ], though sometimes
interrogative as in 1 S. 16², is here exclamatory as in Is. 14⁴ Ez. 26¹⁷
La. 1¹, etc.—17. רַע עַל], as Delitzsch pointed out, is a late expression
parallel to עַל טוֹב of Es. 3⁹ and the similar expression in Ps. 16⁶. It is
an idiom found in the Mishna, see Pirke Aboth, 2¹⁰· ¹² and 4¹². Hit.
endeavors to explain the prep. in רע עַל as "unto," and Gins. as "upon,"
denoting the resting of a burden upon one. Hit. cites Job 10¹ and Ps.
42⁵· ⁶ in support of his view, and Gins., Is. 1¹⁴ Job 7²⁰ Qoh. 6¹ 8⁶ in
support of his. Possibly it originated in the view Gins. advocates, but
it has become simply a late usage.—מַעֲשֶׂה] may refer to cosmic activity
as in 1⁹, or to human activities as in 1¹⁴.—וֹרְעוּת רוּחַ]. Gr. would emend
to רְעָה רוּחַ, on the ground that the verse refers to the world-order, and
it is unfitting to say that it is desiring wind.—This is unnecessary, however, since Q.'s complaint is that the cosmic order, which dooms the wise
to oblivion like the fool, renders the efforts of man toward wisdom a desire of wind.—18. אֲנִיתַ] Kn. derived from ינח, but most recent interpreters have correctly observed that it is from נוח. Cf. הִסִּית from סות,
Je. 38²².—אַחֲרֵי], cf. Kö. §410b.—19. הֶחָכָם], the הֶ- is the interrogative particle. It is used with או in double questions. The more common par-
ticles for such questions are הֲ- ..... אִם, but the combination הֲ- .. אִ֫י,

which we have here, occurs several times, once in the J. document.
c/. Ju. 18¹⁹ 2 K. 6²⁷ Ma. 1⁸ Job 16³ 38²⁸ and Qoh. 11⁶. For the more
usual form see Gn. 24²¹ 27²¹, etc. Cf. Ges.ᴷ· §150g and Kö. §379b.
—סכל]. The root, spelled with a z, occurs, as noted above, in this sense
in the form Zakalu in the code of Hammurabi, col. XXIII, 40.—שלט]
occurs in BH. only in late compositions, Ne. Es. Ps. 119¹³³ and Qoh.
It is frequent in the Aram. portions of Daniel. 𝕲ᴮᴬᴺⱽ read ἐλ ἐξου-
σιάζεται, which represents השלט in Heb. Perhaps as McN. thinks this
was a reading before the time of Aqiba. It is an unnatural reading,
and may have arisen through some mistake.—או סכל]. Ha. regards this as
a gloss, and both he and Zap. reject גם זה הבל as a stereotyped insertion.
These supposed glosses are in the interest of their metrical arrangement.
—שעמלתי ושחכמתי] is, as Zö. and Del. have noted, a hendiadys for "upon
which I toiled wisely."—20. וסבותי]. Some scholars maintain that there
is a distinction between סבב and פנה—that the former means "turn to
do," the latter "turn to see." Del. has pointed out, however, that in
Lv. 26⁹ פנה means "turn to do," while in Qoh. 7²⁵ סבב signifies "turn to
see."—יאש], according to Baer, should be pointed שׁ יָאֵשׁ. Dr. so points it,
and the reading is accepted by Ges.ᴷ· §64e. The form is a Piel inf.
The root occurs outside of this passage but five times in the OT. (1 S.
27¹ Is. 57¹⁰ Je. 2²⁵ 18¹² Job 6²⁶), and always in the Niphal. The Mishna
has the Hithpael of the root, thus vouching for its use in the Piel, see
Aboth, 1⁷, and Kelim, 26⁸.—על כל העמל]. A number of MSS. of 𝕲 read ἐν
μόχθῳ μου = בעמלי. [תחח השמש]. Ha. rejects this as a gloss, which spoils the
symmetry of his metrical arrangement.—21. ארם.....ארם] is a balanced
rhetorical expression, cf. Kö. §34.—בכשרון] occurs only in Qoh., here,
and in 4⁴ and 5¹⁰. Its root כשר occurs in Es. 8⁵ Qoh. 10¹⁰ and 11⁶,
also in NH. Aram. and Syr. (BDB. 506b and Ja. 677b). The root
means "to go well," "prosper;" and the noun, "success."—חלקו] is taken
by No. as the second object of נתן. cf. Ps. 2⁸, Ges.ᴷ· (§131m) takes it
as an appositive to the preceding suffix, Kö. (§340o) regards it as a
predicate acc. חלקו and רעה רבה Ha. excises so that the verse shall
conform to his metrical conception.

22. והוה], the part. of הוה, occurs elsewhere in Ne. 6⁶. The root, Job 37⁶,
has the meaning "fall;" in Gn. 27²⁹ Is.1 6⁴ Ne. 6⁶ and Qoh. 11³ the sense
of היה, "be," which it has here. Ges.ᴮᵘ· (13th ed.) regards הוה, "to
fall," and הוה, "to be," as different roots, but BDB. is probably right in
connecting them, that "which occurs" or "falls out," being that which is
In Aramaic הוה and היה occur side by side in the sense of "be" (see
Dalman, Aram. Gram. §73, and Ja., p. 338). הוה is found in the Aram.
inscr. of Panammu of Zendjirli, which is from the 8th cent. (cf. G. A.
Cooke, North Sem. Inscr., pp. 172, 176). Its occurrence in Aram. led
Hit., No. and others to regard it as an Aramaism, but its occurrence
in an old poem in Gn. 27²⁹ indicates that in Heb. as in Aram. it was at

every period a synonym of היה· This usage occurs in NH. also *cf.*
Aboth, 1⁴ and 2³, and for the idiom Ja. *sub voce*. See also Kö. §326h.—
For לאדם] 𝔊 has ἐν τῷ ανθρώπῳ. Probably there was a pre-Aqiban reading באדם.—רעיון] is not רעות, but probably comes from the same root.
BDB. renders it "longing," "striving." In the Tal. it means "desire,"
"ambition," "greed" (*cf.* Ja. *sub voce*).—שֶׁהוּא] was read שְׂהוּא by Ki
(*cf.* Ges.ᴷ. §36), and is so read by Baer, Del., No. and Vl. *Cf.* שְׁהֶם,
ch. 3¹⁸. כל and השמש.....שהוא] Ha.'s metrical arrangement leads him
to reject as glosses.—**23**. כל ימיו] is regarded by AE., Hit., Gr., Gins.
and McN. as acc. of time, מכאבים being taken like כעס as a pred. of עניו.
This is a possible construction. Del., Wr., Sieg., Ha. and Kö. (*cf.*
§306r) take it as the subj. of a nominal sentence, of which מכאבים is the
predicate.—מכאבים]. Gins. remarks that this is a plural used to express
an abstract idea.—וְכַעַם], see the comment on 1¹⁸ and for עניו, on 1¹³. Del.
and Wr. note that the pointing of *waw* with *kameç* before כעס is done because כעס is a segholate, having its accent on the first syllable, thus bringing the vowel of ו into an open syl. before the tone. For similar cases see
Lv. 18⁵ Is. 65¹⁷ and Pr. 25³. The sentence which begins here is nominal and its pred. is for emphasis placed first. *Cf.* Kö. §338c.—שכב],
literally "lie down," is used for "sleep" (Gn. 28¹³ Ju. 16³ and 1 S. 3¹⁵).
The rendering "rest" is a little free, but gives the sense.—גם]. 𝔚 read
a ו before the last גם. but this is unsupported by the other versions.
—גם זה הבל] Zap. erases as a stereotyped gloss, which disturbs the
metre, but Ha. finds it necessary to the metre here.

24. Sieg., with no good reason, denies the last clause of the vs. to
Q. It is thoroughly consistent with the point of view of such a
Jew as Q. Sieg. is right in saying that in Q. טוב and טובה rarely
denote ethical good (as in 7²⁰ 12¹⁴), but "convenience," "satisfaction,"
as in 2¹· ²⁶ 3¹². ¹³· ²² 4⁶· ⁸ 5¹⁷ 6³· ⁹· ¹² 7⁸· ²⁶ 8¹². ¹⁵ 11⁷. BDB. show that
they seldom have ethical meaning in OT.—באדם] is a corruption from
לאדם, for that is the reading of 𝔊ᴮᴬᶜ, 𝕾 and 𝕳, and the construction
in 6¹² and 8¹⁵.—שיאכל], before this word a מ has fallen out. Gins., Gr., Del.,
Wr., Eur., Wild., McN., Kit. and Kö. (§319h) have taken this view.
משיאכל is supported by 𝔊ᶜ, 𝕾, 𝕷, 𝔊, 𝕶, and by the analogy of 3¹². ²² and
8¹⁵.—וישתה והראה]. Instead the pre-Aqiban reading seems to have been
וישתה ושיראה, for so read 𝔊ᴮᶜᴺ ¹⁶¹⁻²⁴⁸. ²⁵⁴. ²⁹⁸ and 𝕾. Perhaps as McN.
suggests the relative שׁ was dropped by mistake from וישתה because of
its proximity to another שׁ, after which הראה was changed so as to make
the tense conform.—זה], fem.; an apocopation of זאת. *Cf.* BDB., Ges.ᴷ.
§34b and Kö. §45. The form occurs also in 2 K. 6¹⁹ Ez. 40⁴⁵ Qoh. 2². ²⁴
5¹⁵. ¹⁸ 7²³ 9¹³.—מיד האלהים], *i.e.*, God's gift (Del.). היא is replaced by
הוא in some MSS. *Cf.* Baer, p. 62.—באדם and בעמלו] Ha. rejects as
glosses for his metrical arrangement. The whole of vs. 24b (נם.....היא)
he, like Sieg., regards as a gloss, although he finds it in metrical form.—

25. Sieg. and Ha. reject the vs. as a gloss along with vs. 24b. That this is unnecessary has been shown under vs. 24.—יחוש‎]. For this ⅖, Θ and ‍𝔖 read ישתה‎, as in vs. 24. 'A, Σ and 𝔖ᴴ read יחוש‎, or יחום‎, "to suffer," "feel pity," etc., like Syr. *ḥûs*. The authorities last cited prove that the reading of ⅖ and Θ is not primitive, for no one would change in that case to the more difficult reading of 'A and Σ. Modern interpreters since Del. connect it with the Ar. *ḥassa*, "to feel, have sensation, perceive," Aram. חשש‎. As. *ašāšu*, "to feel pain." Thus we have the Syr. *ḥâs*, "perceive," "understand," and Eth. *ḥawâs*, "understanding." Thus Del., Wr., No., *B*DB. and Ges.ᴮᵘ· take it correctly for "perceive," "feel," "enjoy."—חוץ מן‎] does not occur elsewhere in BH., but occurs in Talmud, *e.g.*, *Berakot*, 33b, and *Niddah*, 16b. It is the equivalent of the Aram. בר מן‎, *cf. e.g.*, Targ. to Isa. 43¹¹ 45⁵, etc.—ממני‎], instead ⅖, 𝕷, 𝕶 and 𝔖 read ממנו‎. Of modern scholars, Gr., Zö., Dale, Del., Wr., Bick., Eur., Sieg., Wild., McN., Ha. and Dr. have followed this reading. In this they are undoubtedly right. ממני‎ gives no intelligible meaning.—
26. נתן‎]. Ty.'s notion that the perf. is used to indicate the unalterable character of God's decrees, is foreign to Heb. thought. The perf. is the perf. of actions, which experience proves to be customary, *cf.* Da. §40 (*c*), Ges.ᴷ· §106k.—הוטה‎] is in Q., except in 7²⁶, pointed like the part. of verbs. "ל"ה‎ (*cf.* 8¹² 9²· ¹⁸). On the kinship of verbs "ל"א‎ and "ל"ה‎, *l*, *cf.* Ges.ᴷ· §7500.—נם זה הבל‎] Zap. erases as a gloss, which destroys his metre, while Ha. regards the vs. metrically perfect as it stands.

MAN'S HELPLESSNESS IN COMPARISON WITH GOD (3¹⁻¹⁵).

The burden of this section is that man's activities are limited to certain times and seasons, in which he goes his little round doing what has been done before him; his nature cries out for complete knowledge of the works of God, but the best he can do is ignorantly to rejoice and get good within these limitations.

¹. Everything has a fixed season, and there is a time for every business under the sun.

> ². A time to be born;
> And a time to die;
> A time to plant,
> And a time to uproot what is planted.
> ³. A time to kill
> And a time to heal;
> A time to break down
> And a time to build.

⁴. A time to weep
And a time to laugh;
A time to mourn
And a time to dance.

⁵. A time to scatter stones,
And a time to pick up stones;
A time to embrace,
And a time to refrain from embracing.

⁶. A time to seek
And a time to lose,
A time to keep
And a time to throw away.

⁷. A time to rend
And a time to sew;
A time to keep silence,
And a time to speak.

⁸. A time to love
And a time to hate;
A time of war
And a time of peace.

⁹. What profit has a worker in that in which he toils? ¹⁰. I saw the toil which God has given the sons of men to toil in. ¹¹. He has made everything appropriate in its time; also he has put ignorance in man's heart, so that he cannot find out the work that God does from beginning to end. ¹². I know that there is no good for them except to rejoice and to do good in their life. ¹³. And also every man—that he should eat and drink and see good in all his toil, is the gift of God. ¹⁴. I know that all which God does it shall be forever; unto it, it is not possible to add, and from it, it is not possible to take away, and God has done it that men may fear before him. ¹⁵. What is that which is? Already it has been, and what is to be already is, for God shall seek that which is driven away.

1. *Everything has a fixed season*]. In this ch. Qoheleth reverts to the thought of ch. 1, but treats the application of the thought to human activities in a somewhat different way. His point is that there is a proper or divinely ordered time for all human activities, and that these go on over and over again. Ha. interprets the word "time" here as a "short space of time," and so obtains the meaning for verses 1–9, that all is transient. This gives, however, an unwarranted meaning to the passage. Compare the Arabic proverb: "Everything has its proper time" (Jewett, in JAOS. XV, 92). Verse 1 is probably alluded to in the last clause of

Wisdom, 8⁸.—**2.** *A time to be born*]. Ty. and Sieg. hold that this table (vv. 1–8), of times and seasons, when various actions are appropriate, betrays Stoic influence, since Marcus Aurelius (IV, 32) makes a somewhat similar contrast. They believe this table shows a knowledge of the Stoic principle of living in accord with nature. The proof is, however, not convincing. A Hebrew, by reflecting on life, might have given expression to sentiments like these, though untouched by Stoic teaching. Cf. *Introduction*, §6 (2). Ha. transposes many of the clauses of this table so as to secure a more symmetrical grouping of events. Other transpositions have been suggested (*e.g.*, the transposition of 2b and 3a, and placing 5a before 4a), so as to secure a logical sequence of thought, the order thus obtained being: 1, treatment of landed property; 2, emotions of joy and sorrow; 3, preservation and loss of property in general; 4, emotions of friendship and enmity. (*Cf.* McN., p. 61.) Such artificial arrangements are, however, as McN. well says, foreign to the book. Many suggestions have been made as to the meaning of "be born" and "to die." The former of these is here to be taken in an intransitive sense (see crit. note). Ty. thought it referred to the fact that pregnancy has its fixed period before birth, and that this fact is made parallel to the fact that life has its fixed period before it is terminated by death. Ha. believes that Qoheleth observed that there are periods in human history when the race exhibits great fecundity, as it did after the Black Death (1348–1351), and that there are other periods, like that of the Black Death, when dying prevails. It is doubtful whether Qoheleth's thought is as abstruse as either of these would imply. It is more probable that he simply meant that in every life there is a time to be born and a time to die, and that every agriculturist has a time of planting and a time of uprooting, *i.e.*, life is full of contrasts. At one period we undo what at another period we have done.—**3.** *A time to kill and a time to heal*]. The antitheses of life are illustrated by further examples. There are times when man destroys life, and times when he tries to save it; times when he breaks down old walls, and times when he builds new ones.—**4.** *A time to weep and a time to laugh*]. In illustration of the mourning referred to, *cf.* Zc. 12¹⁰, and in illustration of the

meaning of "times of mourning and of rejoicing," *cf.* Mt. 9[14. 15]
11[16. 17] Lk. 6[21] and Jn. 16[20].—**5.** *A time to scatter stones*]. The
interpretation of the first clause is difficult. The 𝕌 and AE. took it
to refer to scattering the stones of an old building, and collecting
stones for a new structure. Several modern scholars (Kn., Hit.,
Heil., Wr., No., Vl., Wild., and McN.) take it to refer to scattering stones to render fields unproductive (*cf.* 2 K. 3[19. 25]), and pick-
ing up stones to render a field cultivable (*cf.* Is. 5[2]). Pl., taking
a hint from a suggestion of Del., is inclined to regard it as a reference to the Jewish custom, which survives among Christians, of
throwing stones or earth into the grave at a burial. Although he
confesses that this leaves the "gathering" of stones unexplained,
it would refer to the severance of human ties, as "embracing" in
the last clause refers to the opposite. Probably the second interpretation, which refers to fields, is to be preferred, though in that
case there is no logical connection between the two halves of
the verse.—*A time to embrace and a time to refrain from embracing*].
Gr. and Wr. take the last clause to refer to the embraces of men
in cordial friendly greeting. It is true that the word is so used in
Gn. 29[13] 33[4] 2 K. 4[16]. Ty., No. and Sieg. take it to refer to erotic
embraces, comparing Prov. 5[20], and Ct. 2[6], where the word undoubtedly has that significance. On this interpretation the time
"to refrain from embracing" is that mentioned in Lv. 15[23. 24].
This latter view is to be preferred.—**6.** *A time to seek and a time
to lose, a time to keep and a time to throw away*]. The two clauses
of the verse are not exactly synonymous. The first refers to the
acquisition of property as contrasted with losing it; the second,
to guarding what one has in contrast with throwing it away.—
7. *A time to rend*]. Most interpreters see in this verse a reference
to rending garments as a sign of mourning (*cf.* Gn. 37[29] 44[13]
2 S. 1[11] 3[31] Job 1[20] 2[12]), and sewing them up after the sadness
is past, also to keeping silence in sorrow (*cf.* 2 K. 18[36] Job 2[13]
Ps. 39[2. 9]), and to utterance as a sign of joy (*cf.* Is. 58[1] Ps. 26[7]
126[2]). Pl., however, prefers to see in it a reference to rending a
garment as a sign of schism or division, as in the case of Ahijah
(1 K. 11[30]), in which case the sewing would be figurative for the
restoration of unity. He compares the words of Jesus (Mt. 10[34. 35])

to show that there are occasions when schism is necessary, and Is. 58¹² to show that there are times when the opposite is in place. While Qoheleth's principle might be figuratively extended to cover such cases as Pl. supposes, it is far more likely that he had the universal customs of mourning in mind.   On silence and speech compare BS. 20⁶·⁷ in the Heb.—**8.** *A time to love*].   Qoheleth declares here that love and hate as well as their expression in war and peace have their appointed times.   Wr. recalls with reference to vv. 2–8 the words of Marcus Aurelius (xii, 23), τὸν δὲ καιρόν, καὶ τὸν ὅρον δίδωσιν ἡ φύσις—"both the opportunity and the limit nature gives."   As was noted above, Ty. and Sieg. regard these verses as the result of Stoic influence.   Pfleiderer (*Jahrbuch für prot. Theol.*, 1887, 178–182) finds in them traces of the influence of the πάντα ῥεῖ, or universal flux, of Heraclitus.   As Wild. well observes, the fundamental thought of these verses in its connection differs from every known philosophy.   It is, as Cox says, when man thinks himself most free that he is subject to divine law.

9. *What profit, etc.*].   After his extended survey, Qoheleth returns to the crying question of ch. 1³.   The positive question is a negative assertion.   His position is that there has been ordained a time for all these activities, but that no substantial advantage accrues from them to man, though he must go through them.—**10.** *I saw the toil*].   Qoheleth reverts here to the very word which he had used in 1¹³ᵇ.   The verse gives the reason for the denial made in vs. 9.—**11.** *Everything appropriate*].   For a justification of the rendering "appropriate" and "ignorance," see critical notes below.   The verse continues Qoh.'s observations about times and seasons.   Everything, he declares, is suitable to its season, but God has so veiled man's vision that he cannot discover God's work from beginning to end, *i.e.*, its purpose and meaning.   *He has put ignorance in man's heart*—gives us a glimpse of Qoheleth's conception of God.   He thinks of him as a being jealous lest man should become his equal.   It is a Semitic thought.   *Cf.* Gn. 3²²ᵃ, and the story of Adapa, *Keilinschriftliche Bibliothek*, VI, 92 *ff.* The first clause of this verse is recalled in the Heb. text of Sirach, 39¹⁶ ³³.—**12.** *There is no good for them*].   This verse reiterates the

pessimistic conclusion previously drawn in 2²⁴. Qoheleth comes
back to it here after passing in review the activities of human life
in their appropriate times and their futility.—*Do good*]. Ew.,
Heng., Zö., Pl., and Wr. maintain that this means to do good in
an ethical sense. Wherever the phrase occurs in Qoh., however,
it is defined by the context to mean "enjoy life." Del. is probably
right in claiming that it is here equivalent to "see good" of the
next verse.—**13.** *And also*]. The verse continues and completes
the thought of vs. 12. Ginsburg is quite right in maintaining that
"and also" is dependent upon "I know." It is not to be rendered
as an adversative, as Wr. and Vl. maintain. The thought is the
same as that of 2²⁴, but Qoh. approaches it here from a somewhat different line of reasoning. *Every man*] or *"each man"*
stands for "all humanity," though the phrase takes each individual man singly. *Cf.* ch. 5¹⁸ and Ps. 116¹¹.—*Is the gift of
God*]. In Qoheleth's view, God's one good gift to man is the bit of
healthy animal life which comes with the years of vigor. See
below, ch. 11⁹–12⁶.—**14.** *All which God does shall be forever*]. This
vs., introduced like vs. 12 by *I know*, contains a second conviction
of Qoheleth, based on vv. 2–3. This conviction is that man is
caught in the world-order and cannot escape from it. This much
can be seen that the world-order is the work of God, and is
ordained to produce in men the fear of God. As the context
shows, however, this is to Qoheleth not a sufficient explanation.
He longs for some vision of a permanent gain from man's pre-
scribed activities, whereas all that he can see is that man should
eat and drink and enjoy himself. It is probable that he does not
put into the word "fear" a meaning so religious as it often bears in
other passages, as Mal. 1⁶. On the permanence of God's works,
cf. Ps. 33¹¹. The first half of this vs. is quoted and elaborated
in BS. 18⁶.—**15.** *What is that which is? Already it has been*]. Qoheleth now reverts, approaching it from another point of view,
to the thought expressed in 1⁹. Here it is the immutability
of the divine order in which man is caught that oppresses him.
Everything has its time. Nothing can be put out of existence.
Acts and events recur continually, each pursuing the other in a

revolving circle. Tyler compares Ovid, *Metamorphoses*, XV,
179 *ff.:*

> Even time itself glides on with constant progress
> No otherwise than a river. For neither can the river pause,
> Nor the fleeting hour; but as wave is urged by wave,
> The earlier pushed by the one approaching, and it pushes the former,
> So the moments similarly fly on and similarly follow,
> And ever are renewed.

Qoheleth's figure is not, however, a river, but a circle. In this he
conceives of event as chased by event, until it is itself brought back
by God. *Already*], see on 1¹⁰.

1¹. זְמָן] occurs in Heb. only in late books (Ne. 2⁶ Es. 9²⁷· ³¹ and here).
It is used frequently in the Mishna (see *e.g.*, *Erub.*, 6⁷, and *Zebakhim*,
1¹ and 2³. The participle occurs in Ezr. 10¹⁴, Ne. 10³⁵ and 13³¹, in the
sense of fixing calendar dates. The noun means a "fixed or appointed
time." Schechter conjectures that in the Heb. of BS. 4²⁰, בני עת המון
should be בני עת וזמן (see above *Introd.* §11, 1). The Greek of
BS., however, translates simply by καιρόν. The root זמן, having the
same general meaning, is found in Ar., Eth. and Aram. In some of
the dialects of the latter (Syr., Mand., Palmyrene and Samaritan), it is
zabna, or *zibna*. In As. it occurs as *simanu*. In the Aram. of
Daniel it occurs several times in the sense of "appointed time," see
Dn. 2¹⁶· ²¹ 3⁷· ⁸, etc. 𝕲's reading, ὁ χρόνος, indicates the pre-Aqiban
reading was הומן. *Cf.* McN., p. 141.—חפץ], from a root meaning "be
pleased" or "take delight," originally meant "pleasure," see *e.g.*, Is.
44²⁸ 46¹⁰ 53¹⁰ and Job 21²¹. Sometimes in Qoh. this earlier meaning
survives (*e.g.*, in 5³ 12¹· ¹⁰). Here, however, it means "matter," or
"business," *i.e.*, "that in which one is occupied, or takes delight," a
meaning which it also has in ch. 5⁷ and 8⁶. The 𝕲 rendered it by
πράγμα. In the Talmud it meant the same, see Ja. 492b. *Cf.* also on
the word Kö. §80c.

2. לָלֶדֶת]. Hit., Zö. and Sieg. maintain that this is not equivalent
to הֹלִיד, but that it is an act. inf. and is connected with חפץ of the preceding vs., and refers to the act of begetting. With this in part Kö.
(§215b) agrees. The τοῦ τεκεῖν of 𝕲, as Wr. observes, refers it to the
labor of the mother, though from this Kö. (*l. c.*) dissents. Heil., Gins.,
Del., Wr., Wild., Vl., No., McN. and Ha. rightly take it as having an
intransitive or passive sense, as the opposite of מות. Similarly מְלַד is
used for "birth" in Ho. 9¹¹ and לִטְבֹּחַ for לְהִטָּבֵחַ in Je. 25³⁴. The ל in
this and the following expressions seems to express the genitive relation,
cf. Kö. §400b.—לָשַׂעַת] is in some authorities pointed לַשַׂעַת, see Baer,

p. 62, and *cf.* לִמּוֹת, Ps. 66⁹. This form of this inf. occurs only here in BH. The usual form is לִנְטַע or לִנְטוֹעַ, see Is. 51¹⁶ Je. 1¹⁰ 18⁹ 31²⁸. The form without the נ occurs in the Mishna, but as לְטַע, see *Shebi'ith*, 2¹.—עָקַר] is a verb which occurs in the Kal once only elsewhere in BH. (Zp. 2⁴), meaning to uproot. It occurs in the Mishna, see *Aboth*, 3¹⁷, and the references in Ja., p. 1108a. The root also occurs in Aram., Syr., Ar. and Eth., *cf.* BDB., *sub voce*. The Piel is used in BH. in the sense of "hough," "cut the ham-strings," *cf.* Gn. 49⁶ Jos. 11⁶. ⁹ 2 S. 8⁴, 1 Ch. 18⁴.—נטוע] Ha. erases as a gloss, to secure a more evenly balanced metre.—**3.** הרג]. AE., who is followed by Hit., Gins. and Sieg., thought it unfitting to take this in its ordinary sense of "kill," because that did not seem to him a natural antithesis to "heal," he accordingly rendered it "wound." Most recent commentators (Gr., Del., No., Wr., Pl., Vl., Wild., McN. and Ha.) rightly regard the contrast between killing and healing—*i.e.*, destroying life and saving it—as natural and forceful. The 𝔊 restricts the word הרג to killing in war, but as Wr. observes, it more probably refers to the execution of individual offenders.—לפרוץ]. The root means to "break through," "to break down," and is particularly appropriate as an antithesis of בנה in a country like Palestine, where buildings are uniformly constructed of stone. In Is. 5⁵ it is used of breaking down a vineyard-wall.—**4.** ספוד and רקוד]. There is a striking paranomasia between these. ספד is used of mourning, whether public or private, see Gn. 23² 1 S. 25¹ 28³ 2 S. 3³¹ Je. 16⁴ Zc. 12¹⁰. ¹². The root occurs in As. as *sapādu* (derivatives *sipdu* and *sipittu*) in the same meaning. It also occurs in Christian Palestinian Aram. (Schwally, *Idioticon*, 64), and in Amharic with transposed radicals, as "dirge" (*cf.* ZDMG., XXXV, 762).—רקד] means "to leap," "dance." The root occurs in Aram., Syr. and As. with the same meaning. In Ar. in 9th stem it means "to hasten greatly," "to run with leaps and bounds." Probably, as Gins. suggests, the root is used here instead of שמח, "to rejoice," on account of the similarity in sound to ספד.—**5.** שלך]. For the use of this in the sense of scatter or throw away, *cf.* 2 K. 3²⁵ 7¹⁵ Ez. 20⁸, Ps. 2³.—חבק] is used in Kal and Piel without apparent distinction in meaning. לרחק מ־], for another example of the use of רחק with מן, see Ex. 23⁷. אבנים] and מחבק]. Ha., to secure his metre, rejects as glosses.—**6.** בקש], literally "seek," is here apparently used of the acquisition of property, *cf.* Mt. 13⁴⁵. ⁴⁶.—אבד] ordinarily means "destroy," a meaning which it has even in this book in ch. 7⁷. Here, however, it is used in the weaker sense of "lose," BDB., in which it appears in the Mishna, *Teharoth*, 8³. This meaning also appears in Ps. 119¹⁷⁶, where שֶׂה אבֵד is "a lost sheep."—השליך], see note on previous verse. —**7.** לתפר], "to sew," is a comparatively rare word. It occurs in Gn. 3⁷ Ez. 13¹⁸ Job 16¹⁵ and here. It is also found in NH., see *Sabbath*, 13², and *Kelim*, 20⁶.—**8.** מלחמה] and שלום]. The change in 8b from infini-

tives to the nouns denotes, as Pl. has noted, that the series is completed.
9. ‏יתרון‎], see on 1³.—‏העשׂה‎] Bick. emends to ‏העמל‎, but as Sieg. remarks, Q. may well have written ‏העשׂה‎. Ha., who practically rewrites
the book, regards this vs. as originally a gloss to 1³, but there is no evidence whatever to justify us in transferring it thither. It is a refrain
which well expresses Q.'s mood, and has a genuine ring.—**10.** ‏ענין‎], see
on 1¹³. Ha. counts the verse a gloss as he does vs. 9, and with as little
cause.—**11.** ‏יפה‎], in BH. usually means "fair," "beautiful," cf. BDB.,
sub voce, but in NH. it has a much wider meaning. E.g., in Zabim,
2², Makshirin, 5¹⁰, Mikwa'oth, 10⁶, ‏יפה‎ signifies "good." It is interesting to note that when BS. paraphrases our passage (ch. 39¹⁶· ³³), he renders
‏יפה‎ by ‏טוב‎. In Zabim, 3¹, ‏אִילָן יָפֶה‎ means "a strong tree." In Nazir,
7⁴, ‏יפה אמר‎ means "to speak very well." In Zebachim, 8², Shebi'ith, 1¹,
and Terumoth, 2⁴· ⁶, ‏יפה‎ means the "best" (animal for sacrifice), while in
Keritoth, 6⁶, ‏יָפֶה שְׁתֵי סְלָעִים‎ means "worth two Sela's," and ‏יָפֶה עֲשָׂרָה זוּז‎
means "worth ten zuzim." That this later usage had begun as early
as Qoheleth is shown by ch. 5¹⁷, where ‏יפה‎ means "befitting" (so Ha.).
The context in the verse before us demands such a meaning here.
—‏עֹלָם‎] should probably be pointed ‏עֶלֶם‎. To say that "God has put
eternity in their heart, so that they cannot find out the work of God from
beginning to end," makes no sense. Kö. (§392g) would render ‏מבלי אשׁר‎
"only that not," but that makes the thought of doubtful lucidity, and
so far as I have observed gives to ‏מבלי‎ an unwarranted meaning. Gaab,
Kn., Hit., and Heil. derived the word from the Ar. 'aloma, and took it to
mean "knowledge," or "Weltsinn." This, however, makes no better
sense of the passage. Wang., Vaih., Zö., Del., Wr., Cox, No., Gins.,
Wild. and McN. cling to the meaning "eternity," or notion of eternity.
It is true that in Qoh. the word has the meaning "forever," "of old,"
and "eternal" in 1⁴· ¹⁰ 2¹⁶ 3¹⁴ 9⁶ and 12⁵, but that is no reason why in
an unpointed text it might not have another meaning here. Dale and
Sieg. take it to mean "future," while Re. takes it in the later meaning
of ‏עלם‎ for "world." Död., more than a century ago, pointed toward
the right interpretation when he rendered it "hidden," or "unknown."
Gr. saw that it meant "ignorance," while Pl. hesitatingly, and Ha.
more positively, have followed this lead. The root ‏עלם‎ means "hidden,"
"unknown," ‏עֹלָם‎, the unknown of time, hence "of old," "forever,"
"eternity." From this same root ‏עֶלֶם‎, frequently used in the Talmud
(cf. Ja. 1084b), means "that which is concealed," "secret," etc. The
context in our verse compels us to render it "ignorance." 𝕲ᴮᶜⱽ ⁶⁸·
²⁵³· ²⁵⁴ indicate that an early reading was ‏מבלי....‎ .‏לא‎ .‏את כל עלם‎], the
two negatives strengthen the negation. They do not destroy each
other as in Latin and English (cf. Kö. §352x and Ges.ᴷ· §152y).—‏סיף‎] is
a late synonym of ‏קץ‎, cf. BDB., 693a. Sieg. assigns this vs. to the Chasid
glossator. Ha., although he translates it as poetry, also regards it as a

gloss. When its real thought is perceived, however, the vs. fits admirably into Q.'s system of thought. The activities of life may be suited
to their seasons, but they are vain and give no proper return, for man
cannot understand them.—**12.** Sieg. claims that this verse draws the
pessimistic conclusion to vs. 10, and contradicts vs. 11. This view rests
on a misunderstanding of vs. 11. Both are parts of Q.'s pessimistic
conclusion. Ha., for a reason, too, so subjective that I do not appreciate it, regards the verse as a gloss.—בם]. It is probable from the analogy
of באדם in 2²⁴ (which is a corruption of לאדם, see crit. note on 2²⁴) and
לאדם in 8¹⁵, which occur in similar expressions to this, that בם is equivalent to לם (possibly a corruption of it), and refers to mankind. So Gins.,
Zö., Gr., Del., Sieg. and most recent interpreters. Rashbam, Luther,
Coverdale, the Bishops Bible, and Ty. took it as "in them," and referred it to the times and seasons of vv. 2–8. This view is less probable.
—לעשות טוב]. Zirkel, Kleinert, Ty., Sieg. and Wild. regard עשה טוב as a
Græcism=εὖ πράττειν. Del., Wr., McN. and others declare that it is
not necessary to regard the idiom as influenced by Greek, and they are
probably right, since in 2 S. 12¹⁸ we have the opposite עשה רע="do
badly," or "vex one's self," in a book where no Greek influence can be
suspected.—כי אם], "but," cf. Kö. §372i. וְיִשְׂמֹחַ] expresses a subject
clause in a shortened form, cf. Kö. §397a.—**13.** וישתה וראה]is, as it stands,
two instances of waw consecutive with the perfect. The same expression occurs in 2²⁴, where the pre-Aqiban reading was שֶׁ־ with the
imperf. The Versions give no hint of a similar original here. Sieg.
regards this and the following vs. as the work of the *Chasid* interpolator.
but when one sees the sequence of the thought as outlined above, that,
so far as this vs. is concerned, is unnecessary. Ha. rejects the vs. as a
gloss apparently because the thought is strongly expressed in ch. 8¹⁵,
but surely an Oriental could express the same thought more than once
in a writing of this length.—**14.** Sieg. and Ha. regard the whole vs. as the
work of the *Chasid* glossator, and McN. so regards the last clause, re-
marking that the mystery of the inexorable world-order, over which
Q. broods, was no mystery to the glossator. If our view of the preceding
context be correct, Sieg. and Ha. err in denying to Q. the whole vs.
McN. has probably needlessly beheld the hand of a glossator too. To
Q.'s mood God might make a world-order to cause men to fear him,
but this would not constitute a satisfactory explanation of the limitations of human life any more than it did to Job in certain of his moods
(cf. Job 7¹²⁻²⁰).—הוא] takes up the subject again like the Gr. αὐτός or
Latin *idem*, cf. Ges.ᴷ· §141h.—יהיה] is, as Del. remarks, "will be."
—על], on the use of this, in additions, cf. Gn. 28⁹. For אין] with an inf.
to deny a possibility, see 2 Ch. 20⁶.—לגרע and להוסיף], on the inf. as ind.
obj., cf. Kö. §397f.—נרעי], cf. Dt. 4² 13¹ and, for a Gr. equivalent, Rev.
22¹⁸·¹⁹·   עשה ש־], the ש־ expresses purpose, introducing an objective sen-

tence, cf. Kö. §384i, Ges. ᴷ §165b. Such Heb. is the original of ποιεῖν ἵνα, Rev. 13¹⁵ ¹⁶. As Gins. noted the subj. of יראו is אדם, which must be supplied from the preceding vs.—15. אֲשֶׁר להיות], as Del. notes, is equivalent to the Gr. τὸ μέλλον, cf. Gn. 15¹² Jos. 2⁵ Ho. 9¹³ 12³; also Ges.ᴷ §114i and Kö. §399z.—וְהָאֱלֹהִים], the clause has usually been interpreted as though נרדף, "that which is pursued," were to be rendered "that which is driven away," and so simply referred to that which is past. Some, as Gr. and Ha., have noted, however, that the Niph. נרדף usually means "persecuted." It certainly has this meaning in the Talmud (cf. Ja. and Levy, sub voce), they accordingly render יבקש by "looks after," i.e., "God looks after him who is persecuted." These scholars accordingly believe that the clause is out of place, and that it probably belonged originally to vs. 17. If, however, we recognize that Q. is thinking of events as chasing one another around in a circle, and take רדף in its original sense of "pursue," as in Jos. 8¹⁶ Je. 29¹⁸, the difficulty vanishes and the clause fits into its context. The phrase is quoted in the Heb. of Sir. 5³. Ben Sira, like 𝔊, 'A, Σ, 𝔖 and 𝔘, regards נרדף as masc. That, however, is not a decisive objection to the view advocated above, for the masc. may be used to express such concepts. Cf. Kö. §244a. After את we should expect הנרדף. The article is similarly omitted in את לב, ch. 7⁷. On these cases, see Kö. §288g. Ha. regards this verse as two glosses, apparently on the principle that Q. could say a thing but once. Sieg., on the other hand, recognizes it as a part of the work of Q¹.

HUMAN OPPRESSION AND INJUSTICE PROVE MEN TO BE NO BETTER THAN ANIMALS.—3¹⁶⁻²².

16. And again I saw under the sun the place of judgment—there was wickedness, and the place of righteousness—there was wickedness.

17. I SAID IN MY HEART THE RIGHTEOUS AND THE WICKED GOD WILL JUDGE, FOR A TIME FOR EVERY MATTER AND FOR EVERY WORK HE HAS APPOINTED.

18. I said in my heart (it is) on account of the sons of men, for God to prove them and to show that they are beasts. . . . **19.** For the fate of the sons of men and the fate of the beasts—one fate is theirs. As is the death of one, so is the death of the other, and all have one spirit. Man has no advantage over beasts, for both are vanity. **20.** Both are going to the same place; both were from the dust, and both are going to return to the dust. **21.** Who knows the spirit of the sons of men, whether it ascends upward, and the spirit of beasts, whether it descends downward to the earth. **22.** And I saw that there is nothing better than that man should rejoice in his work, for that is his portion, for who can bring him to see what shall be after him?

¶ 6. *Again I saw*]. This vs. begins a new section, which is but loosely connected with the survey of times and seasons. In it Qoheleth expresses his views on the wickedness of men and their lack of superiority to animals. The vs. pictures the corrupt administration of Qoheleth's time. The opening of the vs. is similar to ch. $2^{12.\ 13}$ and 4^1, but contains the word *again*, which is unusual in such connections. Zö. maintains that this refers back to vs. 12, but it seems rather loosely to connect some independent observations of the writer with the preceding.—*The place of judgment—there was wickedness*]. "*Place*" has been regarded by Hit., Gins., Zö., Del., Sieg. and Kö. (§330k) not as the object of "*saw*," but as acc. of place or pred. acc., the former being the favorite view. Gins. urges that it cannot be the obj. of "*saw*" on account of the accent, but, as Wr. points out in Gn. 1^1, we have the acc. occurring in spite of this accent. I agree with Wr. and No. that the simplest construction is to regard it as an acc. here.—*Place of judgment*] is the place of the administration of justice.—*Place of righteousness*] is probably "the place of piety," "righteousness," as Gr. has suggested, being, as in $7^{15.\ 16.\ 20}$ 9^2, equivalent to piety. On this view Qoheleth maintains that wickedness prevails in the administration of government and in the practice of religion. See also critical note.

17. *The righteous and the wicked God will judge*]. This verse interrupts the thought. It is, no doubt, the work of the *Chasid* glossator (see critical note). Del. notes that "judge" has a double meaning, referring to the vindication of the righteous as in Ps. 7^8 26^1, and to the punishment of the wicked. The idea that the righteous are vindicated is entirely out of harmony with the context. This is a strong reason for regarding it as the work of a glossator. On the emendation which underlies our rendering, see critical note.—*A time for every matter*] is a distinct allusion in the verse to vv. 2–8.

18. *It is on account of the sons of men*]. As Graetz observed, this verse connects directly with vs. 16, vs. 17 being, as already noted, an interpolation. Qoheleth's view is that the corruption in civil and religious affairs is God's way of demonstrating that men are, for all their intelligence and assumed superiority, really on a level with

animals. For the phrase, "I said in my heart," see critical note on
1¹⁶. Before *on account of, it is,* is to be supplied. After *beasts* the
Hebrew has some words which were added through a mistake.
The reasons for this view and discussions of particular words are
given in the critical notes.—**19.** *Sons of men—beasts—one fate is
theirs*]. The thought of vs. 18, that men are the same as beasts,
is here more fully developed. For a similar thought, *cf.* Ps. 49²⁰.
On "fate," see critical note 2¹⁴. It is further defined in this very
verse as *death. Spirit*] is here the breath of life as in 12⁷ and Ps.
104³⁰. Men and animals are said to possess the same spirit. In
Job 12¹⁰ man is said to have a spirit and animals a soul, but the
distinction is there largely a matter of phraseology on account of
poetic parallelism. For the rendering *both*, see 2¹⁴. The thought
of this vs. is opposed in Wisd. 2².—**20.** *Both are going to the same
place*]. The thought of the preceding verse is here made more
definite. Men and beasts came from the same dust (Gn. 2⁷· ¹⁹),
and to the same dust they will return (Gn. 3¹⁹). It is a thought
which finds an echo in Job 10⁹ 34¹⁵ Ps. 104²⁹ 146⁴, and is quoted
in BS. 40¹¹ (Heb.) and 41¹⁰ (Gr.). Siegfried refers to Gn. 6¹³ 7²¹ to
prove it equivalent to "all flesh," but this is contrary to the context.
As Del. observes, the "one place" is the earth, which, as in ch. 6⁶,
is conceived as the great cemetery. Qoheleth is not thinking of
Sheol, but of the common sepulchre. Pl. finds the same thought in
Lucretius:

> Omniparens eadem rerum commune sepulchrum.
> (The mother and the sepulchre of all.)

Ginsburg's claim that this verse refers only to the body, because
Qoheleth treats the spirit in the next verse, can hardly be maintained. What Qoheleth says of the spirit indicates that he included it with the body. Genung's claim that Qoheleth was
thinking simply of the present phenomenal life, is probably true,
but at the moment the phenomenal life seemed to Qoheleth to be
the whole. Siegfried's claim, however, that ch. 9¹⁰ must be from
another writer, because it recognizes the existence of Sheol which
this denies, will hardly convince one who knows from experience
to what seemingly contradictory ideas one may, in passing through

transitions in thought, give room.—**21.** *Who knows*]. The interrogative is in reality a strong negation, *cf.* ch. 6¹² Am. 5²⁵ Ps.
90¹¹ Is. 53¹. Apparently, Qoheleth's contemporaries held that
as the breath of man came from God (Gn. 2⁷), so it went back to
God, while the breath of animals went to the earth. This Qoheleth combats. That Qoheleth really held the view that the
spirit (or breath) of man returns to God is shown by 12⁷, though
in his mood of despondent pessimism he seems here to deny it.
He uses "spirit" to mean "the breath of life," BD*B*., and not in the
sense of "soul." The latter was expressed by a different Heb.
word (see Schwally, *Leben nach dem Tode*, 87 *ff.*, 161, 180 *ff.*, and
Frey, *Tod, Seelenglaube und Seelenkult*, 18). This is true, although
in the Talmud it was supposed that Qoheleth was referring to the
souls of men (*cf.* Weber, *Jüd. Theol.*, 1897, 338 *ff.*). Qoheleth
follows up his statement that "both return to dust," by the claim
that no one can make good the assertion that the breath of one has
a different destination than that of the other.—**22.** *There is nothing
better, etc.*]. Qoheleth's train of thought, starting from the corruption in civil and religious life, has, at least for the moment,
convinced him that man is no more immortal than an animal.
From this he draws in this verse the conclusion that man's only
good is to have as good a time as he can in the present life. This
is a fundamental thought of the book, to which Qoh. frequently
reverts (*cf.* 2²⁴ 3¹² 5¹⁷⋅ ¹⁸ 8¹⁵ 9⁷⁻⁹). Here he adds as a reason for it
that no man can know what will happen after him,—a thought
shared by other OT. writers (*cf.* Ps. 30⁹ 88¹⁰⁻¹² Is. 38¹⁸). It is too
great a refinement to try to determine, as some have done, whether
Qoheleth refers to man's ignorance of what will happen on the
earth after him, or to an entire lack of knowledge after death.
The language of some of the Psalmists is as strong as his. In
Qoh.'s mood a complete negation of all knowledge is most fitting,
and grew naturally out of the old Hebrew point of view as to the
future life. Although no reference is made here to eating, or to the
pleasures of the appetites as in 2²⁴, we should not conclude with
Genung that Qoh.'s thought is now centred on work in its nobler
creative aspects. Qoheleth has plainly shown that man's "work"
(what he can do) includes the sensual side. His thought is "Let

a man live to the full the round of life's occupations in every de-
partment, for this is his fated lot—his profit for his toil—and he
has no higher possibility."

16. שָׁמָּה] is an emphatic form of שָׁם. Ordinarily the הִ is used only
after verbs of motion with a locative signification, but in Je. 18² Ps.
122⁵ and here it is an emphatic form of שם, cf. Kö. §330h.—רֶשַׁע]. Gr.
noted that in the two halves of the vs. it is tautological, and conjectured
that instead of the second we should read פֶּשַׁע, transgression, a conjecture which Dr. also makes. This is probably right. Had it any
MS. authority I should introduce it into the text. 𝔊 curiously reads
εὐσεβής for ἀσεβής in all copies. Eur. regards it as an early mistake, but
McN. as an early dogmatic correction in the interest of orthodoxy.

17. Sieg., McN. and Ha. regard this vs. as an interpolation of the *Chasid*
glossator. In this they are right, for the thought is out of harmony with
its context. The opinion of Del. as to the double meaning of שֶׁפֶט is
reinforced by BD*B*. p. 1047b. The opinions of such Hebraists cannot
lightly be rejected. Moreover, vs. 18 joins directly on to vs. 16.—אמרתי].
𝔊ᴮ ⁶⁸· ²⁴⁸· ²⁹⁸ and 𝔖 read ואמרתי.—עַל] is used as in late Heb. in the
same meaning as לְ, so BD*B*., Del., Wild.—שָׁם] has been variously
interpreted. Hit., Heil., Ty., Gins., Zö., Del., Pl., and Wr. take it as
"there," interpreting it as "in that place" (Heil.), "in the appointed course of things" (Ty.), or *apud Deum* (Del. and Wr.). On
the other hand, Houb., Dat., Van d. P., Luz., Kn., Gr., Re., No., Vl.,
Wild., Ha. and Dr. emend to שׂם, as I have done above. 𝔊ᴮ ⁶⁸ omits
it. This has led Sieg. and McN. to do the same. McN. regards it as
a possible corruption of the last two letters of מעשה or the first two of
the fol. אמרתי. As 𝔊 puts it at the beginning of the next verse, it may,
on the other hand, have been omitted for the sake of smoothness.
McN. opposes the emendation שׂם on the ground of awkwardness of
style, but the verb in the first half of the vs. is near the end, and this
clause may well have been inverted in like manner. On the whole, I
prefer the conjectural emendation of the commentators quoted.

18. עַל דברת] is late. Apart from this passage it occurs only in BH. in
Qoh. 7¹⁴ 8² and Ps. 110⁴. The usual form is עַל דבר (cf. Gn. 20¹¹· ¹⁸
12¹⁷ 43¹⁸ Ex. 8⁸), or עַל דברי (cf. Dt. 4²¹ Je. 14¹). It means "for the sake
of." Cf. BD*B*.—לְבָרָם] is, as BD*B*., Gins., Del., McN. and Ges.ᴷ (§67p)
have noted, from ברר, the inf. being formed like רֹד from רֶדֶר, Is. 45¹,
and שַׁךְ from שָׂכַךְ, Je. 5²⁶. It is connected with the As. *bararu*, "to be
bright." 𝔊's διακρινεῖ takes it in the secondary meaning of "choose,"
"select," in which the part. of the stem is used in 1 Ch. 7⁴⁰ 9²² 16⁴¹ and
Ne. 5¹⁸. It has in NH. the meaning "single out," "choose," and "sift"
also, cf. *Kil.*, 2¹, *Maasr.*, 2⁶, *Sab.*, 7², and *Gitt.*, 5⁹. "*Probaret*" (𝔏), and

the similar reading of ⵟ, presupposes a Piel, as in NH. the stem has this
meaning only in the Piel (*cf.* Ja. 197b). The meaning "sift" fits here
admirably. ⵄ's reading ברא is an error (*cf.* Eur. p. 58, and Kamenetzky in *ZAW.*, XXIV, 215).—לְרָאוֹת]. Instead ⵖ, ⵄ and ⵗ read לְרָאוֹת.
Hiph. "to show," which is undoubtedly the true reading. So, Wr.,
No., Eur. and McN. The clause introduced by ל is a clause of purpose, see Kö. §407c.—שֶּׁ֑־]. On the pointing for the relative, see Ges.ᴷ·
§36.—הֵמָּה לָהֶם]. These words have been very differently treated by
different interpreters. Del. and Wr. take them to mean "they in reference to themselves," believing that הֵמָּה was introduced because of its
alliteration to בהמה. Kö. (§36) interprets להם similarly. Sieg. believes
that neither word belongs to the text, holding that הֵמָּה arose by dittography with בהמה, and that להם was afterward added as an explanatory gloss. With reference to the origin of הֵמָּה, Gr. had anticipated
him. McN. agrees as to הֵמָּה, but holds that, because ⵖ begins the following vs. with καὶ γε αὐτοῖς, the ending of this verse was גם להם.
Del. admitted that the last clause contained an unusual fulness. In
reality it is most awkward Heb., and I agree with Sieg. that both these
words are an intrusion in the text.—**19.** לָהֶם] ⵖ, ⵄ and ⵄᴴ bring over
from vs. 18 to the beginning of vs. 19. ⵖᴮ reads οὐ συνάντημα, but
the οὐ is probably a corruption of ὅτι, a translation of כי. Sieg. would
emend כי to כְּ and make the comparison begin here. מִקְרֶה] MT.
points as though in the absol. state, which would compel us to read
"fate are the sons of men, and fate are the beasts,"—a reading which
Heil., Gins., Del. and Wr. follow. ⵖ, ⵄ, ⵗ and ⵟ, however, read
מִקְרֵה, stat. constr., and this is undoubtedly right.—מוֹתֵר] occurs nowhere else in Qoh., who uses יִתְרוֹן or יֶתֶר. ⵖ, Σ and Θ read מי יתר,
making the clause a question, to which אין was the answer. McN.
adopts this reading, and it has much in its favor. Zap. and Ha. erase
כי הכל חבל, and Ha. also הבהמה כי מקרה בני האדם ומקרה, and מן בהמה
on metrical grounds with great arbitrariness.—**20.** ⵖᴮᴺ*ⱽ 68. 147-157-159. 254
omit הולך. McN. accordingly believes that it was absent from the
pre-Aqiban text. Other MSS. of ⵖ as well as the other ancient versions
support it. Ha., for metrical reasons, omits as a gloss הכל הולך אל-
מקום אחר, and suggests the improbable explanation that it was based
on Horace's "Omnes eodem cogimur," which was written about
23 B.C.—שָּׁב] instead ⵖᴮ 68. 159. 254. 261. 296 ⵄᴴ read apparently יָשׁב.
Whether this was a pre-Aqiban reading, or has resulted from a corruption in Gr. MSS., is uncertain.—**21.** הֵ־], before עלה and ירדת, is
rightly taken by ⵖ, ⵄ, ⵗ and ⵟ and by most modern interpreters (Kn.,
Gins., Gr., Zö., Del., Wr., No., Vl., McN. and Kö. §§379aα, 414d)
as interrogative. Geiger, Sieg. and Ges.ᴷ· (§100m) hold that the text
here was intended to be interrogative, but that it cannot be so considered
as at present pointed, and that the ה has been in both cases changed

for dogmatic reasons. This seems to be a mistake, as in some cases
the interrogative particle takes *kameç* before gutturals (see הֶאִישׁ, Nu.
16²²), and in some cases *daghesh forte* before other letters (see הַבְּרַב Job
23⁶, הַבָּאִים Is. 27⁶, and חַיֵּטַב Lv. 10¹⁹).

𝕲, 𝕾 and 60 MSS. (so Dr.) read וּמִי at the beginning of the verse.
—22. שׁוֹב מֵאֲשֶׁר], in the sense of "better than," *cf.* Kö. §392e. הָאָרָם], the
art. is used to denote a class of beings (*cf.* Da. §22 (*c*)).—חֵלִק]. The
context shows that here and in 2¹⁰ 5¹⁷. ¹⁸ and 9⁹ it has the meaning of
"reward," "profit" (*cf.* BDB. 324a).   מִי יְבִיאֶנּוּ], like מִי יוֹרֵע of the
preceding vs., is really a strong denial.—רָאה ב], see crit. note on 2¹.—
אַחֲרָיו] Kö. (§401b) seems to be right in saying that this is equivalent
to אַחֲרֵי מוֹת. Vl.'s interpretation, which limits the lack of knowledge
to what goes on among men on the earth, seems forced.—יְבִיאַנּוּ]
Winckler (AOF., 351) emends to יְבִינֶנּוּ, "cause him to perceive."
This is unnecessary.—מֶה]. Hit., Del., and No. note that the pointing,
seghol, here is due to the influence of the following שֶּׁ-. *Cf.* also Ges.ᴷ·
§102k. Baer notes (p. 63) that two authorities favor the reading מָה.
Sieg. assigns this vs. and its kindred passages cited above to an epicurean
interpolator, claiming that Q¹ knew no joy in work. In support of
this he cites 1³. ¹⁴ 2¹¹. ¹¹ᶠ. ²⁰. ²²ᶠ. This result is reached only by excising
in each part of the context—a process which can be necessary only to
one who is convinced that both Stoic and Epicurean thought mingle
in the book. Against this view, see above, *Introduction*, §6 (2). Ha.
rejects as an unmetrical gloss all of the verse after מֵעֲשִׂי. His basis
is, however, too doubtful.

MAN'S INHUMANITY.

**4¹⁻¹² is a section treating of man's inhumanity to man, and the re-
flections which it caused in the mind of Qoheleth. The subject is
divided into three parts: (1) The oppressions of men by men; (2) The
vanity of rivalry; and (3) The lonely miser's inhumanity to himself.**

    4¹. And again, I saw all the oppressions which are practised under
the sun, and behold the tears of the oppressed! And they had no
comforter. And from the hand of the oppressors (went forth) power,
but they had no comforter.   ². And I congratulated the dead, who have
already died, more than the living who are yet alive.   ³. And (I regarded)
as happier than both of them him who had never been born, who has
not seen the evil work which is done under the sun.   ⁴. And I saw all
the toil and all the skilful work, that it was jealousy of one towards another, also this is vanity and a desire of wind.

    ⁵. *The fool folds his hands and eats his own flesh.*

    ⁶. Better is a palm of the hand full of rest than the hollow of two hands
full of toil and the desire of wind.   ⁷. Again I saw a vanity under the

sun.   8. There is a lone man, without a second, he has neither son nor
brother, but there is no end to all his toil, yea his eye is not sated with
wealth.   And for whom do I toil and deprive myself of good?   This
also is vanity and an evil task.

   9. Two are better than one, for they have a good reward in their toil.
10. For, if one shall fall, the other can raise up his companion, but woe
to the solitary man who shall fall, when there is none to raise him up.
11. Also, if two lie together, then they have warmth, but the solitary
man—how shall he be warm?   12. And if (a man) should attack one,
two could stand against him, and a threefold cord is not easily broken.

4¹. *I saw all the oppressions*].   The observation contained in
this verse is kindred to that in 3¹⁶, though different from it.—*Tears*].
The deep emotion which the tears of the oppressed excited in
Qoheleth is evidence of his profound sympathies with the lower
classes.—*Power*] is taken by several commentators to mean
violence.   Such a meaning would fit the context admirably, but
the word bears such a significance in no other passage.   Undoubtedly the context shows, however, that it means an oppressive use
of power.   The iteration of the phrase *they had no comforter* is for
rhetorical effect.   It heightens the impression of the helplessness
of the oppressed.—**2**. *I congratulated the dead*].   The oppressions
which men suffer make Qoheleth feel that the only happy men are
those who are dead.   This was, however, not his settled opinion
(*cf.* 9⁴).   It was rather a transitory mood, though intense in feeling while it lasted.   For similar expressions, see ch. 7¹ Job 3¹⁻
and Herodotus 1³¹.—**3**. *Happier than both, him who had never
been born*].   The thought of Qoh. here surges onward to the assertion that better even than the dead are those who have never
been born.   For similar sentiments, see ch. 6³⁻⁵ 7¹ Job 3¹³⁻¹⁶
Je. 20¹⁸, and among classical authors, Theognis, 425–428, Sophocles, *Œdipus, col.* 1225–1228, and Cicero, *Tusc.* 1⁴⁸.—*Seen*] is here
not so much "seen" as "experienced."   **4**. *That it was jealousy
of one towards another*].   It springs from jealousy or rivalry.
Qoheleth here passes from consideration of the inhumanity of
oppressors to the inhumanity of competition.   He finds in this
the motive of toil and the arts.

   5. *Folds his hands*], a synonym for idleness, *cf.* Pr. 6¹⁰ 19²⁴ 24³³.
—*Eats his own flesh*], devours his substance through idleness.

This is no doubt a current proverb, which is here quoted. It is out of harmony with the context, however, and was probably added by the *Hokma* glossator.

6. *Palm of the hand*], the slight hollow of the flat up-turned hand.—*Rest*], an Oriental's ideal of enjoyment, *cf.* Job 3¹³.— *The hollow of two hands*], both hands so curved as to hold as much as possible. This, too, is no doubt a current proverb, but it is so in accord with the thought of the context, that it was probably inserted by Qoheleth himself. The thought is similar to that of Pr. 15¹⁷.—**7.** *Again I saw*], Qoheleth now turns from rivalry to consider avarice.—**8.** *Without a second*]. This is explained by the words *son nor brother*. Qoh. means a man without helper or heir, though *second* can hardly mean "wife," as AE. thought.—*No end to all his toil*], activity has become a disease.— *His eyes*]. The eye is frequently used as the organ of desire, *cf.* 2¹⁰ and note.—*Sated*]. An avaricious soul is never satisfied.—*For whom do I toil?*] Qoheleth suddenly drops the indirect discourse and transfers us to the soul of the miser, perhaps to his own soul, for this may be a bit of personal experience. See above, *Introduction*, §13.—*This also is vanity*]. Here Qoheleth reverts again to his own reflections. The sentiment of this verse is repeated in BS. 14⁴.

9–12 are evidently current proverbs. It is an open question whether the proverbs were introduced by Qoheleth himself, or by glossators. See critical note. **9.** *Two are better than one*]. *Cf.* Gn. 2¹⁸. Jewish and classic lore contain similar sentiments, *e.g.*, *Iliad*, 10²²⁴⁻²²⁶.—*A good reward*]. The nature of this is explained in the next vs. It is that they help each other in time of need.—**10.** *If the one shall fall the other can raise up his companion*]. The thought of the vs. is that comradeship is the reward of united toil.—**11.** *If two lie together*]. The reference is not to husband and wife, but to two travellers. The nights of Palestine are cold, especially in the colder months, and a lone traveller sleeps sometimes close to his donkey for warmth in lieu of other companionship (see Barton, *A Year's Wandering in Bible Lands*, p. 167 *ff.*); Del. observes that in the *Aboth* of R. Nathan, ch. 8, sleeping together is a sign of friendship.—**12.** *A man*], the Heb. leaves the reader to gather the subject of the verb from the sentence, but it is clear that a robber is intended.—*Two could stand against him*]. This and the preceding vs. present further proofs of the advantages of companionship.—*A threefold cord*], one of the best-known passages in the book. Genung thinks the phrase means that if two are better than one, three are better still. Probably this is right. The other suggestions that have been made seem fanciful.

4¹. וּשְׁבַתִּי......וָאֶרְאֶה]. This is an instance of waw consecutive with the imperf. An earlier instance occurs in ch. 1¹⁷. Instances of its use with the perf. have been noted in 2²⁴ and 3¹³, though it is rare in Qoh.—וְשַׁבְתִּי, like שׁבתי in 9¹¹, is, as several interpreters have noted, a Heb. idiom for an adverb. It is equal to "again," see Kö. 369r.—עֲשֻׁקִים]. The first occurrence is, as most recent commentators agree, an abstract, as in Am. 3⁹ Job 35⁹. Kö.'s limitation of this usage to the last two passages quoted (Kö. §261d) seems arbitrary. The second עשוקים is the passive part. *Cf.* פרויי, Is. 35¹⁰.—רמעה], though sing. in form, is collective in sense, as in Is. 25⁸ Ps. 39¹³ 42⁴.—אשר נעשׂים]. Ha. excises this Niph. part as a gloss; it does not fit his metrical theory. 𝕭 inserts אין before מיד. which gives the sentence quite a different turn. There is no other authority for this, however, and it is probably a mistake.—מיד עֹשְׁקֵיהֶם כֹּחַ], RV. renders "on the side of their oppressors there was power," making מיד equal to עַל יד. As McN. observes it is simpler to supply some verb like "went forth."—לָהֶם.....לָהֶם]. Ha. claims that the first refers to the oppressed, and the second time to the oppressors; מנחם] he also takes the first time as "comforter," the second as "avenger." In that case the last clause should be rendered, "there was no avenger (for the wrongs done, by them)"—a view which is probably right. Sieg. holds that the last אֵין לָהֶם מְנַחֵם is a mistake, that the words are unsuited to the context, and must have arisen from dittography. On Ha.'s interpretation, adopted above, this objection falls to the ground.—2. וְשַׁבֵּחַ] has caused the commentators much trouble, and has occasioned some emendations of the text. AE., Herzfeld and Gins. regarded it as a verbal adjective. Ges., Kn., Heil., Elst., Del. (hesitatingly) and others regarded it as a participle Piel, from which the מ had been accidentally dropped. מְהֵר in Zeph. 1¹⁴—a form which made Del. hesitate to call שַׁבֵּחַ an inf.—is, as Wr. has pointed out, a verbal adjective. Among more recent commentators Eur. and Sieg. hold that it is a part. They explain the accidental loss of the מ through its similarity to שׂ in the old alphabet. Dr. suggests that possibly the original reading was וּשְׁבַחְתִּי. Both these suggestions, however, lack evidence. Rashbam, Mendelssohn, Ew., Zö., Wr., Heng., Gr., Hit., Vl., Wild., McN., Kö. (§§218b

and 225e) and Ges.ᴷ· (§113gg) regard it as an inf. abs. With this
view I agree. For similar constructions, *cf.* Gn. 41⁴³ Ex. 8¹¹ and Ju. 7¹⁹.
The word in the sense of "praise," "congratulate," is an Aramaism,
and occurs in late books only. It appears in Ps. 63⁴ 1 Ch. 16³⁵, and often
in Aram. as in Dn. 2²³ 4³¹· ³⁴ 5⁴· ²³, and in the Targum on Koh. 4² Ex. 15¹
Ps. 4¹, etc.—כבר], see note on 1¹⁰.—את מתים]. As 𝕲 read את־כל המתים instead, McN. properly regards this as the pre-Aqiban reading. Ha.
regards יכבר מתו and the second חיים as glosses. Of course it is because of his arrangement of the metre.—עֲרָנָה] (pointed thus by Baer
and Dr., but עֲרֶנָה by Hahn) is composed of עַר־הֵנָה or עַר־הֹן. In vs. 3
it is shortened to עֲרֶן. It occurs nowhere else in BH., but *cf.* the NH.
עֲרָיִן.—3. את אשר]. Scholars have differed in their interpretation of the
government of this. Kn., Wr., Vl., Wild., Sieg. and Kö. (§270b) hold
that it is governed by שַׁבֵּחַ of the preceding verse, Gins. and McN. by
שַׁבֵּחַ, to be supplied in thought from the preceding vs. As Del. observed, however, טוב follows שַׁבֵּחַ very unnaturally, and neither 𝕲, 𐍈
nor 𝔘 takes it as the object of such a verb. Del. accordingly suggested
that את may be the equivalent of the Ar. *'ayya*, a sign of the nom. case,
as 𝕲 and 𐍈 render it. He also suggests that קראתי is, perhaps, to be
supplied, since 𝔘 renders *judicavi*. In that case את would be the sign
of the acc. as usual. This is the view taken by No. and, apparently,
by Ges.ᴷ· (§117l). It seems to me the most probable view.—עֲרֶן], see
note on vs. 2. היה] is happily rendered ἐγεννήθη by Σ.—המעשה] refers
here to human oppressions.—את המעשה הרע]. 𝕲, 'A and Θ read את־כל
הרע המעשה, which was probably the reading in Aqiba's time. Ha.
omits הָרָע on metrical grounds. 4. כשרון]= "skill," though in 5¹⁰ it is
equivalent to יתרון, see note on 2²¹. 𝕲 renders it in all three passages by
ἀνδρεία, which does not give quite the thought.—כי]= "that" as in Gn. 1⁴
Job 22¹², *cf.* Kö. §414c.—קנאת], "jealousy" is often used with ל, as in
1 K. 19¹⁰ Nu. 11²⁹, etc., and with כ as in Dt. 32²¹ Pr. 3³¹, etc.—מן.
קנאת איש מרעהו], in this expression the מן is used to express the re-
ciprocal idea, *cf.* Kö. §308b. From 𝕲ᴮ'ˢ reading ὅτι τὸ ζῆλος ἀνδρί,
which Swete adopts in his text, McN. concludes that the true reading
was כי קנאת איש, omitting היא. The point is uncertain, however, since
היא is here a copula and might not be represented in 𝕲.

5. Sieg., McN. and Ha. rightly consider this vs. a proverb inserted by
some glossator. It was probably introduced because the context seemed to
encourage sloth.—חבק] generally in BH. means "to embrace," *cf.* ch.
3⁵ Gn. 29¹³ 48¹⁰, etc. It is connected with Aram. חבק and similar
Mand., Syr. and Ar. stems. The root means "to embrace," except
in Ar., but the Ar. ii stem means to "gather together." Here it
is used figuratively for folding the hands.—אכל בשרו]= "to destroy
one's self," *cf.* Ps. 27² Mi. 3³ Is. 49²⁶ Pr. 30¹⁴. So, correctly, Ty., Kn.,
Hit., Wr., Wild. Gins.'s explanation, "to enjoy a delicate repast,"

which he bases on the analogy of Ex. 16¹⁸ 21²⁸ Is. 22¹³ and Ez. 39¹⁸, is wrong. The sentiment of the verse is that laziness is suicide.

6. קלא], after this נָחַת, and עמל are the acc. expressive of the material, *cf.* Kö. §333d.—חפנים] means the "two hollow hands full." It occurs elsewhere only in Ex. 9⁸ Lv. 16¹² Ez. 10². ⁷ Pr. 30⁴. It is found also in NH. (*Yoma,* 5¹), and is kindred to Syr. *ḥûphnā* and Eth. *ḥafan.*—**7.** ושבתי אני ואראה], a repetition of the phrase of 4¹, in which waw consecutives occur, see note on 4¹.—**8.** אחד], on the use of this, *cf.* Ez. 33²⁴ and Kö. §315n.—גם], according to Kö. §371e, means "neither."—גם בן ואח] **𝕮** and 𝕾ᴴ read גם בן וגם אח, which was probably the pre-Aqiban reading. The pointing וְאֶח with the accent Munah is unusual. In Pr. 17¹⁷ we find וְאָח with Merka. *Cf.* וְצָאן (2⁷) with וְבָקָם (2²³).—עיניו], the *Kt.* is supported by 𝕌 and 𝕳 and is defended by Hit., Heil., Zö., Eur., Ty. and Vl. It has in its favor the fact that the members of the body are frequently mentioned in pairs (*cf.* Mi. 4¹¹ and 1 K. 14⁶. ¹²). The *Qr.* is supported by 𝕮, 𝕷, and 𝕾. As the latter is the reading hardest to account for, it is probably original. Bick., p. 12, regards this verse as the work of a clumsy editor. Zap. rejects גם זה הבל as a stereotyped gloss, Ha. regards גם זה הבל וענין רע הוא as a gloss. These opinions are only convincing to those who hold the peculiar views of their authors. The Hebrew text of BS. (14⁴) expresses the thought of this passage thus:

מונע נפשו יקבץ לאחר ובטובתו יתבעבע זר:

9-12. Sieg., McN. and Ha. regard these vvs. as proverbial additions made by glossators. There can be no doubt as to the proverbial character of the material, but it is an open question whether Qoh. himself may not have introduced them. They explain and give definiteness to vs. 8, but possibly may be epexegetical glosses introduced by others.—**9.** האחד and השני], the art. in these words, as Ty., Del., Wr. and Kö. (§313h) hold, is used because the writer individualizes two persons and one person.—אשר]= "because," or "for," *cf.* ch. 6¹² 10¹⁵ Gn. 30¹⁸ 34²⁷ Dt. 3²⁴ Jos. 4⁷ and Dn. 1¹⁰, also Ges.ᴷ· §157a.—**10.** יִפֹּלוּ]. The plural here denotes an indefinite sing., *cf.* Ges.ᴷ· §157a. Kn. compares ויאמרו איש אל רעהו in Gn. 11³ and Ju. 6²⁹. Dr. suggests that the original text may have been יפל האחד השנ יקום. This is the reading of 𝕾, 𝕳, and 𝕌, and seems probably correct. If so, the corruption of MT. antedates 𝕮, for it is supported by it.—אילו] is taken by 𝕮 and 𝕾 and many Heb. MSS. as= אוי לו. So, among interpreters, Kn., Gr., Del., Vl. and Kö. (§321c).—אוי is regularly "woe," *cf.* Nu. 21²⁹ 1 S. 4⁷ Is. 3⁹ and Ez. 13¹⁸ (where it is spelled הוי). 𝕌 takes it as the Aram. אילו=Heb. לּי, "if." The former view is correct.—אי]="woe" occurs in BH. only here and ch. 10¹⁶, but in NH. it appears as אי, *cf.* Ja., p. 43b.—לו האחד], the אחד is in apposition with the suffix, and the

suffix is anticipatory, the prep. logically governing אחר, so, Hit., Gins.,
Del., No., Eur., McN. and Kö. (§§340 o, 343a and 406a).—וְשִׁפֵל], as
Del. remarks, may be "who falls," or "when he falls."—לְהקִימו] Del.
and No. regard as potential.—11. גם] is often used to introduce a new
thought.—שׁכב] is used regularly for lying down to sleep, see e.g., Gn.
28¹¹.—וְחַם], the conjunction introduces the apodosis, and the construction of the verb is impersonal.—אֵיךְ] is here interrogative; not so in 2¹⁶.—
12. יתקפו] has an impersonal subject, i.e., the reader has to supply
it from the context, cf. Kö. §323c. The suffix וֹ- is instead of the more
common ◌ֵהו, see e.g., Job 15²⁴. The verb itself occurs only in late
Heb., though also common in NH., Aram. (Biblical, Nab. and Syr.),
and in Sabæan. Its ordinary meaning is to "overpower," and Zö.,
Del., Sieg., Wild., McN. and BDB. so take it here. The context, however,
requires here the meaning "attack," so correctly Kn., Wr., Ha. and
Ges.ᴮᵘ. ⑥ read וְתָקֵף, making האחד the subject—a reading which Kn.
regarded as right.—וְנֶגְדוֹ], the suffix refers to the implied robber, the
subject of יתקף. The prep. following עמד is more often in such constructions, בפני as in Jos. 10⁸, or לנגד in Dn. 10¹³.—הַמְשֻׁלָּשׁ], on the use
of שלש and deriv. in BH. and NH., cf. Kö. §312c.—כִּמְהֵרָה] is late Heb.
for מְהֵרָה. It is parallel to the late expression עַד מהֵרָה in Ps. 147¹⁵.

**4¹³⁻¹⁶ set forth the vanity of the popularity of certain young kings
who are not named.**

¹³. Better is a youth poor and wise than a king old and foolish, who
no longer knows how to be admonished. ¹⁴. Though from the house
of the rebellious he came forth—although even in his kingdom he was
born poor. ¹⁵. I saw all the living who walk under the sun with [the
second] youth, who shall stand in his stead. ¹⁶. There was no end to all
the people—all whose leader he was—moreover those who come after
could not delight in him. For this also is vanity and a desire of wind.

13. *Better is a youth poor and wise*]. The word *youth* is applied
to children (1 S. 3¹) and to men at least forty years of age (1 K.
12⁸). In the East great deference has always been paid to age.
This vagueness presents a difficulty in the interpretation of this
vs. Many theories as to whom Qoheleth refers, have been put
forth. The Targum makes it a contrast between Abraham and
Nimrod; the Midrash, between Joseph and Pharaoh, or David
and Saul. Joash and Amaziah, Cyrus and Astyages, the high
priest Onias and his nephew Joseph, have also been suggested.
Graetz believed that the reference was to Herod the Great and
his son Alexander; Hitzig, to Ptolemy Philipator, who, weak and

headstrong, had been beaten by Antiochus III, and Ptolemy
Epiphanes, who came to the Egyptian throne in 205 B.C. at the
age of five; Winckler believes the contrast to be between Antiochus
Epiphanes and Demetrius I; Haupt, between Antiochus Epiphanes and Alexander Balas—a view which would be tempting, if
one could bring the book down as late as Haupt does. Alexander
Balas was a youth of humble origin (cf. Justin, xxxv, 1), who pre-
tended to be the son of Antiochus. Balas was friendly to the Jews
(1 Mac. 10⁴⁷). This would seem very tempting, if the external
evidence did not make it certain that the book was written before
175 B.C. (See *Introduction*, §§11, 15). This evidence makes it
probable that Hitzig was right and that the "wise youth" is one
of the Ptolemies, perhaps Ptolemy V, who in 205 B.C. succeeded
his aged father Ptolemy IV. Ptolemy V was but five years old
when he came to the throne.—**14.** *House of the rebellious*] probably refers to the Ptolemaic dynasty. It is so designated because
Ptolemy IV persecuted the Jews; see 3 Macc. Symmachus, the
Targum, Wang., Del., Wr. and Vl. take the last clause of the
verse to refer to the old king, but it is better with McN. and Haupt
to take the whole verse as referring to the youth.—**15.** *All the living
who walk under the sun*], an hyperbolical expression of popular
enthusiasm upon the young king's succession.—*Second youth*.]
Second is here a difficulty and has been variously explained.
Ewald, whom Marshall follows, thought it analogous to "second"
in Gn. 41⁴³, *i.e.*, it designated a youth who held the second place
in the kingdom and who usurped the throne. Kn., Del. and Wr.
held that the youth is "second," the old king, his predecessor,
being first. Del. cites as analogies the use of "other," Mt.
8²¹, and "others," Lk. 23³². The expression and interpretation are,
however, unnatural. As McN. declares it can only mean a *second*
youth. Bick., Sieg., Ha. and Dr. (the last hesitatingly) regard
second as a disturbing gloss. Erase this, and we have, on Hitzig's
view, a picture of the enthusiasm with which Ptolemy V was
greeted. If *second* is genuine, it would, on our view, be a reference
to the enthusiasm which greeted Antiochus III when he conquered
Jerusalem in 198 B.C. (*cf.* Jos. *Ant.* xii, 3²).—*Who shall stand*],
future, because spoken from the point of view of the moment when

the enthusiasm burst out.—*In his stead*], *i.e.*, if "second" is genu-ine, in place of the first youth.—**16.** *No end of all the people*], hyper-bole again, referring to the young king's accession. *Those who came after*], in a short time the popularity of Epiphanes waned because of the corruption of his advisers. Then Anti-ochus III (200–198) attached Palestine to Syria, and was gladly received by the Jews. See Bevan, *House of Seleucus*, II, 37, and Jos. *Ant.* xii, 3³.—*This also is vanity*], the old refrain. Specific cases have demonstrated the fleeting character even of royal prestige. If these are not the real instances of which Qoheleth was thinking, he had similar ones in mind.

13. שׁוב], *i.e.*, better suited to govern, *cf.* what is said of a high priest, *Horayoth*, 3⁸.—מסכן], *poor*, occurs in BH. only here and in ch. 9¹⁵· ¹⁶. It is not uncommon in Aram., see *e.g.*, the ⅏ of this passage, and to Dt. 8⁹. In Babylonian (Code of Hammurabi) the word occurs as *miskenu* and designates the lowest class of citizens above slaves (*cf. Code*, col. vi, 65, and CT., XII, 16, 42b). The root סכן, "to be poor," occurs in Is. 40²⁰, and מִסְכֵּנֻת, "poverty," in Dt. 8⁹. Just why it should be applied to Ptolemy V, we know too little of the history of the times to tell. Possibly the word is an early gloss added by some one who did not per-ceive that the reference was to a royal youth.—יֶלֶד] is used not only of boys, but of Joseph when 17 years old (Gn. 37³⁰), and of the companions of Jeroboam who were about 40 years old (1 K. 12⁸). Here, however, the reference is to a real boy.—נזהר] is usually explained as from זהר, "to be bright," but this is doubtful (*cf.* BDB. 264a). In Niph. and Hiph. it means "warn," or "admonish," *cf.* ch. 12¹² Ez. 3²⁰ 33⁴·⁶ and Ps. 19¹². 'A, Σ, and Θ render τοῦ φυλάξεσθαι, "to be on one's guard," but this destroys the parallelism.—**14.** הסורים], some MSS. and ⅖, ⅏, read האסורים (see Baer and Dr.). AE., Kn., Heil., Gins., Heng., Del., Wr., No., Vl., Eur., McN., Kam. and Ges.ᴷ· (§35d) hold this to be the true rendering on the ground that in late Heb. א is often dropped. ⅏ and ⅏ give the word a different interpretation, and Ew., Hit., Dale and Ha. take it from סור, "to turn," the derivatives of which may mean "rebels," or "outcasts" (*cf.* Je. 2²¹ 17¹³). This I believe to be nearer the truth.—יצא] is perf. Gr.'s contention that it is imperf., was but a *tour de force* to fit his theory.—כי גם], it is better to take this as "although" with most interpreters (*cf.* Kö. §394f) than as "for" with McN. For the sake of consistency, however, the first כי should be rendered "though."—במלכותו], the suffix probably refers to the "youth," not to the old king as Σ, ⅏, Wang., Del., Wr. and Vl. held.—נולד] prob-ably has here its usual meaning. It is true, as Ty., Gins. and Gr. hold,

that in the Mishna it means "arise" or "become" (*cf. Terumoth*, 8⁸,
Ned., 9³, and *Temurah*, 3⁵), but a more natural meaning is obtained
by taking it in its ordinary sense. It then means that the "youth"
was born poor in the kingdom which he afterward ruled. Possibly
this last clause, like מסכן, is a gloss, though it may possibly refer
to the impoverished state of Egypt at Ptolemy V's accession on
account of political disorders in the preceding reign. Cf. Polybius, V, 107, and XIV, 12.—**15.** המהלכים], the Piel part. The Kal is
more common, *cf.* Is. 42⁵.—שני] is supported by all the Versions, and
is probably not a gloss, as Bick., Sieg., Ha. and Kit. hold.—עם],
"with," in the sense of "on the side of," *cf.* Gn. 21²² 26³.—יעמד], in the
sense of "reign" or "arise," see BDB. 764a. Its imperf. tense is paralleled
2 K. 3²⁷ and Job 15²⁵. תחת is often used of a successor to a throne, see
e.g., 2 S. 10¹ and 2 Ch. 1⁸.—**16.** האחרונים] often means "posterity"
(*cf.* 1¹¹ and Is. 41⁴), but here probably simply "those who come after."
If we are right in our interpretation of the passage, but seven years had
passed.—אשר היה לפניהם]="before whom he was," *i.e.*, whose leader
he was, *cf.* Ps. 68⁸ and 2 Ch. 1¹⁰, thus Ros., Ges., Gins., Del. and Wr.
Ew. misunderstood it and made הם refer to the two preceding kings.
𝔖, 𝔙 and 𝔗 changed הם to י, misunderstanding it also.—וגם] is adversative, *cf.* Kö. §373n.

5¹⁻⁷ (Heb. 4¹⁷-5⁶) treats of shams in religion.

5¹ (4¹⁷). Guard thy foot when thou goest to the house of God, and
to draw near to obey is better than that fools should give sacrifice, for
they do not know (except) to do evil. **2⁽¹⁾.** Do not be rash with thy
mouth and let not thy heart be hasty to utter a word before God, for
God is in heaven and thou on the earth, therefore let thy words be few.

> **3⁽²⁾.** *For dreams come through a multitude of business,*
> *And the voice of a fool through a multitude of words.*

4⁽³⁾. When thou vowest a vow to God, do not delay to fulfil it, for there
is no delight in fools, what thou vowest fulfil. **5⁽⁴⁾.** Better is it that
thou shouldst not vow than that thou shouldst vow and not fulfil.
6⁽⁵⁾. Do not permit thy mouth to make thy flesh to sin, and do not
speak in the presence of the angel, for it is an error, Why should God
be angry at thy voice and destroy the work of thy hands, **7⁽⁶⁾.** (*For in
a multitude of dreams and words are many vanities*), but fear thou God.

5¹ (4¹⁷). *Guard thy foot*]. Do not run to the place of worship
thoughtlessly, or because it is the fashion to go frequently, but consider the nature of the place and thy purpose in going. Interpreted by what follows, this is the meaning.—*The house of God*],

often used in the OT. for the temple, *cf.* 2 S. 12²⁰ Is. 37¹. It probably means that here, though some think it the synagogue. Whether it is to be regarded as temple or synagogue depends upon how we interpret the next clause.—*To obey is better than that fools should give sacrifice*]. The sentiment recalls 1 S. 15²² Am. 5²⁴. ²⁵ Mi. 6⁷. ⁸. If this *sacrifice* is to be taken literally, Qoh. was thinking of the temple; if it is to be interpreted by the following verse as figurative for words, he may have referred to the synagogue. On the whole, it is more probable that this verse refers to the well-known contrast between literal sacrifice and obedience, and that the next verse takes up a new topic, unless we interpret vows as votive sacrifices.—*Know except to do evil*]. They go from their sacrifices with an easy conscience to plunge again into evil.—**2** ⁽¹⁾. *Rash with thy mouth . . . utter a word*]. This is explained in vs. 4 to refer to vows.—*God is in heaven*]. The belief in the transcendence and aloofness of God, Qoheleth shared with his age, *cf.* Ps. 115³. The verse is paraphrased in BS. 7¹⁴.

3 ⁽²⁾. Sieg. and Ha. are right in regarding this verse as a gloss. It is a proverb, kindred to 5⁶ and in reality breaks the connection of the thought here. It was probably introduced because the reference to a fool's multitude of words seemed kindred in meaning to vs. 4⁽³⁾. It has a proverbial form and is apparently the work of the *Hokma* glossator. The sentiment of the first part of the vs. is expressed in BS. 31¹⁻⁴.—*Dreams come through a multitude of business*]. The words apparently mean that one who is worried with cares cannot sleep, but in that case there is little connection with the next clause. Tyler thought the "multitude of business" referred to the multiplicity of images and the confused action of a troubled dream. This would make the parallel with the "words of a fool" closer. If this is the meaning it is not clearly expressed, but not all popular proverbs are clear.

4 ⁽³⁾. *When thou vowest a vow*]. This is taken with as little change as possible from Dt. 23²¹. For other statements about vows, *cf.* Nu. 30³ Ps. 50¹⁴.—*Do not delay to fulfil*]. Hasty vows were not infrequent in later Judaism, and many evasions were attempted, as the Talmudic tract *Nedarim* shows. On vows of the sort here referred to, see Gn. 28²⁰ Lv. 27 Ju. 11³⁰ Jos., BJ.

ii, 15¹; *cf.* also Mk. 7¹¹ Acts 18¹⁸ 21²³.—*There is no delight in fools*].
God has no delight in them. Vows are the favorite resort of the
foolish. They think to bribe Providence.—*What thou vowest fulfil*]. This expresses in another way the meaning of Dt. 23²². ²³. The
verse is quoted in BS. 18²².—**5** ⁽⁴⁾. *Better not to vow*], for one is then
at least honest. Qoheleth's point of view on this point is similar
to that of Acts 5⁴.—**6** ⁽⁵⁾. *Do not permit thy mouth*] by rash vows.—
Thy Flesh]. Flesh here stands for the whole personality; perhaps
it is used here because the Jews thought of punishment as corporal.—
In the presence of the angel]. This has been variously interpreted:
(1) It has been held that *angel* is a later and more reverent way of
alluding to God. This view has in its favor the fact that 𝔊 and
𝔖 actually read "God" here. (2) That angel (literally messenger)
is God's representative—either prophet as in Hg. 1¹³ Mal. 3¹, or
a priest as in Mal. 2⁷—here, of course, a priest. (3) That we
should translate "messenger," and regard it as a temple messenger
who recorded vows and collected the dues. Probably the first interpretation is right.—*Error*], a sin of inadvertence.—*Why should
God be angry*]. Qoheleth has much the same idea of God as that
which underlies our expression, "tempting Providence."—**7** ⁽⁶⁾. *For
in a multitude of dreams and words are many vanities*]. This is another interpolated proverb, corresponding to vs. 3. It interrupts
the connection.—*But fear thou God*]. This is the conclusion to
vs. 6.

1–7. McN. regards these verses as the work of the *Chasid* glossator,
and Sieg. assigns vvs. 1 and 2 to Q⁸—a term which covers a mass of glosses.
One with so keen an eye for glosses as Ha. has, however, regarded
vvs. 1 and 2 as genuine. Really the whole section, except vvs. 3 and 7a,
is Q.'s work. Because he held a Sadducæan point of view, he was not
prevented from speaking of religion.—1 (4¹⁷). [רגליך] is, according to
Qr., רגלך, a reading which is supported by 160 MSS. and 𝔊, 𝔖, and 𝔙,
and is probably right. Analogies can be adduced for the plural (*e.g.*,
Ps. 119⁵⁹) and for the sing. (Ps. 119¹⁰⁵ Pr. 1¹⁵ 4²⁶). So far as the meaning
goes, it is a matter of indifference which reading is followed.—[כאשר=
"when," as in Gn. 18³³. 𝔊, Θ and Tal., Jer., *Berak.*, 4⁴, 71³, and *Megill.*,
71c, *Tosephta*, 17², read באשר by mistake.—[קרוב] was taken by Ros., De W.
and others as an inf. continuing the imperative construction, but recent
interpreters (Kn., Del., Wr., No., Zö., Vl., Ha. and Kö. (§223a) rightly
regard it as an inf. used as the subject.—[זתה], טוב is to be supplied

in thought before this, as in 9¹⁷, cf. Ges.ᴷ· §133e, and Kö. §308c. ⑤, ⑤, and 𝔈 take the word as a noun="gift," but this is an error. —הכסלים זבה] ⑤ read זבח הכסילים רע.—[אינם יודעים לעשות רע] has occasioned much trouble. It naturally seems to mean "they do not know (how) to do evil," which is obviously contrary to Q.'s thought. Kn. understood it "they do not know when they do evil," Del. and Eur. "ignorance makes for evil doing," Re. supplied כי אם before לעשות, while Sieg., whom McN. follows, emends to מלעשות. One of these emendations has to be made, the last is the simplest, as the מ may easily have fallen out after יודעים. The error is older than any of the Vrss., for they all support MT.—2 ⁽¹⁾. [על פי] is a not uncommon expression, see Ex. 23¹³ Ps. 50¹⁶ Pr. 16¹⁰. Parallel expressions are על לשנו Ps. 15³, and על שפתי Pr. 16¹⁰. [לפני האלהים], i.e., where God is, in his house; cf. Ex. 16⁹ 18¹² Dt. 14²⁵ 15²⁰ Is. 37¹⁴.—[יעטים], as a plural predicate (cf. Kö. §334b), occurs elsewhere only in Ps. 109⁸. It is a late and rare usage. This verse is paraphrased in BS. 7¹⁴, see Heb. text.—3 ⁽²⁾. [החלום], the art. is used to make the sing. stand for a class, cf. Ges.ᴷ· §126r.—[ענין], see on 1¹³. Σ read ἀνομίας=עון (iniquity).—[ב ברב] is instrumental, cf. Hb. 2⁴ and Ps. 19¹².—4 ⁽³⁾. [כאשר] corresponds to כי of Dt. 23²².—[אל תאחר] to לא תאחר of the same passage. Ha., for metrical reasons, erases [לאלהים] as a gloss.—[חפץ] means usually "delight," "pleasure." As the "delight" of Yahweh is his "will," also Pl. takes it to mean "fixed purpose," i.e., "there is no fixed purpose in fools"—not enough to fulfil a vow. Such a meaning would be attractive, if it had lexical authority, but it has none. Cf. Is. 62⁴.—[את אשר תדר שלם]. Zap. erases this as a gloss for metrical reasons.—6 ⁽⁵⁾. [נתן], in the sense of "permit," takes an acc. of the object and dat. of the end, cf. Gn. 20⁶ 31⁷ Ex. 3¹⁹ Nu. 22¹³ Ju. 1³⁴ Job 31³⁰. Sometimes ל is omitted as in Job 9¹⁸.—[לחטיא] is for להחטיא, cf. Ges.ᴷ· §53q.—[מלאך], instead ⑤ and ⑤ read אלהים, which was probably the original reading. [שגגה] is often used in Lv. and Nu. for sins of error or inadvertence, BDB., cf., e.g., Lv. 4². ²². ²⁷ and Nu. 15²⁶. ²⁷. ²⁸. ²⁹. Such sins were readily atoned by offerings.—[למה] is used in Heb. idiom as we would use "lest," cf. Kö. §354e.—7 ⁽⁶⁾. The first part of the vs. is a proverbial interpolation, but its text is evidently corrupt. It is probably a variant of vs. 3, and was written on the margin, afterward creeping into the text. The simplest emendation is to suppose that הבלים and דברים have been accidentally transposed. It is thus translated above. ⑤, ⑤, 𝔈, 𝔎, read אתה for את, which reading is to be followed.

5⁸ ⁽⁷⁾.—6⁹ treats of oppression: (1) **Of despotic government, 5⁸, ⁹;** (2) **Of riches, 5¹⁰–6⁹.**

5⁸ ⁽⁷⁾. If thou seest oppression of a poor man and the wresting of justice and right in a province, do not look in astonishment at the matter, for one high officer is watching above another, and there are higher ones above them. ⁹ ⁽⁸⁾. But an advantage to a country on the whole is a king—(*i.e.*) an agricultural land.

¹⁰ ⁽⁹⁾. He who loves silver will not be satisfied with silver, nor who loves riches, with gain; also this is vanity. ¹¹ ⁽¹⁰⁾. When goods increase, eaters of them increase, and what profit has their owner except the sight of his eyes? ¹² ⁽¹¹⁾. Sweet is the sleep of the laborer, whether he eat little or much, but the satiety of the rich does not permit him to sleep. ¹³ ⁽¹²⁾. There is a sore evil which I have seen under the sun,—wealth guarded by its owner to his hurt. ¹⁴ ⁽¹³⁾. And that wealth perished in an unlucky adventure, and he begat a son and there was nothing in his hand. ¹⁵ ⁽¹⁴⁾. As he came naked from the womb of his mother, he shall go again as he came; and nothing shall he receive through his labor, which he can carry in his hand. ¹⁶ ⁽¹⁵⁾. Also this is a sore evil—exactly as he came so shall he go, and what advantage is it to him that he toiled for wind. ¹⁷ ⁽¹⁶⁾. Also all his days he is in darkness and mourning and much vexation and sickness and anger.

¹⁸ ⁽¹⁷⁾. Behold what I saw,—a good that is beautiful is it to eat and drink and to see good in all one's toil which he toils under the sun the number of the days of his life which God gives him, for that is his lot.

¹⁹ ⁽¹⁸⁾. Also every man to whom God has given riches and wealth and has empowered him to eat of it and to take up his lot and to rejoice in his work—this is the gift of God. ²⁰ ⁽¹⁹⁾. For he will not much think on the days of his life, for God occupies him with the joy of his heart.

6¹. There is an evil which I have seen under the sun, and it is heavy upon mankind; ². A man to whom God has given riches and wealth and honor and he lacks nothing for himself of all that he desires, but God has not empowered him to eat of it, but a stranger eats of it—this is vanity and an evil disease. ³. Though a man beget a hundred (children), and live many years and multiplied are the days of his years, but his soul is not satisfied with good, and also he has no burial,—I have seen that an untimely birth is better than he. ⁴. For into vanity it came and into darkness it shall go and with darkness shall its name be covered. ⁵. Yea the sun it saw not, nor had knowledge. This has more rest than the other. ⁶. And if he live a thousand years twice over and good he does not see,—are not both going unto the same place?

> ⁷. All the toil of man is for his mouth,
> And yet his appetite is not satisfied.

⁸. For what advantage has the wise man over the fool, and what the poor who knows how to walk before the living? ⁹. Better is the sight of the eyes than the wandering of desire. This also is vanity and a desire of wind.

5⁸ ⁽⁷⁾. *Oppression*]. The unequal oppressions of life may lead one to pessimism (*cf.* ch. 4¹ᶠᶠ·), but when he considers how an Oriental state is organized and governed he does not marvel at it. —*Wresting of justice and right*]. The constant complaint against Oriental rule, where each official looks out for his own interests, from time immemorial to the present day.—*One high officer is watching above another*], an excellent description of a satrapial system. The appropriateness of this remark to Qoheleth's line of thought lies in the fact that these officials were watching, not, as a rule, that justice might be done to the poor, but to squeeze revenue out of the petty officials under them. As each officer was an oppressor, no wonder that the poor peasant—the lowest stratum of the heap—should be squeezed.—*Higher ones above them*]. This is perhaps an impersonal allusion to the king.—**9** ⁽⁸⁾. *An advantage to a country on the whole is a king*]. Qoheleth thinks that, after all, monarchy has some advantages. Others have thought that even kings like Herod had some good points (*cf.* Jos. *Ant.* xvi, 9¹), in that they prevented plundering raids and rendered agriculture secure.

10 ⁽⁹⁾. *He who loves silver*], perhaps this reflection was suggested by the rapacity of the officials referred to in vs. 8. It serves as the starting-point for some reflections upon the vanity of riches.—*Will not be satisfied*]. The miser is always poor, because his desire is not satisfied.—**11** ⁽¹⁰⁾. *What profit has their owner except the sight of his eyes?*]. One can really enjoy but a limited amount of wealth, he who has more, has only the pleasure of seeing others consume it. For similar sentiments, *cf.* Herod., I, 32; Horace, *Satires*, I, 1⁷⁰ᶠ·, and Xenophon, *Cyroped.*, VIII, 3³⁵⁻⁴⁴. A part of the last passage (§40) is particularly in harmony with our text: "Do you think, Sacian, that I live with more pleasure the more I possess? Do you not know that I neither eat, nor drink, nor sleep, with a particle more pleasure than when I was poor? But by having this abundance I gain merely this, that I have to guard more, to distribute more to others, and to have the trouble of taking care of more."—**12** ⁽¹¹⁾. *Sweet is the sleep of the laborer*]. Qoheleth recognizes that the healthy out-door life of the peasant has some blessings which money not only cannot buy, but which it destroys.—**13** (12). *Wealth guarded by its owner to his hurt*], *i.e.*, guarded at the expense of anxiety and sleeplessness.— **14** (13). *Unlucky adventure*], such as speculation in a caravan which robbers capture.—*He begat a son and there was nothing in his hand*]. After all his anxiety he has nothing to leave his offspring. **15** (14). *As he came naked*]. Probably, as Del. remarked, Qoheleth has Job 1²¹ in mind. For similar thoughts, see Ps. 49¹⁰ and 1 Tim. 6⁷.—**16** (15). Both this vs. and the preceding were suggested by "father" in vs. 14.—*What advantage*], perhaps, refers back to the father, as Graetz thought.—*Toiled for wind*], a figurative expression for nothingness, only in late writings. *Cf.* Is. 26¹⁸ Pr. 11²⁹.—**17** (16). *All his days he is in darkness*]. The vs. refers to the self-denial and mental distresses of those who are bent upon the accumulation of wealth. Qoheleth's thought reminds us of that in 1 Tim. 6⁹, "They that desire to be rich fall into a temptation and a snare and many foolish and hurtful lusts."

18 (17). *A good that is beautiful is to eat*]. In contrast to the evils incident to the accumulation of wealth given in vs. 17, Qoheleth advocates the enjoyment of life as one goes along, claiming that this is the order of life appointed man by God. It is an iteration of his fundamental philosophy. The sentiment probably refers to rational enjoyment of present good, in contrast to miserly self-denial for the sake of hoarding.—**19** (18). *This is the gift of God*]. This expresses the same thought as vs. 18 in a different way. The way in which Qoheleth dwells upon the idea shows how heartily he was in favor of getting rational enjoyment as one goes along. The vs. is quoted and opposed in Wisdom 2⁹.—**20** (19). *Will not much think*]. One will not brood over life's brevity, if it is full of proper enjoyment. Qoheleth sees no very bright ray illuminating life, but believes in being content with such satisfactions as God has allotted to man. On the sentiment, *cf.* Hor. *Epist.* I, 4, 7:

Di tibi divitias dederunt artemque fruendi.

6¹. *There is an evil*]. The phrase introduces the following verse.—**2.** *Has given riches and wealth and honor*]. This description is almost identical with that in 5¹⁹, where Qoheleth described what he regarded as the right course of life for a prosperous man.

The description is purposely repeated here in order to set forth what in Qoheleth's judgment is one of life's greatest misfortunes.— *God has not empowered him to eat of it*]. "To eat" is used in the sense of "enjoy," *cf.* Is. 3¹⁰ Je. 15¹⁶. Perhaps he does not enjoy it through worry, or because in the hard processes of obtaining it he has lost the power of enjoyment.—*A stranger eats of it*]. He has not even a son to inherit it, its real enjoyment is obtained by another.—**3.** *Though a man beget a hundred children*]. A numerous offspring was to the ancient Hebrew an object of great desire, and its possession regarded as a great blessing, *cf.*, *e.g.*, Gn. 24⁶⁰ and Ps. 127²⁻⁵.—*A hundred*] is simply a round number, *cf.* Gn. 26¹² 2 S. 24³ and Pr. 17¹⁰.—*And live many years*]. Long life was also regarded as one of the most desirable blessings, *cf.* Ex. 20¹² Dt. 11⁹· ²¹ and Pr. 28¹⁶.—*Soul is not satisfied with good*], *i.e.*, he does not obtain that enjoyment praised in 5¹⁹.—*Also he has no burial*]. The ancient Semites, like the ancient Greeks, attached great importance to proper burial. At the end of the *Gilgamesh* epic are the following lines (*cf.* KB., VI, 265):

> He whose dead body is thrown on the field,
>   Thou hast seen, I see,
> His spirit rests not in the earth.
> He whose spirit has no caretaker
>   Thou hast seen, I see,
> The dregs of the pot, the remnants of food,
> What is thrown in the street, must eat.

This idea prevailed widely among the Greeks. Much of the plot of the *Antigone* of Sophocles turns upon it. It also prevailed among the Hebrews, *cf.* Is. 14¹⁹· ²⁰ Je. 16⁴· ⁵ Job 21³²· ³³ Tobit 1¹⁸ 2⁴· ⁵ 1 Mac. 7¹⁷ 2 Mac. 5¹⁰ 13⁷, see also Schwally, *Leben nach dem Tode*, 48–51, and 54–59. Plumtre's idea that the importance attached to burial here is due to Greek influence, is quite wrong.— *Untimely birth*], *cf.* Job 3¹⁶ Ps. 58⁸.—**4.** *Into vanity it came*], *i.e.*, into a lifeless existence.—*With darkness shall its name be covered*]. As Delitzsch observes, it really has no name. The Hebrew way of saying this is the above. As in Job 3¹⁶ and Ps. 58⁸, the untimely birth is an example of something that has no sensations either of good or evil, and which leaves no memory behind it. It can be

conscious of no loss or suffering, hence in comparison with the unfortunate in question, Qoheleth regards it fortunate.—**5.** *Yea the
sun it saw not*]. The lifeless fœtus escaped all sensation.—*Nor
had knowledge*], did not come to consciousness.—*This has more
rest than the other*], freedom from the toil and worry of life. Rest
is an Oriental ideal, and Qoheleth in this expression approaches
the Buddhistic appreciation of Nirvana.—**6.** *A thousand years
twice over*], twice the length of an antedeluvian patriarch's life.—
And good he does not see], misses the one redeeming feature of
mortal existence, which in 5¹⁸ Qoheleth has recognized to be such.—
Are not both going unto the same place?]. Both the lifeless fœtus
and the man whose life has been long but wretched, are destined
to Sheol, and the lifeless fœtus is to be congratulated because it
reaches the goal by a shorter and less agonizing way.—**7.** *The
man*], here the long-lived individual referred to in vs. 6.—*Mouth
and appetite*] are probably used symbolically. One toils all his
life for a satisfaction which he never attains.—**8.** *What advantage
has the wise man over the fool?*]. The idea that the lifeless fœtus
has an advantage over a prosperous man prompts a repetition of
the thought of ch. 2¹⁴ᶠ.—*What, the poor who knows how to walk
before the living?*]. This evidently means, as McN. has seen,
"what advantage has the poor man, who has got on in the world
by knowing how to walk prudently and successfully, before his
fellow-men?" This, like the question about the wise and fools, is
suggested by the comparison of the prosperous, long-lived man
with the lifeless fœtus.—**9.** *Better is the sight of the eyes*]. The
last clause shows that this expression means "better is the enjoyment of what one has."—*Wandering of desire*], desires for various
unattainable things.

5⁸ ⁽⁷⁾. Sieg. and Ha. regard this verse as the work of a glossator—
Sieg., of Q⁴, his *Chasid* glossator. Sieg. misinterprets the text, however,
taking חמה in the sense of σκανδαλίζεσθαι in Mt. 13²¹, emending שֹׁמֵר
to וְשָׁמַר, and following Kn., Heil., Zö., BD*B*. and Ges.ᴷ· (§124h), in
taking גבהים, plural *majestatis*, referring to God. It is better with Hit.,
Ew., Del., Wr., Wild., Gins., Pl., Vl. and McN. to interpret it of a
hierarchy of officials, as we have done above. It then becomes thoroughly harmonious with Q.'s point of view.—וְזֵל מִשְׁפָּט], *cf.* גֵּזֶל מִשְׁפָּט.
Is. 10².—מדינה], in the sense of "Province," occurs frequently in the

late books, Ezr., Neh., Est., Dn., La., and Qoh. Outside of these books, only in 1 K. 20¹⁴· ¹⁵· ¹⁷· ¹⁹ and Ez. 19⁸.—תהמה] on חמה, in the sense of "look with astonishment," see Is. 13⁸ 29⁹ Je. 4⁹ Ps. 48⁶ Job 26¹¹. —חפץ="business" in Is. 58¹³ and Pr. 31¹³, it has here passed from that to mean "matter," or "thing," BDB., as in the Talmud, cf. Ja. 492b.—
9 (8). This verse has been a crux to interpreters. The various renderings from that of Död. to that of Sieg. are, when compared, an eloquent testimony to the difficulty of the verse.—שׂדה] Död. emended to יׂשׂרי, rendering, "Superior land, whose king is a servant of the Almighty." Ewald and Zö. rendered, "A king set over a land"; Kn., Ges., Vaih., "A king who is served by the land"; 𝔗, Ra. and AE., "A king who is subject to the land"; Del., Heng., Wr., "A king devoted to arable land," and Wild., "King of a kingdom which is served." McN. and Ha. have correctly rendered substantially as it is rendered above. Ha. alone seems to have correctly seen that שׂדה is epexegetical of ארץ. McN. and Kö. (§286d) hold that they cannot refer to the same thing. McN. correctly observes, however, that the accents show that נעבד is to be construed with שׂדה and not with מלך. The article in בכל expresses totality, cf. Gn. 16¹² 2 S. 23⁵ 1 Ch. 7⁵ and Kö. §301a. 𝔊 and Σ read ἐπὶ παντί. Perhaps, as McN. suggests, the scribe thought it referred to the hierarchy of officials in vs. 8.—שׂדה], literally "field," i.e., land for pasturage or tillage.—נעבד]. This Niphal occurs only in Dt. 21⁴ and Ez. 36⁹· ³⁴, and always means "till."

10 (9). אהב כסף] was regarded by Zirkel as a Græcism=φιλάργυρος, a view which McN., p. 41, has sufficiently refuted. See above, Introduction, §6 (1). כסף was among the ancient Semites the specific word for money.—ב אהב. ב- occurs with אהב only here. It strengthens the idea. It is parallel to ב חפץ in Nu. 14⁸ 2 S. 15²⁶, etc.—מי] is used in the sense "whoever," cf. Ex. 24¹⁴ 32²⁶ Ju. 7³ Is. 44¹⁰ Pr. 9⁴· ¹⁶, also Kö. §382b.—המון] usually means "multitude," being derived from a root, "to roar," or "murmur." Sometimes it has as here the meaning "wealth," cf. Is. 60⁵ Ps. 37¹⁶ 1 Ch. 29¹⁶. Dr. thinks the original reading may have been ממון, since that is the reading of 𝔖 and 𝔗. The ב before המון he regards as due to dittography.—גם זה הבל] Zap. regards as a stereotyped gloss, while Ha. refers the whole verse to a glossator. —11 (10). ברבות] affords an example of a common Sem. method of denoting time by a prep. and an infinitive. Cf. the As. ina kašadiša="when she approached," IV, R., 31, 12; KB., VI, 80, and also cf. Ges.K· §114e. —השובה] is another way of referring to המון of the preceding vs.—כשׂרון], see on 4⁴. It primarily means skill, but is here equivalent to יתרון. —בעליה]. בעל is frequently used in the pl. form with a sing. sense, but always before a suffix, cf., e.g., Ex. 21²⁹ Is. 1³ and Kö. §263k.—ראות] is probably to be read with Qr., though Eur. takes the opposite view. Cf. Dr., in loco, and BDB. p. 909.—12 (11). עבד] 𝔊, Σ, θ and 𝔎 read

עֶבֶד, "slave." MT. is, however, supported by 𝕾, 𝖁, 𝖀, and is probably right. As AE. noted, Gn. 4² and Pr. 12¹¹ make it probable that the expression is shortened from עֹבֵד אדמה, and refers to an agricultural worker. —אם‥‥אם], usually without ן, mean "either"... "or"; cf. Kö. §371r. For שבע, in the sense of "satiety," cf. Dt. 33²³. The construction of the word is a case of *casus pendens*, cf. Da. §106.—מניח], Hiph. part. of נוח, followed by ל, and meaning "permit." The inf. is usually used in such constructions, see Kö. §289d.—לישׁון], from ישׁן, is one of the rare forms of the inf. made after the analogy of the strong verb, cf. Ges.ᴷ §69n.—13 ⁽¹²⁾. רעה חולה]. חולה is part. of חלה, used adjectively. It means "sore," or "deep-seated" (so Del., Wr. and BDB.). 𝕾 reads ἀρρωστία="sickness," in which it is followed by 𝕾, which leads McN. to conjecture that the pre-Aqiban reading was יש רע חלי, "there is an evil sickness." 𝖁 and 𝖀 support MT., however, and its reading is so much more intelligible that it can but be regarded as the original. Then, as Kn. long ago observed, in Qo. the adj. regularly follows the noun. The Niph. of חלה has a similar meaning, cf. Je. 14¹⁷ Na. 3¹⁹. For the use of the passive followed by ל to express agency, see Gn. 14¹⁹ and Kö. §104.—בעליו] see on vs. 12. Ha., on account of his metrical theory, erases תחת השׁמשׁ and לרעתו as glosses.—14 ⁽¹³⁾. ענין רעה], most interpreters agree that the phrase means "a bad business," or "venture." —ענין] see on 1¹³.—בידו]. Interpreters differ as to whether the suffix י refers to the father or the son. Kn., Gins., Heil. and Pl. hold that it refers to the former, while Gr., Vl., No. and Sieg. refer it to the latter. Wild. rightly remarks that it may refer to either. Ha., for his usual reason, regards העשׁיר ההוא and מאומא as glosses.—15 ⁽¹⁴⁾. כאשׁר] is frequently used in comparisons, cf. Ges.ᴷ §161b and Kö. §388h.— וישׁוב ללכת]="go again." On account of its poverty in adverbs, שׁוב is often used to express an adverbial idea, cf. Ges.ᴷ §120d.—וישׂא], literally "take up," "carry," is here used in the sense of "receive," as in Dt. 33² 1 K. 5²³ Ps. 24⁵.—בעמלו], the ב expresses instrumentality.— שֶׁיֵּלֵךְ was read by 𝕾 and Σ שֶׁיֵּלֶךְ. Kö. (§194b) regards ילך here as probably a Kal, but it is better to regard it as a Hiph. Jussive. Wr. notes that it is one of the few Jussives in the book. Other instances he believes occur in 10²⁰ (יגיר) and 12⁴ (יקום).—16 ⁽¹⁵⁾. רעה חולה], on this, see on 5¹³ ⁽¹²⁾. כל־עמת שׁ־] is variously regarded by different scholars. Geiger, who is followed by Wild., McN., and Ges.ᴮᵘ·, regarded it as a compound of כ, ל, and עמת, comparing 1 Ch. 25⁸. Kö. (§§277l, 339r and 371n) seems to favor this view. On the other hand, Del., who is followed by Wr., Sieg. and BDB., regards the expression as an imitation of the Aram. כל קבר ד־ (Dan. 2¹⁰), and accordingly as an Aramaism. This view is correct.—יתרון] 𝕾 read יתרונה=περισσεία αὐτοῦ.—17 ⁽¹⁶⁾. The MT. of the verse is obviously corrupt; a translation of the present text is impossible. Many attempts have been made to explain בחשׁך יאכל].

Some, as Del., taking it literally; others, as Wr., taking it figuratively like ישב in Mi. 7⁸. ⵮, however, reads καὶ ἐν πένθει= וַאֲבֶל, the preposition being carried over from בחשך. This is the best solution of the difficulty, and with Gr., Kn., Sieg., McN., and Ha. we adopt it.—נָעַם]
is to be corrected to בַעַם, and taken as a noun with No., Eur., Sieg., McN. and Ha. The ו of חליו is untranslatable. It should be omitted as an error (cf. 6²), (so Kn., Gr., No., Eur., Wild., Sieg. and McN.), which, as Kn. and McN. have observed, arose by an accidental doubling of the following ו. We thus obtain a verse which by supplying a copula at the beginning contains a series of nouns all governed by ב in בחשך. Ha. regards חליו וקצף as a gloss to the rest of the vs. because it spoils the metre. He unnecessarily denies the whole vs. to Q¹.

18 ⁽¹⁷⁾. This verse contains no Athnah. As Del. notes, it is to be compared in that respect with Gn. 21⁹ Nu. 9¹ Is. 36¹ Je. 13¹³ 51³⁷ Ez. 42¹⁰ Am. 5¹ 1 Ch. 26²⁶ 28¹ 2 Ch. 23¹. The phrase טוב אשר יפה is difficult. In interpreting it, the Massoretic accents must be disregarded. Gr., Pl., Wild. and Sieg. regard this as a translation of the Greek καλον κἀγαθόν. That, however, would be טוב ויפה. Del., who is followed by Wr., McN. and Kö. (§§414m, 383a), noted that the one parallel is in Ho. 12⁹ עָוֹן אשר חֵטְא="iniquity which is sin." As there can be no suspicion of Greek influence in Hosea, the phrase is not a Græcism. —מספר] is acc. of time, cf. Kö. §331a. חיו is an accidental misspelling of חייו. Cf. Dr., ad loc. Sieg. holds that the vs. is the work of the Epicurean glossator. Ha. also regards it as the work of a secondary hand, but as we have interpreted it, it belongs naturally in the sequence of the thought.—**19** ⁽¹⁸⁾. כל האדם]. ⵮ πᾶς ἄνθρωπος=כל אדם. The pre-Aqiban reading apparently lacked the article.—נכסים] is an As. or Aram. loan word, cf. As. nikasu, "possessions," "treasure," Syr. nekse. It occurs in Heb. only in late works (Jos. 22⁸ ⁽ᴾ⁾ 2 Ch. 1¹¹·¹² and Qoh. 6²), though common in Aram., see e.g., Ezr. 6⁸ 7²⁶.—הִשְׁלִיט]="to empower," has an Aramaic coloring, cf. Dn. 2³⁸·⁴⁸. The only Heb. passage in which the meaning approximates is Ps. 119¹³³.—הוא] is a good example of the copula, cf. Ges.^K· §141h. Sieg. and Ha. regard the verse as the work of the later hand. There is little convincing reason for this. The only ground would be that it might be regarded as a doublette of the preceding verse, but that is not in this case convincing.—**20** ⁽¹⁹⁾. מענה]
has caused interpreters much difficulty, and Dr. would emend to עֹנֶה. The root ענה may be (1) עָנָה, "occupy" (Ar. 'anā, Syr. 'enā), or (2) ענה, "answer." Ew., Del., No., Wr., and McN. take it from the latter root, DeJong, Sieg., Wild. and Ha. (cf. JBL., XIX, 71) from the former. McN. notes that the reading of ⵮ περισπᾶ αὐτόν=מענהו, which was the pre-Aqiban reading, but fails to see that this supplies the desired object of the verb, so that if we take the verb from ענה (1) as ⵮ and 𝔚 both do, we need to make no further change in the text and

obtain the most satisfactory sense. In that case ענה is probably an
Aram. loan word (BD*B*.). Ha., in JBL., XIX, 71, proposed to amend
in accord with 𝔙 to בשמחה לבו, so that לב could be the object, but 𝔊
is a much older authority, its reading is simpler and gives the better
sense. It is also supported by 𝔖 and 𝔄. If vs. 17 is genuine, as I believe, it carries with it this vs. Ha. and Sieg. wrongly make this a gloss.

6¹. יש] is several times used by Q. (4⁸ 5¹² 8¹⁴ and 10⁵) to introduce a
new topic or example, but not always so used; *cf.* 8⁶, and perhaps 2²¹.
Dr. notes that 20 MSS. add after רעה], חולה, as in 5¹². ‎־על......רבה]=
"be great," *i.e.*, "heavy upon"; *cf.* its use in 8⁶.—**2.** נכסים], see on
5¹⁹ ⁽¹⁸⁾.—איננו]. The suffix is pleonastic as in Gn. 30³³.—חסר] may in form
be either as a vb. or an adj. Del. takes it here rightly as an adj. and
compares 1 S. 21¹⁶ 1 K. 11²² Pr. 12⁹.—מן is partitive after חסר, *cf.*
Gn. 6² and Kö. §81.—נפשו] "himself," *cf.* 2²⁴ BD*B*.—נכרי] ordinarily
"foreigner," but as Gins., Wr., Vl. and Sieg., it here signifies one of another family—not a regular heir.—חלי רע]= "evil disease," is peculiar. If
the reading is genuine, Q. must have varied the text from 5¹² purposely,
perhaps because he regarded the thing in his mind as an incurable disease in human affairs (*cf.* 1 Ch. 21¹² ᶠ, which may have been in his mind).
Ha., for metrical reasons, regards האלהים] in both its occurrences in
this vs. as glosses; also זה הבל וחלי רע הוא.—**3.** אם]= "although," *cf.* Is.
1¹⁸.—מאה] carries with it after יוליר the idea of בנים, *cf.* 1 S. 2⁵. 𝔊, 𝔖
and 𝔄 support MT. in its reading, while 𝔙, 𝔗 and 𝔎 supply בנים.
Hit. follows the latter, but most recent interpreters take it as above.
—שנים רבות], as Del. observes, is interchangeable with שנים הרבה; *cf.*
11⁸ and Ne. 9³⁰. ־ש] seems, as Wr. noted, pleonastic, but Kö. (§387k)
regards it as an *iterative* of אם. Dr. thinks the original reading may
have been רבים יהיו. One is tempted with Ha. to regard ורב שיהיו
ימי שניו as a gloss, it seems such a repetition, but as McN. observes,
it may have been inserted by Q. for emphasis. In late Heb. this would
not be strange.—שבע], with מן, *cf.* Is. 66¹¹.—וגם קבור לא היתה לא]. Ha.
regards it as a gloss. By eliminating this and the gloss mentioned
above, he makes poetry of it. Del. and Pl. think that the vs. refers in
part to Artaxerxes Memnon, who had, according to Justin (X, 1), 115
sons by various concubines, besides three begotten in lawful marriage,
and in part to Artaxerxes Ochus, who had no burial, his body being
thrown to the cats. Possibly some such tales floating through the centuries, influenced Q.'s expression. Gr. takes the last clause to refer to
Hyrcanus II (*cf.* Jos. *Ant.* xv, 6²), but this is an idle fancy.—**4.** שמו], שם
is frequently= זכר, *cf.* Dt. 9¹⁴ 1 S. 24²¹ 2 S. 14⁷ Ps. 72¹⁷.—**5.** שמש] elsewhere in Qoh. has the article, but is frequently used in BH. without it,
cf. Je. 31³⁵ 43¹³ Ez. 32⁷ Jo. 2¹⁰ 4¹⁵, etc.—שמש ראה]=ראה אור of Job
3¹⁶.—ידע] is construed by several interpreters like ראה, as governing שמש.
Σ makes it govern נחת, but Wild. is right in taking it in the sense of the

Lat. *sapĕre*="to have knowledge" or "discernment," *cf.* Is. 44⁹ 45²⁰
56¹⁰ Ps. 73²² 82⁵ and Job 13².—נחת], a segholate noun from נוּחַ, is held by
some to be used here as in the sense of "better," as it is in two passages
in the Talmud (*cf.* Ja. 886b), but as McN. observes it must have the
same meaning as in Job 3¹⁷ as well as Qoh. 4⁶ and 9¹⁷.—זה . . . . . זה, *cf.* ch.
3¹⁹ and Kö. §48.—מזה]. This use of מן is very common, *cf.* 1 S. 24¹⁷ Ps. 52⁵
Hb. 2¹⁶.—6. אִלּוּ (=אֵן לוּ=אִין לוּ) is an Aramaism (*cf.* Ja. 48b). It
occurs elsewhere in BH. only in Est. 7⁴. *Cf.* אם לא, Ez. 3⁶ and Kö.
§390y.—פַּעֲמָיִם], the dual="two times," is usually understood to double
the preceding numeral, but in Is. 30²⁶ we have the analogous expression,
שִׁבְעָתַיִם, which 𝔊 explains as equal to 343, *i.e.*, 7×7×7. Ha., who
strangely assigns the verse to a glossator, rejects—לא] after טובה as
a still later gloss, but he misses the point of Qoheleth's thought. It is
only the man who has had no enjoyment in life, whose lot is worse than
that of a lifeless fœtus. There is a limit to Q.'s pessimism.—טובה]
refers to the enjoyment of life, *cf.* 5¹⁷. שאול=מקום, *cf.* 9¹⁰ and 11⁸.
—הכל]="both," see on 2¹⁴.—7. McN. and Ha. regard this verse as a gloss,
but it can so easily be interpreted to fit admirably into the context, that
I think we should so interpret it. It is true the poetical form of the
saying suggests a proverb, but it is a proverb so appropriate that it may
well be introduced by Q. himself.—האדם]. The article is by most interpreters taken to be the generic art., but Gins. is right in regarding it as
the art. which refers to a subject recently introduced (Da. §21(a)).
Here it refers to the man mentioned in vvs. 3 and 6, the הנפש לא תמלא]
corresponding to נפשו לא תשבע of vs. 3.—לפיהו], not to be taken with
Zö. and No. in contrast with נפש, nor, as some have thought,="according to his measure," or "proportion" (*cf.* Ex. 12⁴ Gn. 47¹²), but in its
ordinary meaning. It is used to represent all the consumptive desires
of an individual. The reading of 𝔖, 𝔘 and 𝕷—בפיהו—is a corruption.
—וגם] is concessive, *cf.* Kö. §373n.—נפש]= "appetite," *cf.* Is. 5¹⁴
29⁸ Pr. 16²⁶, also *Ḥullin*, 4⁷. In this latter passage נֶפֶשׁ הַיָּפָה="good
appetite," see BDB.—8. Sieg. assigns this verse to his *Hokma* glossator, and Ha. breaks it up into two glosses, but both seem to lack sufficient warrant. It fits well into the development of Qoheleth's theme.
Gins., whom Dr. follows, would supply מן before יודע] from the first
clause, and make the meaning, "what advantage has the poor man over
one who knows," etc. Del., Wr. and McN., however, take יודע as
an attributive without the art. Del. compares Ps. 143¹⁰ (רוחך טובה),
but as Br. points out (Psalms, *ad loc.*), the words are taken from Neh.
9²⁰, where טובה has the art. It is easier to disregard the pointing of
MT. and suppose that לעני] is without the art., then יודע can be attributive without the art. also (*cf.* Kö. §411c).—להלך], for the strong inf.
instead of ללכת, *cf.* Ex. 3¹⁹ Nu. 22¹³. ¹⁴ Job 34²².—חיים] is not="life" (Kn.,
Hit., Wild.), but "living" (so Gins., Del., Wr., McN., Ha.).—9. Schol-

ars differ as to the genuineness of this vs.   Ha. regards it as Q.'s, except
the words—[גם זה הבל].   Sieg. attributes the couplet to Q²—his *Hokma*
glossator—and the last clause to his R¹.   McN. assigns it to his proverbial glossator—the part which Sieg. attributes to Q³, but regards
the last clause as genuine.   As in the case of vs. 7, if vs. 9a is a proverb,
why may not Q. have introduced it himself?—[מראה ע׳] has been compared by many scholars to Ps. 35²¹ Gn. 3⁶, etc., but the comparisons are
really inapt.—[מראה] is here used to denote the power of seeing and enjoying a meaning which is found in late Heb. only (*cf.* BDB. 909b).
It occurs again in ch. 11⁹ and in *Yoma*, 74b (*cf.* Ja. 834b) in this sense.
—[הלך], again the strong form of the inf. as in the preceding vs.—[הלך נפש]
="wandering of desire."   Compare ῥεμβασμὸς ἐπιθυμίας="roving of
desire," in Wisd. 4¹².—[גם זה הבל], etc. is, if the first part of the vs.
be assigned to a glossator, said of vs. 8.   If, however, the first part of the
vs. Q. inserted himself, it applies to the roaming of desire.

6¹⁰⁻¹². Puny man against Fate.

    ¹⁰. That which is, its name has already been called, and it has been
known what man is, and he will not be able to contend with Him who
is stronger than he.   ¹¹. For there are many words which increase vanity.
What advantage has man?   ¹². For who knows what is good for man in
life, the number of the days of his vain life, for he spends them like a
shadow: for who shall tell man what shall be after him under the sun?

   6¹⁰. *Its name has already been called*].   It has already existed.
The phrase is perhaps influenced by the Babylonian, in which
"to name a name" is equivalent to saying that the thing named
exists.   When, at the opening of the Babylonian Creation
epic, the poet wishes to refer to a time before the existence
of the heavens and the earth, he says (see King's *Seven Tablets
of Creation*, I, 1):

> When in the height heaven was not named,
> And the earth beneath did not yet bear a name.

Cf. also Is. 40²⁶.—*It has been known*], *i.e.*, foreknown, and so
foreordained.—*He will not be able to contend with Him*], with his
Creator, who ordained his fate.   The thought of the vs. is similar
to that of Is. 45⁹ 46¹⁰ and Rom. 9²⁰.—**11.** *Many words which increase vanity*].   As Del. saw, this refers to the "contention" spoken
of in vs. 10.   Delitzsch and Wright held that the verse contained
a reference to the disputes between the Pharisees, Sadducees and

Essenes, as to how far fate controls the actions of men, the Pharisees contending that it controls some of their actions, the Sadducees
that it controls none of them, and the Essenes that it controls all
(see Jos. *Ant.* xiii, 5⁹; xviii, 1³⁻⁴ and BJ. ii, 8¹⁴). To what extent these disputes were carried on as early as the time of Qoheleth,
however, we do not know. We cannot clearly trace the sects
mentioned in his time. Qoheleth maintains that man is so powerless against his Creator that discussion of the matter is futile.
—*What advantage has man*], in his powerless position.—**12.**
Who knows what is good for man]. The positive question is a
negative assertion. No one knows what is really good, for power,
possessions, sensual enjoyment, and wisdom have been shown to
be vanity.—*The number of the days of his vain life*]. This reminds
the reader of the verdict on life which Qoheleth has repeatedly
reached.—*Like a shadow*]. The thought that human life is as
unsubstantial as a shadow finds expression several times in the
OT., as 1 Ch. 29¹⁵ Job 8⁹ Ps. 102¹¹ and 144⁴. Pl. cites an
expression of the same sentiment from Sophocles:

> In this I see that we, all we that live,
> Are but vain shadows, unsubstantial dreams.
>
> (*Ajax*, 127 *ff.*)

The thought expressed by Qoheleth is rather that human life flits
like a shadow. It is more nearly akin to ch. 8¹³ Job 14² Ps.
109²³.—*What shall be after him*]. The uncertainty of the future
creates a part of the difficulty of telling what is good for man.

6¹⁰. אשר], *i.e.*, what sort of creature man is, *cf.* Ex. 14¹³. Perhaps, as
Ty. thought, the words were shaped by a reminiscence of Gn. 6³, בשגם הוא
בשר.—לדין עם], used in the sense of ריב, occurs only here (*cf.* BDB.
192b), though נדון="be at strife," occurs in 2 S. 19¹⁰. The nearest
parallel is in Gn. 6³, though there probably was the original reading did not
contain ידון (*cf.* BDB. 192b). Ty. thought this text an allusion to
Gn. If that had been corrupted into its present form by the time Q.
wrote, perhaps Ty. was right.—שהתקיף], Qr. שתקיף is probably, as
Dr. conjectures (in Kit.'s BH.), a corruption of שהוא תקיף, *cf.* שהוא עמל.
ch. 2²². Some have taken the Kt. as a Hiph., but that is not so probable,
as elsewhere its Hiph. does not occur in Heb.—רַקיף] is an Aramaism,
cf. Dn. 2⁴⁰⋅⁴² 3³³ and the cognate Syr.—11. רברים] was taken by Kn.
and Gins. as "things," as 𝔗 takes it, but 𝔊, 𝔖, 𝔚 and 𝔄, which render it

"words," are rightly followed by most recent interpreters. On הרבה],
cf. Kö. §318e. 𝔊 adds after the words of MT. in this vs. *majora
se querere* (=לִבְקֵשׁ חֵקֶף ? Cf. Est. 9²⁹). Zap. (*Kohelet*, p. 14) thinks
that the metre makes it necessary to adopt an equivalent for these words
of 𝔊, to fill out the line. The words are an ancient gloss supplied to
relieve a supposed abruptness in the sentence, but their absence from
all other versions attests that they were a late addition to the text.
—12. מספר], an acc. of time, cf. Kö. §331a, also ch. 5¹⁷.—חיי הבלו], an
attrib. gen., cf. Da. §24 (c).—וַיְעֲשֶׂם]; עשׂה, in the sense of "spend time,"
is without parallel in BH., but occurs in *Midrash Tillim* (cf. Ja. 1125a).
𝔊, in Pr. 13²³, shows that the LXX had before them some such reading
there, while ποιήσαντες δὲ χρόνον (Acts 15³³ 18²³) and ποιήσομεν ἐκεῖ
ἐνιαυτὸν (Jas. 4¹³) preserve the same idiom (cf. also Acts 20³ 2 Cor.
11²⁵ Tob. 10⁷ Jos. *Ant.* vi, 1⁴). The idiom is found in both Greek and
Latin, and is claimed by Zirkel and Gr. as a Græcism. McN. would
avoid this conclusion by making כצל complete the meaning of the verb,
thus, "seeing that he makes them like a shadow." It seems more natural
to take the words as a Græcism. Such an idiom may have been borrowed after a few years of Macedonian rule, even if Q. was not influenced by Greek philosophy.—אשׁר]="because"; does not differ from
כי when מי follows, cf. Dt. 3²⁴. It is causal in Q., also in ch. 4⁹ 8¹¹ and
10¹⁵, cf. Kö. §389a. Sieg. makes the verse a gloss, Ha. four separate
glosses, but I see no reason for so doing.

7¹⁻¹⁴.—A Variety of Proverbs.

1. *A good name is better than good ointment,*
   And the death-day, than the birth-day.
2. It is better to go to the house of mourning
   Than to the house of feasting,
   For that is the end of every man,
   And the living will lay it to heart.
3. *Better is grief than laughter,*
   For through sadness of countenance it is well with the heart.
4. The hearts of wise men are in the house of mourning,
   But the hearts of fools, in the house of mirth.
5. *It is better to hear the rebuke of a wise man*
   Than for a man to list to songs of fools.
6. *As the crackling of nettles under kettles,*
   So is the laughter of fools.
         [*This also is vanity.*]
7. *For oppression makes mad a wise man,*
   And a bribe corrupts the heart.
8. *Better is the end of a thing than its beginning;*
   Better is patience than pride.
9. *Do not hasten in thy spirit to be angry,*
   For anger lodges in the bosom of fools.

¹⁰. Do not say: "Why is it that the former days were better than these?" For thou dost not ask in wisdom concerning this.

¹¹. *Wisdom is good with an inheritance,*
And an advantage to those who behold the sun.
¹². *For the protection of wisdom is as the protection of money,*
And the advantage of knowledge is, wisdom makes its possessor to live.
¹³. Consider the work of God;
For who is able to straighten
What he has made crooked?

¹⁴. In the day of prosperity be joyful, and in the day of adversity consider; even this God has made to correspond to that in order that man should not find anything (that is to be) after him.

7¹. *A good name is better than good ointment*]. This is a proverbial phrase which has no relation to the context. Sieg. and McN. believe it to have been added by a glossator. This may be right, but it is difficult to divine what motive can have induced a glossator to add it. Ointment is, in hot climates, highly valued, *cf.* 2 S. 12²⁰ Am. 6⁶ Ps. 45⁷ Pr. 7¹⁷ Ru. 3³ Dn. 10³. In Ct. 1³ it is a simile for a good reputation. The thought of this line, however, is "honor is better than vanity."—*The death day*]. This has the true ring of Qoheleth, *cf.* 6⁴ᶠ.—**2.** *House of mourning*]. The mourning at a death lasted seven days, see Gn. 50¹⁰ BS. 22¹², those who sat round about sought to comfort the mourners, see Je. 16⁷ Jn. 11¹⁹· ³¹.—*The living will lay it to heart*]. The thought is similar to Ps. 90¹².—**3.** *Better grief than laughter*], *i.e.*, sorrow than wanton mirth.—*It is well with the heart*]. The idea is similar to the Greek proverb, "to suffer is to learn." A similar thought is expressed in Job 33¹⁹⁻²³. The thought is, however, foreign to Qoheleth, who never seems to grasp a moral purpose in suffering. The verse as Ha. has seen is a proverb added by a glossator. —**4.** *House of mourning ... house of mirth*]. The vs. reverts to and enforces the thought of vs. 2. McN. and Ha. are wrong in regarding it a gloss. Its thought is "like attracts like."—**5.** *Hear the rebuke*], *cf.* Pr. 13¹· ⁸, from which the expression is borrowed.— *Songs of fools*], probably mirthful drinking songs, such as are mentioned in Am. 6⁵. This proverb is probably also a gloss. Its thought is out of harmony with Qoheleth, as Sieg., McN. and Ha. have perceived.—**6.** This vs., like several which follow, is a proverb added by a glossator.—*The crackling of nettles*]. There is a word-play in the original, which our English rendering imitates. In the original, however, the word rendered *nettles* means "thorns." In the East charcoal was commonly used for fires (*cf.* Ps. 18[8] 120[4] Is. 47[14] Jn. 18[18]), as it is to-day. It burns slowly in a brasier (*cf.* Je. 36[22. 23]), and gives out considerable heat. Thorns (Ps. 58[9]), or even stubble (Is. 47[14]), might be burned by the hasty, but the result was noise, not heat.—*The laughter of fools*] is alike noisy, but valueless.—*This also is vanity*]. This clause spoils the symmetry of a poetic couplet, and as Sieg., McN. and Haupt agree, is a still later gloss.—**7.** *For oppression makes mad a wise man*]. This clause has no connection with the preceding. Del. supposed that two lines had fallen out, and proposed to supply them from Pr. 16[8]. As Sieg., McN. and Ha. have noted, the vs. is a gloss, introduced by the hand which inserted so many of these proverbs; it is vain, therefore, to seek for connection of thought, or to suppose that another couplet is necessary.—*A bribe corrupts the heart*]. This is an echo of Ex. 23[8] and Dt. 16[19]. Heart in Heb. includes "understanding" (Ho. 4[11]), and the moral nature also. In Hebrew thought, wisdom and goodness go together, and folly and wickedness.—**8.** *Better is the end of a thing*]. This is a proverb quite in Qoheleth's mood. Sieg. and McN. regard it as a gloss, but Haupt is right in seeing in it Q.'s hand. It is too pessimistic to be true without qualifications, as Pr. 5[4] 23[32] show.—*Better is patience than pride*]. This last has no connection with Q.'s theme, but it belonged to the proverb which he quoted, so he introduced it. Its presence led a glossator to add the next verse.—**9.** *Do not hasten . . . to be àngry*]. This is a proverb out of harmony with Q.'s thought, it was introduced because of the suggestion of vs. 8b.—*Anger lodges in the bosom of fools*]: a sentiment set forth in Pr. 12[16] and Job 5[2].

10. *Why is it that the former days were better?*]. This is always the plaint of an old man. Sieg. and McN. regard this also as a gloss, but it is not in the form of a proverb, and is in thorough harmony with Qoheleth's thought, see ch. 1[9. 10].—**11.** *Wisdom is good with an inheritance*]. Compare the saying in *Aboth*, 2[2], "Beautiful is knowledge of the law with a secular occupation";

also 1 Tim. 6⁶. It does not imply that wisdom without an inheritance is of no value, but that with an inheritance it makes an especially happy combination. The vs. is, as Gr., Sieg., McN. and Ha. have seen, a proverbial gloss.—*Those who behold the sun*], the living, *cf.* Ps. 58⁸.—**12.** *For the protection of wisdom is as the protection of money*]. Money ransoms a life (Pr. 13⁸), while wisdom may deliver a city (Ec. 9¹⁵). The verse is a gloss by the same hand as the last, and gives a reason for it.—**13.** *Consider the work of God*]. Qoheleth has not given up belief in God, though he is a pessimist. This vs. followed vs. 10. Vvs. 11 and 12 have been interpolated.—*Who is able to straighten what He has made crooked?*]. This is an iteration in other words of the thought of 1¹⁵. Sieg. and Ha. unnecessarily regard it as a gloss. It is certainly Qoheleth's thought, and he could as easily repeat himself as a modern writer.—**14.** *This God has made to correspond to that*]. He has made good and evil correspond to each other.—*Not find anything that is to be after him*]. God has so mingled good and evil that man cannot tell what the future will be. *Cf.* 3²². Here, as there, "after him" refers to what will be in this world.

7¹. שוב] is best regarded as pred. adj. with Gins. and Del., not as attributive (Kn. and Hit.).—שם] is used in the sense of שם טוב as in Ez. 39¹³ Zp. 3¹⁹· ²⁰ Pr. 22¹.—הֻזְּלָדוֹ] 𝕲ᴺᴮ and 𝔖 omit the suffix, which is here meaningless. Ec. 5¹⁷ 8¹⁶ and Is. 17⁵ are sometimes cited to show that וֹ‎ here means "one's," but they are really not parallel, as in each case the accompanying verb implies an agent. Probably the original reading was הֻיָּלֵר (McN. and Dr.), or הֻלֶּרֶת (Bick.).—**2.** מִשְׁתֶּה], lit. "drinking bouts." In vs. 4 we have בית שׂמחה. In Est. 9¹⁷ we find יום משׁתה ושׂמחה, which shows the close association of the words.—בַּאֲשֶׁר]= "because," *cf.* Kö. §389e.—הוּא]= "that."—זה would have been inappropriate, for it refers to the thing first mentioned. Del. remarks that הוא follows the gender of סוף.—הַחַי], the art. here is rightly pointed with ־ bef. ח. Exceptions to this rule occur in Gn. 6¹⁹ and Is. 17⁸.—ישׂם אל=[יתן אל לב, 2 S. 13³³.—על לב occurs with שׂים in Is. 42²⁵ 47⁷ 57¹· ¹¹ and בלב in 1 S. 21¹³. All these expressions are syn.—**3.** כעס], *cf.* on 1¹⁸.—רֹעַ], an inf., so Del.—רֹע פנים], *cf.* Ne. 2², and the expression רע לב = "sad heart," which it contains.—וייטב לב], if used in the meaning attaching to it in ch. 11⁹, makes no sense; if used with a moral signification, it contradicts Q.'s whole thought. As the first half of the vs. makes a moral signification imperative, the vs. must be a late gloss—late, because the

expression everywhere else in the OT. has the non-moral meaning, *cf.*
Ju. 18²⁰ 19⁶·⁹ 1 K. 21⁷ Ru. 3⁷ Ec. 11⁹.—4. אֹבֵל]. Del. remarks that the Zakef
Katon on אבל divides the vs. instead of Athnah, because none of the
words after אבל are tri-syllabic. *Cf.* for the opposite vs. 7.—5. נערת],
"rebuke," occurs in Q. only here, but is used in Ps., Job, Is. and Pr.
frequently. *Cf.* the Targ. on Zc. 3².—מאיש שמע]. Gins. held that the
normal form of expression would be טוב לאיש לשמע ..... משמע, but
Del., Wild. and McN. maintain that איש is introduced before שמע because the two hearings are supposed to be the acts of different individ-
uals.—6. סירים], a rare word for "thorns." It occurs in Is. 34¹³ Ho. 2⁸
and Na. 1¹⁰, also with plural in ־וח in Am. 4² in the sense of "hook." In
Sabæan it is found as a proper name (*cf.* Hommel, *ZMG.* xlvi, 532). It is
used here for the sake of the paranomasia.—קול] stands for all sorts of
sounds.—7. עשק] is connected with the As. *ešku*, "strong," the same stem
in Ar. means "roughness," "injustice," and in Syr., "slander." It often
means "extortion," *cf.* Ps. 62¹¹ Is. 30¹² 59¹³. Ew. emended to עשר and Gr.
to עקש, but later comm. have realized that no emendation is necessary.
—מחנה] disagrees with its vb. יאבד in gender, *cf.* Ges.ᴷ· §145a.—[יהולל]
Polel of הלל, "to shout," "boast." It occurs in Is. 44²⁵ Job 12¹⁷ in
the sense it has here. *Cf.* the noun הוללות in 1¹⁷ 2¹², etc.—מתנה] is here=
שחַר, so Del., *cf.* 1 Mac. 2¹⁸. Some of the Vrss. had a different reading,
but there seems no reason to change the MT., *cf.* Eur., p. 82.—את] is
interpretative of another's words acc. to Kö. §288g.—8. אחרית] occurs also in Pr. 25⁸ in the sense of "end." Sieg. takes the word as
evidence that this *mashal* is not from Q¹, since he has used סוף for
"end" in 3¹¹. In so small a work, however, arguments from mere vocabulary have little weight.—דבר], 𝕲 דברים. Perhaps the final ם was
accidentally dropped before the following מ.—ארך רוח]. ארך is usually
coupled with אפים in the sense of "long suffering" or "patience," *cf.*
Ex. 34⁶ Pr. 14²⁹ 15¹⁸ 16³². With this the Talmudic usage agrees, *cf.*
Ja. 121a. In Pr. 14²⁹, however, קצר רוח is used for the opposite, and
in 16³², משל ברוחו, as a parallel.—גְּבַהּ], constr. of נְבֹהַּ (*cf.* BDB. 147a),
not נָבַהּ (Bö.).—9. כעס ..... לכעוס], *cf.* on 1¹⁸. Sieg. notes that כעס has a
different meaning than in vs. 3, and makes the difference an argument
for difference of authorship. I agree as to difference of authorship, but
this word is no argument for it, since the Semites naturally employ the
same word to express "anger" and "sorrow," both of which are expressed in the modern dialect of Jerusalem by *za'lān.*—בחיק ..... ינוח],
cf. בלב ..... תנוח, Pr. 14³³.—10. מה] used in the sense of למה, as in Ct.
8⁴.—מחכמה]. 𝕲, 𝔖 and 𝔄 read נחכמה, which was probably the original
reading.—שאל על] is a late idiom, *cf.* Ne. 1². In earlier Heb. it was
שאל ל־, *cf.* Gn. 43⁷, and 1 S. 22¹³.—11. עם], with the use of this
prep., *cf. Aboth*, 2², יפה תלמוד תורה עם דרך ארץ.—נחלהם. 𝔖 has apparently connected it mistakenly with the root חיל.—ראה השמש],

cf. שמש חזו בל אשת נפל Ps. 58⁹, and אור ראה Ps. 49²⁰ Job 3¹⁶.—**12.** - .. כצל‎ _
כצל] is a corrupt text. 𝕲, 𝕾, Σ, 𝕷, 𝕳, 𝕶, 𝕿, all support the reading כצל in the second instance, while in the first instance all, except 𝕲,
support the same reading. The text, therefore, was כצל . . . . . . כצל, analogous to Gn. 18²⁵ and Ho. 4⁹. If MT. be retained, כ must be regarded
as ב _essentiæ,_ cf. Ges.ᴷ· 119i. On צל‎ = "protection," cf. Nu. 14⁹
Je. 48⁴⁵ and Ps. 91¹.—**13.** ראה], as Del. observes, is not = הִנֵּה, but means
"thoughtfully consider," cf. ch. 1¹⁰ 7²⁷· ²⁹ 9⁹.—תקן], an Aramaism, cf.
on 1¹⁵.—עות], see also on 1¹⁵.—**14.** בטוב היה]. Del. notes that when שוב is
used of persons, it carries with it the idea of לב, cf. Je. 44¹⁷ Ps. 25¹³.
𝕲, 'A, Θ, 𝕶, and 𝕾ᴴ read חיה for היה, an easy corruption of the text.
—לְעֻמַּת] = "corresponding to," cf. 1 Ch. 24³¹ 26¹².—על דברת ש], an Aramaism (cf. על דברת די, Dn. 2³⁰ 4¹⁴) for the Heb. למען or למען אשר. See
Kö. 396p.—מאומה] was mistakenly resolved into two words by Σ and 𝕳.

7¹⁵–10³.—ANOTHER ARRAIGNMENT OF LIFE.

7¹⁵⁻²².—Uselessness of going to extremes.

7¹⁵. Both have I seen in my vain life,—
>   There is a righteous man who perishes in his righteousness,
>   And there is a wicked man who prolongs his life in his wickedness.

¹⁶. Be not greatly righteous and do not show thyself excessively wise;
why shouldst thou ruin thyself? ¹⁷. Be not excessively wicked, nor be a
fool; why shouldst thou die before thy time? ¹⁸. It is good that thou
take hold of this, and that thou refrain not thy hand from that.
FOR HE THAT FEARS GOD SHALL BE QUIT IN REGARD TO BOTH.
¹⁹. _Wisdom strengthens the wise more than ten rulers who are in a city._
²⁰. For there is not a righteous man in the earth who does good and
sins not. ²¹. Also to all the words which they speak do not give heed,
lest thou hear thy servant curse thee. ²². For even many times thy heart
knows that thou also thyself hast cursed others.

7¹⁵. _Both have I seen_]. Qoheleth here drops the Solomonic
mask.—_Vain life_] is equivalent to "short life."—_Righteous man
who perishes in his righteousness . . . a wicked man who prolongs
his life in his wickedness_]. Qoheleth here takes issue with two
orthodox OT. doctrines—(1) That the righteous have a long
life (Ex. 20¹² Dt. 4⁴⁰ Ps. 91¹⁶ Pr. 3²· ¹⁶ 4¹⁰), and (2) That the wicked
shall not live out half their days (Ps. 37¹⁰ 55²³ 58³⁻⁹ 73¹⁸).—**16.** _Be not
greatly righteous_], probably a reproof of the excessive legal ob-
servances of the _Chasidim._—_Do not show thyself excessively wise_].

The world often hates its greatest men and makes marks of them.
In one sense it is not good to be ahead of one's time.—**17.** *Be not
excessively wicked*]. Some interpreters, as Del., hesitate to admit
that Qoheleth really implies that one may sin to a moderate degree.
That, however, is what he undoubtedly implies. It is true that
he was led into this statement by the necessity of an antithesis,
but there is no reason to believe that the thought was repugnant
to him.—*Nor be a fool*]. Righteousness and wisdom are to Qoheleth kindred terms, while wickedness and folly form a counter-
balancing couplet.—*Why shouldst thou die before thy time?*]. In
spite of the fact that Qoheleth had seen many men prolong their
lives in their wickedness (vs. 15), he recognizes that debauchery
ends in premature death.—**18ᵃ.** *This . . . that* refer to "righteousness" and "wickedness" of the two preceding verses. Qoheleth
here sums up his thought, advising the avoidance of extremes in
either righteousness or wickedness. *Cf.* Horace, *Virtus est
medium viatorum et utrimque reductum* (*Epist.* I, 18, 9), and
Ovid, *Medio tutissimus ibis* (*Met.* II, 137).

18ᵇ. *For he that fears God shall be quit in regard to both*]. This is
a gloss added by some orthodox Jew, probably a *Chasid.*—**19.** *Wisdom strengthens the wise*]. It is impossible to find any intelligent
connection for this verse with the preceding context. It is undoubtedly an interpolation by the glossator who was interested
in proverbs (so Gr., Sieg., McN. and Ha.).—*Ten rulers*]. Gins.,
Ty. and Plumtre took "ten" as a round number, Delitzsch thought
it referred to some definite situation, such as the archons at Athens.
Wright, with more probability, compares the Mishna (*Megilla*, 1ᵃ),
which says that "every city is great in which there are ten men of
leisure." The idea here is similar, only the "men of leisure" are
represented as "rulers."

20. *For there is not a righteous man in the earth*]. This connects
with vs. 18a, from which it is now separated by two interpolations,
and gives the reason for it. It is a quotation from 1 K. 8⁴⁶. There
is no good reason for regarding the vs. as a gloss, as Siegfried and
Haupt do.—**21.** *The words which they speak*]. "They" is indefinite, referring to men in general. The way in which men talk about
one another is further proof that all sin.—*Lest thou hear thy servant*

curse thee]. One loses peace of mind and often gains nothing by seeing "oursel's as ithers see us."—**22.** *Many times*]. The words are placed in the first part of the sentence for sake of emphasis.—*Thy heart*]. The Hebrew had no word for conscience, and so used "heart," which stood for the whole inner nature. Conscience (συνείδησις) occurs first in the *Wisdom of Solomon*, 17¹⁰. —*Thou also thyself hast cursed others*]. The verse is an appeal to one's conscience to enforce the maxim of the preceding verse. One knows how little meaning attaches to many of his own idle words, and should not, therefore, listen to the idle words of others.

7¹⁵. הכל]= "both," *cf.* on 2¹⁴.—כימי הבלי], *cf.* 6¹² and Job 27¹².—מאריך].
ימים is to be supplied in thought as in Pr. 28². It is often expressed, as in Dt. 4²⁶, ⁴⁰ 5³⁰ Jos. 24³¹ and Pr. 28¹⁶.—**16.** חתחכם]= "to show one's self wise," *cf.* Ex. 1¹⁰. See also similar use of Hith. in התחזק, 2 S. 10¹²,
2 Ch. 13⁷; in התאנף, Dt. 1³⁷ 4²¹, and התנכל, Ps. 105²⁵. Sieg. would render it "play the Rabbi," citing התנבא, Ez. 13¹⁷, "play the prophet," as a parallel.—ויתר], *cf.* on 2¹⁵.—חשׁומם], a Hithpolel. The ת is assimilated as in הפינן, Nu. 21²⁷, and הזכה, Is. 1¹⁶. *Cf.* Ges.ᴷ· §54d.—**17.** עת לא עתך].
with suffix means the proper or fitting time for a thing, *cf.* Ps. 1³ 104²⁷ Pr. 15²³, hence לא עת means "untimely," or an unfitting time. יום is frequently used like עת in such expressions, *cf.* Is. 13²² Ps. 37¹³ Job 18²⁰.
—**18.** שׁב אשׁר], *cf.* on 5⁴.—תאחז ב־], *cf.* Dt. 32⁴¹.—יצא], as Del. has pointed out, is used as in the Mishna in the sense of "be quit from," or "guiltless of," *cf. Berakoth*, 2¹: היה קורא בתורה והגיע זמן המקרא, אם כון לבו יצא, אם לאו לא יצא.
𝔖 renders יצא, nᵉqeph, "to adhere" or "follow closely," but this is an accidental error for nᵉphaq.—**19.** תעז ל־] probably = "be strong for the wise." Ps. 68²⁹ proves that עז may be used transitively. If it has a transitive force here, ל would be used as in Aram. as sign of the direct object. Since עז, like As. *ezezu*, usually means simply "be strong," it is unnecessary to assume an Aramaism.—עשרה] is taken by Gins. and Pl. as a round number= "many," but the parallels cited (Gn. 31⁷ Nu. 14¹² Job 19³) do not bear out the interpretation. Wild. takes the word in the sense of "wealth," but the versions are all against this.—**20.** אדם אין צדיק], *cf.* חבן אין נתן, Ex. 5¹⁶.—**21.** אשׁר ידברו] is regarded by Zap. and Ha. as a gloss for metrical reasons.—ידברו] is impersonal, *cf.* Ges.ᴷ· §144f. 𝔊, 𝔖, 𝔄 and 𝔗 add רשׁעים, but this is really an unnecessary interpretation.—חתן לבך], *cf.* on 1¹³.—מקלל]
Σ= λοιδοφοῦντες, "revile," which is a happy rendering. On the meaning, *cf.* Lv. 19¹⁴ 2 S. 16⁵. The part is used here after a vb. of hearing, *cf.* Kö. §410d.—אשׁר לא] (*cf.* שׁלא of 7¹⁴)= פן of earlier Heb. *Cf.* Est. 1¹⁴ 2¹⁰.—**22.** ס׀]. Gins. held that this belongs to אתה, but because so far

removed, another was inserted. Sieg. regards it as a dittograph. It is
better with Wr. to take it with לכך‎, cf. Ho. 6¹¹ Zc. 9¹¹ Job 2¹⁰.—פעמים‎
רבות‎], the acc. of time. The construction has been inverted for sake
of emphasis as in vs. 20, also 3¹³ 5¹⁸.—רבות‎] Ha., for metrical reasons,
regards a gl.—ידע‎]. 𝕲 and 'A read ירע‎ here, which is evidently a blunder,
for it makes no sense. The present reading of 𝕲 is conflate, that of 'A
having been combined with it (so Montfauçon and Wr.).—אַתְּ‎], Qr.
אַתָּה‎, correct.

7²³⁻²⁹.—**The search for wisdom leads to a severe judgment of
women.**

²³. All this I have tested by wisdom. I said "I will be wise," but it was
far from me. ²⁴. Far off is that which exists and deep, deep; who can
find it? ²⁵. I turned in my heart to know, to search and to seek out
wisdom and (its) sum, and to know that wickedness is foolishness; and
folly, madness. ²⁶. And I found a thing more bitter than death—a
woman who is snares and nets are her heart, and her hands fetters.
HE THAT IS GOOD BEFORE GOD SHALL ESCAPE FROM HER, BUT A
SINNER SHALL BE CAUGHT BY HER. ²⁷. See this I have found, *says
Qoheleth*, (adding) one to one to find the sum. ²⁸. Which again and
again my soul has sought and I have not found. One man out of a
thousand I have found, but a woman among all these I have not found.
²⁹. ONLY SEE WHAT I HAVE FOUND, THAT GOD MADE MEN UPRIGHT,
BUT THEY HAVE SOUGHT OUT MANY CONTRIVANCES.

7²³. *All this I have tested by wisdom*]. "All this" refers to the
preceding. The writer, as he passes to a new theme, assures us
that the preceding maxims have been tested.—*I said "I will be
wise," but it was far from me*]. Though Qoheleth could by wisdom test some things, he declares that he had found it impossible
to become actually wise. The verse really forms a transition to a
new topic.—**24.** *Far off is that which exists*]. "That which exists"
seems here to refer to the true inwardness of things, the reality
below all changing phenomena. This is "far off," man can never
grasp it.—*Deep, deep*]. The repetition is for emphasis.—*Who
can find it?*]. On the thought of the verse, compare Job 11⁷· ⁸
28¹²⁻²⁸ BS. 24²⁸· ²⁹ Bar. 3¹⁴⁻²³· ²⁹⁻³¹ and Rom. 11³³.—**25.** *To search and
seek out*], cf. 1¹³.—*To know that wickedness is foolishness; and
folly, madness*]. Although it is impossible to find out the ultimate
reality, as Qoheleth has just said, he could ascertain that wickedness is folly, and that folly is madness.—**26.** *More bitter than death*].

Death is frequently thus spoken of, *cf.* 1 S. 15³² Pr. 5⁴ BS. 28²¹ 41¹.—
A woman who is snares and nets are her heart, and her hands fetters].
The Hebrews held that the sin and wretchedness of man entered
the world through woman (*cf.* Gn. 3 6¹⁻⁵ BS. 25²⁴), but Gins. is
wrong in thinking that is the thought here. Qoheleth is inveigh-·
ing against bad women in the vein of Pr. 5¹· ²²· ²³ 7²²· ²³ 22¹⁴. He
does not mean to say that all women are destructive, for in 9¹⁰
he encourages honorable marriage as a source of happiness.—*He
that is good before God*]. This and all that follows to the end of vs.
McNeile regards a *Chasid* gloss.—**27.** *Adding one to one to find
the sum*]. This is an expression which impresses the reader with
Qoheleth's laborious and thorough process of investigation. Perhaps Qoheleth was thinking of the experience of Solomon as described in 1 K. 11¹ᶠ. *Cf.* BS. 47¹⁹.—**28.** *Again and again my soul
has sought*]. He does not say simply "I have sought." It was no
mere curious inquiry of the intellect, but a heart search.—*One
man out of a thousand*]. Possibly the number was suggested by
the number in Solomon's *harem* (*cf.* 1 K. 1³), but this is uncertain,
as "a thousand" is often used as a round number, see Ex. 20⁶
34⁷ Dt. 1¹¹ Job 9³ 33²³ Ps. 50¹⁰ 84¹⁰ 90⁴ 105⁸ Is. 30¹⁷ 60²².—*A woman
among all these I have not found*]. This implies that Qoheleth
was something of a misogynist. He had apparently had some
bitter experience with a member of the opposite sex. He is more
than reflecting the Oriental view that women are more prone to
sin than men. Chrysostom, *Hom. Ad. Cor.* 28, represents the
Oriental view when he says, "Satan left Job his wife, thinking she
would further his purposes." Qoheleth is saying "perfect men
are rare, perfect women are non-existent."

29. Sieg. and McN. are right in regarding this verse as the work
of a *Chasid* glossator.—*God made men upright*], probably a reference to Gn. 1²⁶· ²⁷.—*They have sought out many contrivances*].
The point of view here is that of the writer J. in Gn. 4²¹ᶠ 6⁴ᶠ.
Perhaps the *Chasid* intended to suggest that the *harem* was one of
man's wicked contrivances.

23. נסיח בחכמה], *cf.* חור בחכמה, 1¹³.—אמרתי אחכמה] is omitted as a gl.
by Zap. and Ha. for metrical reasons.—אחכמה is the only instance
of a cohortative in the book. It expresses strong resolve.—**24.** מה שהיה]

was misinterpreted by 𝕲 and 𝕾. Probably their text had been corrupted to משהיה.—שהיה] usually means events or phenomena which exist (1⁹ 3¹⁵ 6¹⁰), but the context makes it necessary to understand it here as that which underlies phenomena.—עמק עמק], an ancient expression of the superlative by means of repetition, cf. Ges.ᴷ· §133k and Kö. §309m.—**25.** ולבי] is difficult. Gins. renders "I and my heart," taking it as a separate subj. AE., Herz., Moses, Stuart, Del. and Wr. construe with what follows: "I turned and my heart was to know." 79 MSS., Σ, 𝕿, and 𝕳, however, read בלבי, and as Winckler and McN. have seen, this must have been the original text, cf. 2¹.—חשבון], an Aram. word="reckoning," "sum," cf. Ja. 509a. It occurs in BH. only here, in vvs. 27 and 9¹⁰. On its formation, cf. Barth, Nominalbildung, §202a.—רשע כסל]. McN., on account of 𝕾 and a reading of Jer. and some peculiarities of 𝕲, holds that the original reading was כסל רשע. MT., as it stands, gives, however, a more climactic and clearer thought, and should be followed.—הסכלות הוללות], cf. on 1¹⁷. Sieg. and Ha. regard the vs. as a gl., the latter as a double gl.—**26.** מוצא], in late Heb. the part. is used instead of various forms of the verb, and here is equivalent to a perfect, cf. Kö. §239g. In late Heb. verbs "לא are often confused with verbs "לה, as here (cf. Ges.ᴷ· 75rr). Del. points out that in the Talmud (*Yebamoth*, 63b) it is said to have been common in Palestine to inquire after a wedding מצא או מוצא—"happy or unhappy?" One ref. was to Pr. 18²², the other to this passage.—היא] is here the copula, cf. Gn. 7².—מצורים] 𝕲 read מצור (sing.).—האשה אשר היא מצורים]="the woman who is nets." Cf. ואני תפלה, Ps. 109⁴. Sieg. regards the vs. as genuine, while Ha. looks upon it as a double gloss. Ha. declares that Qoh. was no misogynist, but favored happy marriage, and refers for proof to ch. 9¹⁰. It is difficult to escape the conclusion, however, that the words here employed are sharpened by a bitter personal experience with some woman. The passage referred to (ch. 9¹⁰) urges enjoyment with a woman, not the placing of trust in her.—**27.** אמרה קהלת] is the only place where קהלת occurs with a fem. vb. Cf. 1² 12⁸ 12¹⁰. In 12⁸ we have אמר הקהלת, and the majority of scholars so take it here (Grot., Houb., Mich., Durell, Van der P., Stuart, Elst., Heil., Wr., Wild., Ges.ᴷ· §122r, Kö. §251d, and Dr.).—**28.** אשר] Perles would change to אשה, but nothing in the versions supports this. Kö. (§383a) regards אשר far more effective.—עוד] as in Ru. 1¹⁴ here= "again and again."—אדם] is explained by Gr. and Sieg. as a Græcism for ἄνθρωπος, but as McN. has noted אדם is opposed to אשה in Gn. 2²². ²³. ²⁵ 3⁸. ¹². ¹⁷. ²⁰. ²¹ (J.), where there can be no Greek influence.—אשה]. Perhaps Q. is thinking of the אשת חיל of Pr. 31¹⁰.—**29.** לבד], "alone," then "only," occurs here in an unusual sense. Its occurrence in Is. 26¹³ is kindred, but not quite parallel.—האדם], generic="mankind," as המה shows.—ישר]= "honorable," "morally upright," cf. 1 S. 29⁶.—חשבנות],

a rare word, occurring only here and in 2 Ch. 26¹⁵. It means "contrivances," "devices." In Ch. it is applied to engines of war.

8¹⁻⁹.—Reflections on despotism.

> 8¹. *Who is like the wise man ?*
> *And who knows the interpretation of a matter ?*
> *The wisdom of a man illumines his face*
> *And the coarseness of his countenance is changed.*

². Observe the command of a king, EVEN ON ACCOUNT OF THE OATH OF GOD. ³. DO NOT RASHLY GO FROM BEFORE HIM, NOR STAND IN AN EVIL MATTER, for what he will he does. ⁴. For the word of a king is supreme, and who shall say to him: what doest thou?

> ⁵. A COMMANDMENT-KEEPER SHALL KNOW NO HARM
> AND TIME AND JUDGMENT A WISE HEART KNOWS.
> ⁶. FOR EVERY MATTER HAS A TIME AND JUDGMENT.
> *For* the misery of man is great upon him.

⁷. For there is no one who knows that which shall be, for when it shall be, who shall tell him? ⁸. No man has mastery over the wind, to restrain the wind, nor is he ruler in the day of death, nor is there a furlough in war, nor will wickedness effect an escape for its owners. ⁹. All this I have seen and have applied my heart to all the work that is done under the sun, at a time when man has power over man to his hurt.

8¹. *Who is like the wise man*]. This verse which consists of two gnomic sayings, has been rightly regarded by Sieg. and McN. as from the hand of the *Hokma* glossator.—*Illumines his face*], gives it graciousness and power to inspire (*cf.* Nu. 6²⁵ Ps. 4⁶), enables it to express courage (*cf.* Job 29²⁴), and intelligence (*cf.* Ps. 19⁸).—*The coarseness of his countenance is changed*], such is the transforming power of character.

2. *On account of the oath of God*], probably the oath of allegiance taken at the king's coronation, *cf.* 1 Ch. 11³ 29²⁴ Jos. *Ant.* xv, 10⁴; xvii, 2⁴. McN. rightly assigns this clause to the *Chasid* glossator. Qoheleth's statements are greatly strengthened when the glosses are removed. Sieg. and Ha. needlessly assign the whole section to glossators.—**3.** *Do not rashly go from before him*], rebel against him or renounce his service.—*Stand in an evil matter*]. This is ambiguous. It may mean (1) "Linger not in," (2) "Enter not in" (*cf.* Ps. 1¹ 106²³ Je. 23¹⁸), or (3) "Stand" (as king) (*cf.* Dn. 8²³ 11²⁰). Probably the second meaning is nearer the writer's thought, at least the context favors the interpretation "enter not into opposition to him." See, however, crit. note.—*For what he will he does*]. It is accordingly folly for a puny subject to oppose him. This bears out the interpretation we have given to the preceding clause.—**4.** *For the word of a king is supreme*]. This is given as an additional reason for the preceding exhortation.—*Who shall say to him, what doest thou?*], a thought which is several times expressed concerning God (*cf.* Is. 45⁹ Job 9¹² Wisd. 12¹²), but is here purposely used to describe the autocratic power of a king.

5. *A commandment-keeper shall know no harm*]. This statement is brought in in such a way that the "commandment" seems to be that of the king previously referred to—a fact which has led many interpreters to compare it to Rom. 13¹⁻⁵. The word for command is usually applied to commands of Yahweh (see crit. note), and the thought contradicts vvs. 6b and 7. McNeile is accordingly right in regarding the vs. as from the *Chasid* glossator.—*Know no harm*], "know" is used in the sense of "experience," as in Ez. 25¹⁴ Ho. 9⁷.—*Time and judgment*], *i.e.*, the final end and determination.—*The wise heart knows*], *cf.* Ps. 90¹².—**6ᵃ.** *For every matter has a time and judgment*]. This remark is also from the *Chasid* annotator, and gives his reason for the preceding remark.

6ᵇ. *For the misery of man is great upon him*]. This, except the word "for" which is editorial, is a remark of Qoheleth himself. and connects immediately with the statement of vs. 4, concerning the irresponsible character of the king, though it has now been removed from it by the glossator's interpolations. It is the beginning of Qoheleth's reflections upon the evils of tyranny.—**7.** *No one who knows that which shall be*]. This is not as in 3²² and 6¹² simply a reference to the fact that the future is unknown, but to the fact that one never knows what an irresponsible despot will do. The writer blends, however, his statement of the impossibility of knowing what a despot will do with a statement of the inscrutable character of the future.—*When it shall be*]. Neither can one tell when the despot will choose to do it. The uncertainty causes misery.—**8.** *No man has mastery over the winds*], *cf.* ch. 11⁵.

Qoheleth illustrates the powerlessness of man to know the future by examples of his powerlessness in other respects. He cannot control the winds. The wind is one of God's grandest creations (Am. 4¹³), and a symbol of his power (Na. 1³), the control of which is in his own hands (Pr. 30⁴).—*Nor is he ruler in the day of death*], a second example of man's powerlessness.—*Nor is there furlough in war*]. This statement seems to contradict Dt. 20⁵·⁸ 25⁵. According to 1 Mac. 3⁵⁶ Judas Maccabæus conformed to one of these laws. John Hyrcanus (135–104 B.C.) employed foreign mercenaries (*cf.* Jos. *Ant.* xiii, 8⁴). No soldier in such ranks could obtain a discharge when his employer had a war on hand. Such mercenaries had been employed freely in Egypt from the time of the XXVIth dynasty (*cf.* Breasted's *History of Egypt*, p. 569 *ff.*), and by the Persians in all periods of their history; so that it was in Qoheleth's day no new thing. The allusion is probably to such soldiers, and thus becomes a third illustration of Qoheleth's point.—**9.** *All this I have seen*], the power of the despot described in vvs. 1–8.—*Applied my heart to all the work*], thoughtfully considered, or investigated.—*When man has power over man to his hurt*]. This is an apt description of the injustices of an Oriental despotism. Such injustice has existed under every Oriental monarchy, the allusion accordingly affords no clue to the date. "To his hurt" is ambiguous. 𝕲, 𝕾 and 𝕿, which are followed by Kn., Gins., Zö., Del. and Wild., make it refer to the second man. Σ and Hitzig and Ha. take it to refer to the first man. The first of these views is the correct one. The retribution to which allusion is made at the end of vs. 9 is often delayed, and meantime the subjects of the tyrant suffer.

8¹. כהחכם] for the more common כהכם. The full writing of the article occurs not infrequently in later Hebrew, *cf.* Ges.ᴷ· §35n.—שׁרפ], an Aram. loan word, occurring only here in BH., but frequently in Aram. (*cf.* Dn. 2⁴· ⁵· ⁶· ⁷· ⁹· ¹⁶· ²⁴· ²⁵· ²⁶· ³⁰· ³⁶· ⁴⁵ 4⁴· ⁶· ¹⁵· ¹⁶· ²¹ 5¹²· ¹⁶, etc.—רבד] here = "thing," "matter," as in 1⁸ and 7⁸.—חאיר פניו], *cf.* Nu. 6²⁵ Ps. 4⁷ Job 29²⁴ Pr. 16¹⁵ and BS. 13²⁵ (Heb.) for אור with עינים, Ps. 19⁹.—עֹז פנים]. The Versions read עַז the adj., not עֹז the noun. This should be adopted. It is used of "shamelessness," "impudence," or "coarseness," *cf.* Dt. 28⁵⁰ Pr. 7¹³ 21²⁹ Dn. 8²³.—ישׁנא] for יְשֻׁנֶּה. א"ל and ה"ל verbs are often confused in the later books, *cf.* Ges.ᴷ· §75rr and 2 K.

25²⁹ with Je. 52³³ and La. 4¹. Some of the Rabbis interpreted this as
fr. שׁנה = "change," others fr. שׂנא= "hate" (so 𝕲 and 𝔖), see the discussions cited by Del. and Wr. from the Talmud, *Shabbath*, 30b, and
Taanith, 7b.—**2.** אני] is difficult. Heil., Gins., Del., Wr., Sieg. and
Ha. supply אמרתי as in 2¹· ¹⁵, etc. These passages are, however, not
parallel, for in the nine cases in which Q. uses this expression he presents
the products of his observations, which is not the case here. Wild.
conjectures that the reading was בני, as so often in Prov. 1–9, but
this is purely conjectural. 𝕲, 𝔖, 𝔘 and 𝔄, which Eur. follows, read
אֶת, which is probably the correct reading.—פי] by metonomy for "command," *cf.* Gn. 45²¹ Ex. 17¹ Lv. 24¹² Nu. 3¹⁶ Job 39²⁷.—מֶלֶךְ], Sieg. contends, is used in Qoh., without the art., in a definite sense like βασιλεύς,
but it does not seem necessary so to regard it.—על דברת], *cf.* on 3¹⁸.—
שׁבעות יהוה]=שׁבעות אלהים of Ex. 22¹⁰ 2 S. 21⁷ 1 K. 2⁴³. The genitive relation is used instead of בְּ, *cf.* Kö. §336t β.—**3.** תבהל], is taken by 𝕲, 𝔖 and
𝔄, which Dale, Sieg. and McN. follow, with the preceding verse. Two
verbs may be combined, however, in a single idea, as is frequent in Heb.,
cf. Gn. 19²² 1 S. 2³ 3⁵ Zc. 8¹⁵, etc., one of them having an adverbial force.
Wild.'s objection that one of them must be in the inf. with ל, does not
hold for all cases. *Cf.* Da. §83(c).—דבר רע] Dt. 17¹ 2 K. 4⁴¹, etc.

4. באשר]= "for," "because," *cf.* on 2¹⁶ (בְּשֶׁ־).—שׁלטון], a noun, meaning "master," "ruler." It occurs in BH. only here and vs. 8. It is an
Aram. loan word, occurring frequently in Jewish Aram., *cf.* Ja. 1581b *ff.*
It is here used adjectively.—**5.** מצוה] may be used either of a king, as
1 K. 2⁴³ 2 K. 18³⁶, or a man, as Je. 35¹⁴· ¹⁶· ¹⁸, or of God, as Ezr. 10³, and
frequently in D., *e.g.*, Dt. 8¹· ². *Cf.* also Ps. 19⁹. The *Chasid* introduced here a phrase coined concerning God, and made it apply ambigu-
ously to a king.—דבר רע], if this has the same meaning as in vs. 3, it
means he will "know no wrong," *i.e.*, will be innocent, but Zö. and
Sieg. are right in taking it in the sense of רע of Ps. 101⁴.—**6.** חפץ]=
"matter," "business," *cf.* on 3¹, also Kö. §80.—רעת], 𝕲, Θ and 𝔄 read
דעת, but this gives no intelligible thought here, and must be an early
corruption.—**7.** שׁיהיה], 𝔖 and 𝔘 add בסום or לסום, but it is clearly
an explanatory addition and not original.—כאשר] was interpreted by
Kn., Hit., Heil. and Zö. as "how," but Gins. and Del. rightly oppose
this. It always means "when," even in Qoheleth, *cf.* 4¹⁷ 5³ and 8¹⁶.
—**8.** שׁלֵיט], an adj., *cf.* BDB. 1020b and Barth, NB. §35. Elsewhere the
word is a noun. On the root שׁלט, see on 2¹⁹.—ל־] points to a conse-
quence, *cf.* Kö. §406a.—לכלא את הרוח] is regarded by Zap. and Ha. as
a gl., on account of their metrical theory.—שׁלטון], see on vs. 4.—משׁלחת],
a late word, occurring elsewhere in BH. only in Ps. 78⁴⁹. It is found in
Aram. in the Midrash to Numbers, *cf.* Ja. 855b.—במלחמה], 𝕲 read
ביום מלחמה. Possibly this is the correct reading, though as McN.
suggests, it may be a corruption arising from an accidental doubling of

the מ in במלחמה.—בעליו], see on 5¹⁰.—**9.** ונתון], an inf. abs. used as a finite verb, cf. ch. 9¹¹ Gn. 41⁴³, also Ges.ᴷˑ §113z, Da. §88(a), and Kö. §218b.—נתון לב], cf. on 1¹³.—עֵת], acc. of time, cf. Je. 51³³ and Kö. §331b. Others, as McN., take it as the beginning of a new sentence= "there is a time."

8¹⁰⁻¹⁵. Results of righteousness and godlessness the same.

8¹⁰. And then I saw wicked men buried, carried even from the holy place, and they used to go about and be praised in the city because they had done so. This also is vanity.

¹¹. BECAUSE THE SENTENCE AS TO AN EVIL DEED IS NOT ACCOMPLISHED QUICKLY, THEREFORE THE HEART OF THE SONS OF MEN IN THEM IS FULLY (GIVEN) TO DO EVIL. ¹². ALTHOUGH A SINNER DOES EVIL EX-CEEDINGLY, AND PROLONGS HIS DAYS, NEVERTHELESS I KNOW THAT IT SHALL BE WELL WITH THOSE WHO FEAR GOD, WHO FEAR BEFORE HIM. ¹³. AND IT SHALL NOT BE WELL WITH THE WICKED, NOR SHALL HE PRO-LONG HIS DAYS LIKE A SHADOW, BECAUSE HE DOES NOT FEAR BEFORE GOD.

¹⁴. There is a vanity which is done upon the earth, that there are righteous men to whom it happens according to the work of the wicked, and there are wicked men to whom it happens according to the work of the righteous,—I say that this also is vanity. ¹⁵. And I praised glad-ness, because there is no good for a man under the sun, but to eat and to drink and to rejoice, and it shall attend him in his toil the days of his life, which God gives to him under the sun.

10. *Wicked men buried*], *i.e.*, pass away in honor. Not to be buried was to be greatly dishonored, *cf.* Je. 16⁴ˑ ⁵ 22¹⁹. See also on 6³.—*Carried even from the holy place*]. For the reasons for this rendering, see critical note. These wicked men had passed their lives even in the temple, where they ought never to have been toler-ated. The holy place is the sanctuary, *cf.* Lv. 7⁶.—*They used to go about and be praised*], for the justification of this rendering, see critical note.—*In the city*], probably Jerusalem.—*Because they had done so*], *i.e.*, had ruled over others to their hurt, *cf.* vs. 9, the end. The verse is a further confirmation of the fact that retribution does not always quickly overtake the "possessors of wickedness."

11. *Sentence as to an evil deed is not accomplished quickly*]. The *Chasid* glossator here takes up the thought of Qoheleth that retri-bution is sometimes delayed. So correctly, Sieg., Ha. and McN.—*The heart of the sons of men is fully given to do evil*], *i.e.*, men are governed by childish evasions of penalty, *cf.* Ps. 73⁹⁻¹¹.—**12.**

Although a sinner does evil exceedingly and prolongs his days], is not prematurely cut off from those blessings which that age regarded as the peculiar rewards of the righteous, *cf.* on 6³. For the basis of the rendering "exceedingly," see critical note. This vs. is also a comment of the *Chasid* glossator.—*I know that it shall be well with them that fear God*]. The sinner, in the view of this annotator, runs the risk of disastrous retribution, but the religious man, although his actual lot may be no more prosperous than that of some rich men, is nevertheless free from this risk.—*Who fear before him*]. This is, for metrical reasons, regarded by Zap. and Ha. as a gloss. It is probably simply a tautology of the late period of the language, *cf.* ch. 4². ⁸ and 6³.—**13.** *It shall not be well with the wicked*]. This reflects the orthodox Jewish doctrine, see Pr. 10²⁵. ²⁷ 14²⁷ 16³¹ Job 5²⁶ 15³² 20⁵. ⁷ 22¹⁶ Is. 65²⁰ Ps. 39⁶ 102¹¹ Wisd. 4⁸. —*Nor shall he prolong his days*]. This seems to contradict vs. 12. Probably the *Chasid* glossator (for the verse clearly reflects his hand, so Sieg., Na. and McN.) meant to state his conviction that, generally speaking, the wicked man did not prolong his days, and that the concession made in the preceding vs. represents the exception rather than the rule.—*Like a shadow*]. There are three ways of explaining these words: (1) With RV. and McN. we may take them as an emblem of transitoriness, expressive of the rapidly fleeting life of the sinner, *cf.* RV., "His days *which are* as a shadow." This interpretation has in its favor the fact that the figure elsewhere in the OT. has this force, *cf.* on 6¹². (2) 𝕮, 𝕾, 𝕳, followed by Hit. and others, divide the vs. differently, rendering "like a shadow are those who do not fear God," taking the figure to indicate the transitoriness of the sinners themselves. (3) The rendering we have followed takes the figure differently, and makes the point of the illustration the fact that at evening the shadows become long, and implies that sinners never reach the evening of life. Although not used in that sense elsewhere, there is no good reason why it may not be so used here.

14. *Righteous men to whom it happens according to the work of the wicked*]. In Job 21⁷ this fact is stated as in passionate grief, here with a calmness which indicates that it had become a part of the recognized order of things, though one of the proofs of the "vanity " of life.   Or is the difference one of artistic expression, the poet in Job speaking in the character of an acute sufferer, while Qoheleth speaks as a reflecting thinker?   " Work " is used as the fruits of work, or "wages."—**15.** *I praised gladness*].   The reflections of Qoheleth bring him back to the thought expressed in 3²² and 5¹⁸.   It runs like a refrain through the book.   It is a materialistic point of view, but it kept the writer from despair.   Life is out of joint, the rewards of goodness and wickedness are often reversed, no ray of light falls on the future, but make the most of the present; eat, drink and have a good time while one can, perhaps on the ground that God even could not rob one of pleasures actually enjoyed.

10. בכן made up of ב and כן, a combination which occurs besides in BH. only in Est. 4¹⁶, but is common in Aram. (*cf.* B*D*B. 486a, and Ja. 170a, 647b).   It is an Aramaism.   𝕲 correctly renders it τότε.—ובאו] should be emended on the authority of 𝕲, 𝕶 and 𝕾ᴴ to מובאים.   The text of M. is here meaningless, as the various renderings which ובאו has received at the hands of interpreters prove—some having taken it to mean "entering into the world" (Kn., Gins. and Wr.); others, "enter into life" (Ew.), and still others, "enter into rest" (Zö., Wild., Sieg., Ha.).   The emendation makes a translation possible.   On the construction of מובאים, *cf.* Kö. §411a.—מקום קדש] naturally means temple (*cf.* Lv. 7⁶ Mt. 24¹⁵).   This natural meaning suits our emended text.   The difficulty of rendering it with באו has led some to render "grave" (Ew., Marsh.), others "Jerusalem" (Hit., Wild.), while Del. and Kö. (§305d) rightly take it as "holy place."—יְהַלֵּכוּ] is, as the text stands, difficult.   To take it as= a Hiph., as many do, is also unsatisfactory.   Elsewhere the Piel is not used for the Kal.   On the basis of 𝕲, 𝕾ᴴ, 'A and Θ we should emend to ויהלכו.   For the force of the Piel, *cf.* ch. 4¹⁵ 11⁹ and Job 24¹⁰.—וישתכחו] is difficult.   It, too, should be emended, according to 𝕲, 'A, Θ, 𝕶, 𝕷, 𝕳, 𝕾ᴴ and 20 MSS., to וישתרבחו (so Kn., Winck., Marsh.), which is here pass. and not reflexive, *cf.* Kö. §101.—כן] is to be taken in its ordinary sense of "thus."   The difficulties of translating MT. as it stands led Kn., Gins., Del. and Ha. to take כן=עשׂו "to do right," and to suppose that two classes are referred to in the verse.   כן has this meaning in 2 K. 7⁹, but here it should be akin to בכן in some way.   The original text, as the versions testify, made allusion to but one class, Σ alone taking this as Del. does.—**11.** וְנַעֲשָׂה], Zö., Wild. and Albrecht (*ZAW.* XVI, 115) would point וְנַעֲשֶׂה, but Del. and Wr. take it as fem. part. (not 3d sing. fem.) as it stands, regarding פתגם a fem. as well as masc. in gender.   This is probably right.—פתגם]

is a Persian word, in old Persian *patigāma*, late Pers. *paigâm*, Armenian *patgam*. In BH. it occurs elsewhere only in Est. 1²⁰, but frequently in Aram., *cf.* Dn. 3¹⁶ 4¹⁴ Ezr. 4¹⁷ 5⁷· ¹¹ 6¹¹.—In post-BH. it occurs in BS. 5¹¹ 8⁹.—מעשה הרעה], 𝕲, 𝔘, 𝔖 and 𝔄 read מעשי הרעה. The analogy of 5⁶ La. 4² and Ct. 7² is in favor of MT. as it stands.—מהרה] here, as usually in BH., an adverbial acc., *cf.* Nu. 17¹¹ Dt. 11¹⁷ Jos. 8¹⁹ 10⁶ 23¹⁶, etc.—מלא לב] is a late Heb. expression, *cf.* ch. 9³ Est. 7⁵ and Ex. 35³⁵ (Ps.). In Aram. (Targ. of On.) it means "comfort the heart," *cf.* Ja. 789b. Here it means that the thoughts (לב) are fully occupied with evil plans.—בהם] is a pleonasm, not uncommon in late writing. —**12.** חמא] for חמא. On the mixture of verbs ל״א and ל״ה, *cf.* on 7²⁶.—מאה-], 𝔘 supplies שנים. One has to supply this, or ימים or פעמים. The last is favored by Zö., Del., Wr. and McN. The omission of the noun is harsh and unusual. The Vers. had different readings, showing the text to be corrupt. 𝕲, 𝔖ᴴ and 𝔏 read מאז (ἀπὸ τότε). 'A, Σ and Θ read ἀπέθανεν=מֵת or מֵית, while 𝔎 has a conflate of both readings. 𝔘, 𝔖 and 𝔘 support MT. As McN. observes (p. 148), none of these are satisfactory. It is necessary to presuppose an original which will account for all readings. McN. suggests two possibilities: (1) A scribe began to write ומאריך, but having accidentally omitted ו, discovered his mistake when he had written מאר and wrote the word again. Then מארומאריך became מאז רמ׳, and later מאת ומ׳ and מת ומ׳. (2) The original text had מאר, which would similarly give rise to the variants. The latter seems the more probable and has been adopted above in the translation.—מאריך]; ימים is to be understood in thought, *cf.* on 7¹⁵. —כי גם]. Kö.'s "wenn auch" (§394f) does not suit the context. Heil.'s "tamen" or McN.'s "surely also" is much more probable.—יהיה טוב]. The thought is similar to the D. point of view (*cf.* Dt. 6²⁴) and the *Chasid* (Ps. 37³⁷). Zap. and Ha. for metrical reasons regard אשר יראו מלפניו] as a gloss. It is tautological, but not more so than the book is elsewhere. —**13.** כצל], 𝕲 read בצל. כצל makes much better sense, and the variant is probably due to an early corruption.—**14.** על הארץ], a variant for רחת השמש, which is more common.—אשר] Ha. regards as a gloss.—מגיע אל־]= "to happen to," *cf.* Est. 9²⁶ Ps. 32⁶, also Kö. §323d. 𝕲ᴮ read מגיע על־ here.—מעשה], for the peculiar use of this word, *cf.* 1 S. 25².—שגם], *cf.* on 1¹⁷.—**15.** והוא] begins a new clause.—ילונו], "cling to" or "accompany" one, *cf.* BDB. 530b. It takes an acc. like דבק in Gn. 19¹⁹. For metrical reasons, Ha. regards תחת השמש and נתן לו האלהים as glosses.— כי אם = "but," *cf.* Kö. §372i.

8¹⁶–9¹. Knowledge cannot be obtained, yet Qoheleth, knowing this, makes the effort.

8¹⁶. When I gave my heart to know wisdom and to see the toil that is done upon the earth—for both day and night he sees no sleep with his eyes—¹⁷. then I saw all the work of God, that man is not able to fathom the work that is done under the sun; for as much as man may toil to search, but he will not fathom it, and even if the wise man think he is about to know, he will not be able to fathom it. 9¹. For all this I took to heart, and my heart saw all this, that the righteous and the wise and their works are in the hand of God; also men do not know love or hate; all before them is vanity.

16. *When I gave my heart*].   This is the protasis, the apodosis of which occurs in vs. 17, the last part of vs. 16 being a parenthesis.— *Toil that is done upon the earth*].   This recalls ch. 1¹³, in which the toil of men is described by the same graphic Hebrew word.—*He sees no sleep*].   "He" refers to man.   In 1¹³ the toil is called the toil of man, and the writer here presupposes that man as the victim of the toil is lying in the background of the reader's thought as in his own.   "To see sleep" is an unusual figure, but is used by Cicero, *Ad Familiares*, vii, 30: "*Fuit enim mirifica vigilantia, qui suo toto consulatu somnum non viderit*"; also Terence, *Heautontimorumenos*, III, i, 82: "*Somnum hercle ego hac nocte oculis non vidi meis.*"   Ordinarily in the Bible the thought is expressed differently, *cf.* Gn. 31⁴⁰ Ps. 132⁴ Pr. 6⁴.   It is, however, simply a bold metaphor which anyone might employ, and no dependence on extra Hebrew sources need be suspected.—**17.** *He may toil to search, but he will not fathom it*].   This is a stronger expression of the thought than that in 7²⁴.   The unsearchable nature of divine things is similarly proclaimed also in Job 11⁶⁻⁹ and Rom. 11³³.—*Even if the wise man think he is about to know, he will not be able to fathom it*].   Qoheleth had seen, apparently, the inutility of many systems and the inefficacy of many universal panaceas.—**9¹.** *I gave my heart*].   The heart, as so often, is used for the whole inner nature including the mind.—*And my heart saw*].   For the justification of the text on which this translation rests, see critical notes.—*The righteous and the wise and their works are in the hand of God*].   Qoheleth, as so often, recognizes God's supreme sovereignty over human affairs.—*Men do not know love or hate*], probably God's love or hate, *i.e.*, they can never tell, from what they do, whether God is going to treat them as though he loved them or hated them   The occurrences of life accord so ill with character, that whether God

loves or hates an individual is one of the inscrutable things mentioned in the preceding vs., which man cannot fathom.—*All before
them is vanity*]. For the text of this rendering, see crit. note to
vs. 2. The meaning is, all before men is a blank, they can gain
no knowledge of God's attitude toward them or of the future.

16. כאשר]= "when," *cf.* Gn. 12¹¹ 18³³, etc.—נתחי את לבי], *cf.* on 1¹³.
—העינין], *cf.* on 1¹³.—כי גם], as RV., Wild., Sieg., McN., etc., have noted,
begins a parenthesis.—שנה] is the object of the act. part. ראה.—בעיניו] is
regarded by Ha. as a gl., because of his metrical theory.—17. וראיתי].
ו introduces the apodosis.—מעשה האלהים], as Wild. notes this is=
אשר נעשה and shows that Q. ascribes all activities to God. Ha.
erases the words as a gl.—למצוא] is used in an intellectual sense, *cf.* ch.
3¹¹ 7²⁹ Job 11⁷ and Je. 2⁵.—בשל אשר], Kn., Ew., Hit., Heil. and Dr.
(hesitatingly) emend to בכל following ⑤. Del., Wr., Eur. and others
hold that כל is due to an early correction, בשל being parallel to the
Aram. דבריל-, which occurs in Targ., Onk., Gn. 6³. In Jonah 1⁷ we
find בשלמי, and 1¹² בשלי. Such compounds are late and influenced by
Aramaic. *Cf.* Ja. 140a and Kö. §§389e and 284e.—ים אב] corresponds
to Ph. אם אם, *CIS*. No. 3⁶, *cf.* Kö. §394f.—אמר ל-] applies to
thought, *cf.* Ex. 2¹⁴ and 2 S. 21¹⁶.—9¹.—ולבור] is taken differently by
different scholars. Hit., Heil., Gins. and Zö. take it as from בור,
which in the Mishna is used as "prove," etc. (*cf.* Ja. 197b), and regard it as an inf. used instead of the finite verb, *cf.* 1 S. 8¹², Je. 17¹⁰ 19¹²
2 Ch. 7¹⁷ (*cf.* for constr. Kö. §413s). Del., Wr. and Wild. take it from
the same root, but supply הויתי with it, as היה is used in 3¹⁵ with להיות.
Gr. and Kö. (§413s) emend with 𝔅, 𝔘 and 𝔄 to ולתור. ⑤, 𝕶 and ⑨,
which are followed by Bick., Sieg., McN. and Ha., read ולבי ראה את כל זה,
which is probably right. This reading has been adopted above.—אשר=
"that" as in 8¹², *cf.* BDB. 83a.—עבר]. *a.λ.* in BH. It is an Aramaism,
cf. Syr. *ʿḇāḏā* and BDB. 714b. Ha.'s theory of the book leads him to
break this vs. into four glosses and scatter it to different parts of the work.
—הכל], vs. 2, was read הבל by ⑤, 𝕶, ⑨ and 𝔄, and attached to vs. 1.
This is rightly followed by Dale, Sieg. and McN., and has been
adopted above.

9²⁻⁶.—The hopelessness of humanity's end.

9². Inasmuch as to all is one event, to the righteous and to the wicked,
to the clean and to the unclean, to the sacrificer and to him who does not
sacrifice; as is the good, so is the sinner; he who swears is as he who
fears an oath. ³. This is an evil in all that is done under the sun, that
one fate is to all, and also the hearts of the sons of men are full of evil,
and madness is in their hearts while they live, and after it,—to the dead!
⁴. For whoever is joined to all the living, there is hope (for him), for

verily a living dog is better than a dead lion. ⁵. For the living know that they shall die, but the dead know not anything; they have no longer a reward, for their memory is forgotten. ⁶. Also their love as well as their hate and their jealousy have already perished, and they have again no portion forever in all that is done under the sun.

2. *Inasmuch as*]. For justification of this text, see critical note. —*To all is one event*], death, *cf.* 2¹⁴ 3¹⁹. As Qoheleth had no faith in anything beyond death, this seemed to him to reduce good and bad to one level regardless of moral distinctions.—*To the clean and to the unclean*]. The words might have either a moral or ceremonial content, but as *righteous* and *wicked* have disposed of the moral class, it is probable that reference is now made to ceremonial cleanness and uncleanness.—*He who swears*]. The analogy of the series, in which the bad character uniformly comes first, compels us to take this of profane swearing which was prohibited (Ex. 20⁷, *cf.* Mt. 5³⁴), and not with Plumtre, of that judicial swearing which was commended (Dt. 6¹³).—*He who fears an oath*], he who observes his oath by God as in Is. 65¹⁶ Ps. 63¹¹.—**3.** *This is an evil in all*]. Many scholars regard this as equivalent to a superlative, *i.e.*, "the greatest evil among all," *cf.* Ob. 2 and La. 1¹. For details, see the critical note. Whatever determination one may reach about the Hebrew method of expressing the superlative, the writer surely means to say that the evil which he is about to mention, is of special prominence.—*Hearts of the sons of men are full of evil*], full of discontent and unsatisfied longing.—*Madness is in their hearts*]. Life, according to Qoheleth, consists of vain strivings, fond hopes and wild desires, *cf.* 1¹⁷ 2¹².—*To the dead*]. The broken construction gives dramatic vividness to Qoheleth's gloomy outlook.—**4.** *Whoever is joined to all the living*]. The peculiar introduction of "all" gives emphasis to Qoheleth's lack of belief in a future life.—*There is hope from him*], hope that he may eat and drink and get some enjoyment out of life, *cf.* 2²⁴ 5¹⁸.—*A living dog*]. The dog is an object of contempt in the East, see 1 S. 24¹⁴ 2 S. 3⁸ 16⁹ Mt. 15²⁶ Rev. 22¹⁵.—*A dead lion*]. The lion was a symbol of regal power, and is used metaphorically of Jacob (Gn. 49⁹) and of God (Job 10¹⁶ Is. 38¹³ La. 3¹⁰ and Ho. 13⁷). Death reduces the kingly lion to a level below that of the living dog, because it reduces him to a state of nothingness.—**5.** *For the living know that they shall die*]. The clause presents a reason for the statement of the preceding verse, but the reason betrays a strange mood of pessimism.—*The dead know not anything*]. To have power to perceive that one must die is to be greater than the dead, who have no knowledge. Qoheleth's eschatology is that of Ps. 88¹⁰ and 115¹⁷.—*For their memory is forgotten*]. That a dead man would be forgotten seems to have been taken for granted by the Hebrews, *cf.* Ps. 9⁶ 31¹² 41⁵. This fact constitutes for Qoheleth one of the great tragedies of life, *cf.* 1¹¹ 2¹⁶. This verse is quoted and opposed in Wisd. 2⁴.— **6.** *Their love as well as their hate and their jealousy have already perished*]. The strongest passions are hushed in the calm of death. —*No portion forever . . . under the sun*]. The dead are denied participation in the only world of which Qoheleth knows, this to his mind makes the pathos of death a tragedy.

9². הכל]. See on vs. 1. כאשר], ⅏, Σ and 𝔙 apparently read באשר (*cf.* McN. 149). This is rightly followed by Zap. and McN., and has been adopted above.—לטוב] is a supernumerary in the text. Gins. held that it was introduced before לטהור and לטמא to show that these referred to moral, not ceremonial, qualities; it not only makes awkward Heb., but the moral qualities have been included in the preceding pair. ⅏, 𝔙 and 𝔄 added לרע to make another balanced pair, but ⅏ omits לטוב altogether, and is rightly followed by Bick., Wild. and Sieg. ⅏ has apparently preserved many pre-Aqiban readings in this passage, and this one has been adopted above.—ירא . . . . . . כטוב], for rhetorical effect the structure of the last two pairs is varied.—**3.** רע בכל]. Kn., Hit., Gins., Ew. and Del. take this as a way of expressing the superlative, comparing Jos. 14¹⁵ Ju. 6¹⁵ and Ct. 1⁸. Wr. points out, however, that in these cases the adj. is accompanied by the article, and that this is really parallel to Ob. 2 and La. 1¹, where the adjs. do not have the art., and where it is doubtful whether the writers intended to express a superlative or not.—מקרה אחד], *cf.* on 2¹⁴ and 9².—מלא] may, as Del. and Wr. note, be either an adj. or a verb, but is probably a verb. Everywhere, except in Je. 6¹¹, it takes an acc. of material as here, *cf.* Dt. 6¹¹ 33²³ 34⁹.—והללות], *cf.* on 1¹⁷. Perhaps to be pointed הוללוּת.—אחריו], ⅏ read אחריהם, using the pl. suf. to refer to אייס. Σ read אחריתם. The suffix of MT. need not, however, be altered.—אל מתים], Gins. insists that in translation הלכים must be added, but it is better with McN. to regard the expression as an abbreviated and forceful exclamation.—**4.** מי אשר] is, as Del. observed, = "whoever." *Cf.* Ex. 32³³ 2 S. 20¹¹. Kö. (§390e) regards it as = "when."—יבחר]

does not fit the context. The Qr., 20 MSS. and ⑥, ⑤, 𝔅, 𝔗, read יְחָבַּר,
which should undoubtedly be adopted into the text, as has been done
above.—בִּטָּחוֹן], an יוֹן– formation from בטח, occurring elsewhere in
BH. only in 2 K. 18¹⁹=Is. 36⁴, but found also in the Mishna and Talmud,
cf. Ja., 156b.—לְכְלֶב], ל may be taken as the prep. standing before the
casus pendens (Kö. §271b), or as an emphatic particle=Ar. "la,"
As. "lu" (cf. Haupt, *Johns Hopkins Circular*, XIII, 107; Budde, *ZAW.*,
IX, 156; Ges.ᴷ· §143e and Kö. §351d). The analogies are very evenly
balanced, but seem to me slightly to preponderate in favor of the latter
view.—**5.** שׂכר] forms a paronomasia with זכר.—**6.** גם.....גם.....גם], cf.
Is. 48⁸.—כבר]= "already," cf. on 1¹⁰.

9⁷⁻¹⁶.—A restatement of Qoheleth's philosophy of life.

9⁷. Come eat thy bread with joy and drink thy wine with a glad heart,
for already God has accepted thy works.   **⁸.** At all times let thy garments
be white, and let not oil be lacking for thy head.   **⁹.** Enjoy life with a
woman whom thou lovest all the days of thy vain life which he gives
thee under the sun, for it is thy lot in life and in thy toil which thou toilest
under the sun.   **¹⁰.** All that thy hand finds to do, do with thy might, for
there is no work nor reckoning, nor knowledge nor wisdom in She'ol
whither thou art going.   **¹¹.** And again I saw under the sun, that the
race is not to the swift, nor the battle to the valiant; also there is no bread
for the wise as well as no wealth for the intelligent and no favor for those
who have knowledge; for time and chance shall happen to them all.
¹². For even man knows not his time; like fish which are caught in an
evil net, or like birds taken in a snare,—like them are the sons of men
taken at an evil time, when it falls upon them suddenly.   **¹³.** Also this
I have seen as wise under the sun and it appeared great unto me.   **¹⁴.** There
was a small city and few men in it, and there came against it a great king
and surrounded it and built siege-works against it.   **¹⁵.** And one found
in it a poor, wise man and he delivered the city by his wisdom, but no
man remembered that poor man.   **¹⁶.** And I said wisdom is better than
might, but the wisdom of the poor man is despised and his words are
not heard.

¹⁷. *The words of the wise heard in quiet (are better) than the cry of a
prince among fools.*

¹⁸. *Wisdom is better than implements of war, but one sinner greatly
destroys good.*

10¹. *Dead flies corrupt the perfumer's ointment;
    More valued is a little wisdom than the great glory of folly.*

². *The heart of a wise man is for his right hand,
    But the heart of a fool is for his left.*

³. *Also when a fool walks in the way his heart is lacking and he says
of every one, he is a fool.*

9⁷. *Come eat thy bread with joy*]. The sudden transition leads Siegfried to find the hand of another author here. That, however, seems unnecessary. Qoheleth, like other men, could come under the influence of various moods or various systems of thought. Each could possess him in turn without preventing the return of the other. Life has no outlook, its problems are insoluble, death will end all, but enjoy sensation and the sunshine while it lasts, this is his philosophy, *cf.* 2²⁴ 3¹². ²² 5¹⁸ 8¹⁵. When a modern man realizes how many different conceptions and moods he can entertain, he finds fewer authors in a book like Qoheleth.—*Bread . . . and wine*]. These are often taken as the means of subsistence or of hospitality, *cf.* Gn. 14¹⁸ 27²⁸ Dt. 33²⁸ 1 S. 16²⁰ 25¹⁸ Neh. 5⁵ La. 2¹² Tobit 4¹⁵⁻¹⁷.—*Already God has accepted thy works*]. The thought apparently is, God, by the constitution of the world, has left this as the only source of enjoyment, and this is evidence that such a course is acceptable to Him. As Hubert Grimme pointed out (*Orient. Literaturzeitung*, VIII, col. 432 *ff.*), vvs. 7–9 are strikingly paralleled in a fragment of the Gilgamesh epic, published by Meissner in the *Mitteilungen der vorderasiatischen Gesellschaft*, 1902, Heft 1. The passage (col. III, 3 *ff.*) reads:

> Since the gods created man,
> Death they ordained for man,
> Life in their hands they hold,
> Thou, O Gilgamesh, fill indeed thy belly,
> Day and night be thou joyful,
> Daily ordain gladness,
> Day and night rage and make merry.
> Let thy garments be bright,
> Thy head purify, wash with water;
> Desire thy children, which thy hand possesses,
> A wife enjoy in thy bosom,
> Peaceably thy work (?). . . .

The argument here is so closely parallel to that of Qoheleth that one can scarcely doubt but that he was influenced by the passage. The Gilgamesh epic can have been influenced neither by Stoic nor Greek thought. This passage shows that the combination of pessimism and brightness which we find in Qoheleth, is thoroughly Semitic, and, to the Semitic mind, congruous. See further above, *Introduction*, §6 (2).

8. *Let thy garments be white*]. "White" corresponds to "bright" of the Babylonian epic. Bright colors and white were the colors for the clothing of courts, *cf.* Est. 8¹⁵, and of festivals (see the Gilgamesh fragment above). Horace (*Sat.* II, 2⁵⁹⁻⁶¹) shows that white garments were also in Rome the attire for enjoyment:

> *Ille repotia, natales, aliosve dierum*
> *Festos albatus celebret.*
> (Clothed in white he celebrates banquets,
> Birthdays or any other festal days.)

The Talmud (*Sabbath* 114a) lays a similar stress on white garments. —*Oil . . . for thy head*]. This takes the place of "thy head purify" in the Babylonian epic. Among the Hebrews oil was also a symbol of joy, *cf.* Ps. 23⁵ 45⁷ 104¹⁵ Pr. 27⁹ Am. 6⁶. The verse is quoted and opposed in Wisd. 2⁷⁻⁸.—**9.** *Enjoy life with a woman whom thou lovest*]. Interpreters have noticed the absence of the definite article before "woman" and have drawn various inferences from it. Gins. saw in it a command to embrace whatever woman pleased one, and so gain the "delights of the sons of men" alluded to in 2⁸—a view which Plumtre opposes. The analogy of the Babylonian, which seems to be freely reproduced here, tends to confirm Ginsburg's view (see crit. note). Moreover, the passage was quoted and opposed in Wisd. 2⁹, where it seems to have been understood of voluptuousness (*cf.* Wisd. 3¹⁴ 4¹). Viewed thus, the passage presents no contradiction of ch. 7²⁶⁻²⁸.—*It is thy lot*], *cf.* 5¹⁸ 8¹⁵. The author of Wisdom was, however, a fierce opponent of Qoheleth (see above, *Introd.* §12), and possibly found in his words a more sinister meaning than Qoheleth intended.—**10.** *All that thy hand finds to do*]. This context refers to methods of enjoyment.—*Do with thy might*], earnestly, or to the extent of thy ability, *cf.* Gn. 31⁶.—*For there is no work . . . in Sheol*], *cf.* Is. 14⁹⁻¹¹ Ez. 32¹⁸⁻³², and the Babylonian poem of "Ishtar's Descent to the Underworld." This last describes it as:

> A place where dust is their food, their sustenance, clay,
> Light they do not see, in darkness they dwell,
> Its clothing, like birds', is a covering of wings;
> Over door and bolt dust is spread.

For the full poem, see *Babylonian and Assyr. Lit.*, Aldine ed., p. 408 *ff.*, or KB., VI, p. 80 *ff.*, or Dhorme, *Choix de textes religieux*,

p. 326 ff.—**11.** *Again I saw*]. This introduces a new phase of the
subject. In vs. 1 Qoheleth declared that righteous and wise are
subject to the same fate as the wicked. He has proved it for the
righteous, and now turns to take it up for the wise.—*Under the
sun*], in this writer a frequent synonym of "in this world."—*The
race is not to the swift*]. Here are examples of the fact that the rewards of this life are not given in accordance with ability or merit.
Plumtre believes that this illustration indicates a late date, when
Greek exercises had been introduced into Jerusalem. This was
done in the reign of Antiochus Epiphanes, 174–164 B.C. (*cf.*
1 Mac. 1¹⁴ 2 Mac. 4⁹⁻¹⁴). He forgets, however, that there were
occasions in every age for competition in running, *cf.* 2 S. 18¹⁹ᶠᶠ.
—*No bread for the wise*]. Three terms are used to describe intellectual power, "wise," "intelligent," and "those who have knowledge."—*Time*], a reference to 3¹⁻⁸. The seasons appointed by
God roll over humanity relentlessly, among them the time of death.
—*Chance*] is here "evil chance" or "misfortune." It is not quite
the thought of 2¹⁴·¹⁵ 3¹⁹ and 9³, for a different Hebrew word is used
(see crit. note), but it borders closely upon it.—**12.** *Knows not his
time*]. "Time" is here ambiguous, it may mean the time of misfortune or the time of death. For similar uses, see Ct. 2¹² Ez. 30³.
The similes of fish caught in a net and birds taken in a snare make
it probable that the time of death is meant.—**13.** *I saw as wise*].
"I noted as an instance of wisdom." "Wisdom"="wise act,"
just as "vanity"="vain pursuit."

14. *A small city and a few men in it, and there came against it a
great king*]. Various conjectures have been made concerning this
city. Hit. thought the siege of Dor by Antiochus III in 218 B.C.
(Polybius, V, 66) was meant; Pl., the siege of Dor by Antiochus
VII (Sidetes), (Jos. *Ant.* xiii, 7²); Wr., the siege of Abel-Beth-
Maacah (2 S. 20¹⁵⁻²²); and Ha., the siege of Beth-sura by Antiochus V
(1 Mac. 6³¹ 2 Mac. 13⁹). Ewald thought reference was made to
Athens and Themistocles, and Friedländer to the siege of Syracuse by the Romans in 212 B.C. There is no certainty that any
of these conjectures is right, and the conjectures of Pl. and Ha. are
ruled out by the dates, and that of Friedländer by the fact that
Syracuse was taken; but more can be said in favor of Abel-Beth-

Maacah than of any of the others, for we do not know why the
other sieges were raised, but Abel-Beth-Maacah was relieved because of the action of a wise woman. Wr. believes the "wise
woman" was changed to "poor man," because it fitted better the
sentiment of vs. 11.—*Siege-works*]. For the reasons of this rendering,
see critical note.—**15.** *One found in it*], for "there was found in it."
—*He delivered the city by his wisdom*]. Pl. admits that the parallel
to Abel-Beth-Maacah (2 S. 20) is particularly strong, but the
"poor wise man" instead of the "wise woman" strangely seems to
him an insuperable objection to the identification.—*No man remembered that poor man*]. The popular fancy is fickle, and public
servants, then as now, were often unrewarded.—**16.** *The wisdom of
the poor man is despised and his words are not heard*]. McN. holds
that this contradicts vs. 15 if that is rendered as we have translated it, and consequently takes the preceding vs. to mean "he
would have delivered the city by his wisdom." Such a view attributes to Qoheleth too exact a use of language. In vs. 15 he
was describing some actual, though to us unknown, incident; here
he is stating the ordinary attitude of the world toward words of
wisdom. See also critical note. The writer has established his
assertion (9¹) that the wise as well as the righteous meet an un-
worthy fate.

9¹⁷–10³ are interpolations of the *Hokma* glossator, suggested
by the "wise man" of the closing incident of the section.
17. The verse is, as Sieg., Ha. and McN. have perceived, clearly a
proverb.—*Words of the wise heard in quiet are better than the cry of
a prince among fools*],—a strong contrast between the quiet strength
of wisdom and the loud pretense of sham. Pl. is reminded of the
English proverb, "Great cry and little wool."—**18.** *Wisdom is better
than implements of war*],—a proverb suggested by the anecdote
with which the preceding section closed.—*One sinner greatly destroys good*]. "Sinner" comes from a root which means "to
miss" or "go wrong," and probably refers here to intellectual or
moral slips. It is the contrary of the Hebrew ideal of "wisdom."
Perhaps Qoheleth thought of some incident like that of Achan
in Jos. 7. Many illustrations of the principle will readily occur
to any one. Often the brilliant plans of a leader, faithfully fol-

lowed by many, have been brought to nothing by the stupid in-
competence of one man.—**10**¹. *Dead flies corrupt the perfumer's
ointment*]. Flies in the East are a great pest, they penetrate everywhere. Entangled in oil, they would of course die, and decaying
would spoil the ointment's odor. The proverb continues the idea
of the preceding utterance.—*More valued is a little wisdom*].
The connection of this with the preceding aphorism is not very
obvious. If the reading adopted is right, a contrast with the
first part of the verse is presented. Perhaps, however, the text is
corrupt; see critical note. The verse is to be regarded with Sieg.
and McN. as from the hand of the *Hokma* glossator. **2.** The
verse is another proverb introduced as a gloss.—*The heart of a
wise man*]. "Heart" is used for "intelligence," "moral percep-
tion" or "will." Perhaps it includes all three.—*Is for his right
hand*], *i.e.*, tends toward the right or fortunate direction or issue.
"Right hand" has this moral meaning in the Talmud. See critical note.—*Heart of a fool is for his left*], *i.e.*, tends in the wrong
direction.—**3.** *When a fool walks in the way*], *i.e.*, when he goes
out for a walk.—*His heart is lacking*], *i.e.*, his sound intelligence
or right judgment.—*He says of everyone, he is a fool*]. In his
jaundiced view all other men are wrong.

---

7. לב טוב] = "glad heart," *cf.* Est. 5⁹ and *cf.* יטב לב, ch. 7ᵇ 1 K. 21⁷.
It is the opposite of לב רע, Pr. 26²³. It is probable, from the contrast
with this last expression, that there is an element of "good conscience"
in the phrase.

9. ראה חיים] = "enjoy life," *cf.* 2¹. חיים is left indefinite as in Ps.
34¹³.—אשה אשר אהבתה] seems like a translation of the Bab. *mar-ḫi-tum*,
"wife," perhaps from *rîḫu*, "to love" (*cf.* MA. 588a). The line of
the Babylonian epic runs: *mar-ḫi-tum li-iḫ-ta-ad-da-am i-na su-ni-ka*,
"A wife enjoy in thy loins,"—which favors Ginsburg's understanding of
the passage. It does not indicate that Qoh. was more sensual than other
Semites of antiquity, that with such frankness he alludes to such things.
—אשר], after הבלך, probably refers to ימי as its antecedent, as in 5¹⁷ and
8¹⁵. If, as some have supposed, it refers back to אשה, Gn. 2²² was in the
writer's mind. That is not so probable.—כל ימי הבלך], where it occurs the second time, is omitted by 𝔖, and is with Eur., Sieg., McN. and
Ha. to be regarded as an accidental gloss.—כי הוא]. Oriental MSS.
read כי היא, which might make it refer back to אשה. *Cf.* on the point
Kö. §350b.—**10.** יירך], *cf.* on its use, Ju. 9³³ 1 S. 10⁷ 25⁸.—בכחך] 𝔊 read

כּכֹחֵ֫ך, but the reading is not so good. בכחך is best construed with עשׂה, contrary to the Massoretic accents.—וחשבון [חִשָּׁבוֹן], cf. on 7²⁵.—בכשאול], וֹרעת וחכמה is for metrical reasons regarded by Zap. as a gloss.—בכשאול], on its use as a proper name, cf. Kö. §293c.—אשׁר אתה הלך שׁם] Ha. regards as gl., for metrical reasons. On the vs. as a whole, cf. Heb. text of Ben Sira 14¹¹· ¹².—11. שׁבתי וראה], a Heb. idiom for "again I saw," cf. on 4¹ and also Kö. §369r.—וראה] is an inf. absol. used instead of the finite verb, cf. Kö. §218b. So most interpreters. Sieg. would emend on the analogy of 4¹ to וָאֶרְאֶה.—מרוץ], this masc. form is used only here. The usual form is מרוצה, cf. 2 S. 18²⁷ Je. 8⁶ 22¹⁷. Wr. thought that the masc. form might indicate a late date, but the fem. form is used in NH. (see Ja. 839).—[וָרֶגַע]= "accident," occurs in BH. only here and in 1 K. 5¹⁸, though found in NH. (cf. Ja. 1135). It may represent either a good or bad occurrence. In 1 K. 5¹⁸, רע is added to it to express the meaning "misfortune." Here it has that meaning without רע. [יקרה] is masc. to agree with פגע.—12. [ייקשׁים] is generally taken as a Pual part., the מ being omitted, and the vowel lengthened to compensate the absence of the doubled consonant (cf. Ges.ᴷ· §52s and Kö., Vol. I, p. 408). Other examples are אֻכָּל Ex. 3², יוּלַד Ju. 13⁸, and לֻקַּח 2 K. 2¹⁰. Dr. suggests נוקשׁים as the original reading.—[כשׁתפול =כאשׁר תפול. [מצורה רעה]. Sieg. regards רעה as a dittograph from the succeeding רעה. Ha. regards the same רעה, as well as כי at the beginning of the verse and פ־אם at the end, as glosses, which mar the metrical form of the vs., but see above, Introd. §9. With reference to the vs. Rabbi Aqiba remarks (Aboth, 3¹⁵), הכל נתון בערבון ומצורה פרוסה על, כל החיים:, i.e., "All is given on pledge, and a net is spread over all the living."—13. [זֹה], fem. Put in the same gender as חכמה, cf. 5¹⁵.—גדולה אלי [היא], cf. גדולה לאלהים Jon. 3², and גדולה ליהודים Est. 10³. Σ correctly renders μεγάλη δοκεῖ μοι.—14. [עיר קטנה], יש or היתה must be supplied in thought.—[מלך גדול]. Del. thinks this a reference to the king of Persia. The phraseology is that used of Persian kings, but it lasted on into the Greek period. It might be used by the writer to designate king David or any other powerful monarch.—סבב] means "surround" as in 2 K. 6¹⁵, not "walk around" as in Jos. 6⁴.—מצורים] evidently means "siege-works," a meaning which it has nowhere else in BH. Two MSS. read מצורים, and this reading is supported by 𝔊, 𝔖, Σ, 𝔙, 𝔄. This reading we adopt with Winck., Dr. and McN.—15. מצא] is here impersonal, so Kn., Hit., Heil., Wild., and Sieg., cf. also Kö. §323c. Wr.'s contention that מלך גדול of the preceding vs. must be the subject, does not commend itself. It is not grammatically necessary, and does not give good sense.—מסכן], see on 4¹³. Dale's contention that it means a wage-worker and not a beggar does not seem well founded, for it occurs in BH. only here, in the fol. vs. and in 4¹³, but often in Aram., and in the Sin. Syr. of Lk. 16²⁰ is used of Lazarus.—וּמִלַּט־הוּא],

as Del. observes, ־ of the Piel reverts to its original ־ on account of the
following Maqqef. Another instance occurs in 12⁹. Del. also notes
that in the earlier language this would have been—יַמְלֵט. McN.
would render this "would deliver" on the analogy of Ex. 9¹⁵ and 1 S.
13¹³, taking the clause as an apodosis with protasis suppressed. The
contradiction which seems to him to render this necessary, does not
seem to me to exist. See above.—אדם], as Del. says, would in the older
language have been איש. Perhaps it is used here because איש immediately precedes, but in 7²⁰ we find אדם. Zap., for metrical reasons,
would follow 𝔐 and supply אחר after אדם.—16. [בזויה and [נשמעים
are participles of continuous or customary action, cf. Da. §97, rem. 1.
Ha. regards—אני טובה] and all that comes after גבורה] as glosses. On
the sentiment, cf. BS. (Heb.) 13²²ᶜᵈ.

17. [בנחת], not ("heard) in wisdom," but ("uttered) in wisdom," the
reference being to the speaker, so Wr. and Wild.—נשמעים] is erased
by Bick., who renders:

> Der Weisen Wort ist ruhig;
> Die Thoren überschrei'n es.

This is arbitrary. MT. is supported by all the versions.—זועקה].
טובים is understood before מן as in 4¹⁷, cf. Ges.ᴷ· §133b and Kö.
§308c.—מושל בכסילים]="an arch fool," wrongly considered by some
a Græcism. Cf. 2 S. 23³ Job 41²⁶ and Pr. 30³⁰.—18. [קרב], in the older
language, would have been מלחמה. The word occurs in Zc. 14³ Ps. 55¹⁹
68³¹ 78⁹ 144¹ Job 38²³. It is found in Aram., Dn. 7²¹ and frequently
in the Talmud, cf. Ja. 1411. Cf. also the Syr. stem and As. *qarabu*,
all with the same meaning. The substitution of קרב for מלחמה was
probably due to Aramaic influence.—חוטא] is pointed like a "לח stem,
as in other parts of Q. 𝔖 read חֵטְא, which better corresponds to חכמה.
This reading is favored by Kn., Del., Sieg., Winck. and Dr.—הרבה],
used adverbially, cf. Kö. §318e. Ha. regards—חכמה מכלי קרב] as a
genuine phrase of Q., and all the rest of the verse as a gloss. This is
arbitrary, and spoils a good proverb.—1. [זבובי מות] is taken by 𝔊 (unless that is corrupt, as McN. thinks) and by Del. and Wr. as="death
bringing" or "poisonous flies." The last claims "dead flies" would
be זבובים מתים. חבלי מות in Ps. 18⁵ 116³ shows by analogy that this
can="dead flies," which suits the context much better.—יבאיש], a
sing. with a pl. subject has been explained in various ways. AE., whom
Gins. and Del. follow, held that the vb. was sing. because Qoheleth
thought of each fly. Winck., McN. and Dr. emend to יבאישו, while
Kö. (§349g) holds that the sing. מות makes the idea sing. Each of
these solutions is possible. It is also possible that Qoheleth was careless
and wrote bad grammar.—יביע] is omitted by 𝔊, 𝔖, Σ, 𝔙, and should,
as McN. and Dr. have seen, be erased.—רוקח], on the meaning, cf.
Ex. 30³⁵ 37²⁹. Beginning with—יקר], the text is probably corrupt.

𝕲 suggests that the original reading was יקר מעט חכמה מכבוד סכלות רב.
This was transformed in 𝔖 into יקר מחכמה ומכבוד רב סכלות מעט.
𝔅 read the same except that it omitted רב, while MT. went a step
further and omitted ו. The original reading of 𝕲 presented an antithesis to the first half of the verse, the Rabbinic revisers present in 𝔖, 𝔅
and MT. a thought in harmony with the first half verse. (*Cf.* McN.,
p. 150 *ff.*, who has worked this out).—**2.** לב] was taken by Mich. in an
anatomical sense. He held the verse to mean that wisdom is as rare
as a man with the heart on the right side of the body. It is better with
Del. to take לב="thought" or "will" (*cf.* ch. 7⁷ and Ho. 4¹¹).—ימין]
is taken by Del., Wr. and Wild. correctly to have a moral significance
kindred to that in the Talmud, where ימן is used as a vb., which in
some forms means "to do the right thing," *cf.* Ja. 580b. There is no
need with Pl. to call in Greek influence to explain the figure.—שמאל]
is similarly used with a moral significance="errors." *Cf.* Ja. 1591b
for kindred Talmudic usage.—**3.** וגם בדרך כשסכל הלך] is inverted for
emphasis from וגם כשסכל בדרך הולך, *cf.* 3¹³.—דרך] is rightly taken
by Kn., Hit., Gins., McN., etc., in the literal sense="when the fool
takes a walk." Wr., with less probability, takes it to mean "the common path of life."—כש=[כאשר, a temporal particle, *cf.* 8⁷ and Kö.
§387f.—חסר] is a verb (so Del., Wr., McN.), and not an adj. (Gins.).
It occurs with לב eleven times outside of this passage, *cf.* Pr. 6³² 7⁷.
—אמר] is taken by Del. and No. to mean "he (the fool) says to every
one by his actions that he is a fool." This gives to אמר an unusual
meaning. This renders—לכל] "to every one." It is better with McN.
to take לכל="concerning every one," and so give to אמר its usual
meaning.—סָכָל], a noun, not an adj.

10¹⁻²⁰.—Advice concerning one's attitude toward rulers. (Largely interpolated.) The genuine portions are 10⁴⁻⁷·¹⁴ᵇ·¹⁶·¹⁷ and ²⁰.

10⁴. If the anger of the ruler rise against thee, do not leave thy place,
for soothing pacifies great sins. ⁵. There is an evil that I have seen under
the sun like an unintentional error which proceeds from the ruler.

> ⁶. He places the fool in high positions often,
>   But the nobles dwell in low estate.
> ⁷. I have seen slaves upon horses,
>   And princes, like slaves, walking on the ground.
> ⁸. *He who digs a pit shall fall into it,*
>   *And he who breaks through a wall, a serpent shall bite him.*
> ⁹. *He who quarries stones shall be hurt by them,*
>   *And he who cleaves wood shall be endangered thereby.*
> ¹⁰. *If the iron be dull,*
>   *And he do not sharpen its edge,*
>   *Then he must strengthen his force;*
>   *But the advantage of wisdom is to give success.*

11. *If the serpent bite for lack of enchantment,*
    Then there is no advantage to the charmer.
12. *The words of the mouth of the wise are favor,*
    But the lips of the fool shall devour him.
13. *The beginning of the words of his mouth is folly,*
    And the end of his speech is wicked madness.

14. *The fool multiplies words:—*
[Man does not know that which shall be, and what shall be after him
who can tell him?]

15. *The toil of fools shall weary him*
    Who knows not how to go to town.
16. Woe to thee, O land, whose king is a child,
    And whose princes feast in the morning!
17. Happy art thou, O land, whose king is well born,
    And whose princes feast at the (proper) time,
    For strength, and not for drinking!
18. *Through great idleness the beam-work sinks,*
    And through falling of hands the house drips.
19. *For laughter they make bread,*
    And wine to make life glad;
    And money answers both.
20. Do not even in thy thought curse the king,.
    Nor in thy bed-chamber curse a rich man;
    For the bird of heaven shall carry the voice,
    And the owner of wings shall tell a thing.

10¹. The section begins with genuine words of Qoheleth. It
is the beginning of his advice concerning one's conduct before
rulers.—*The anger of the ruler*], an oft recurring calamity under
a despotic government.—*Do not leave thy place*], *i.e.*, throw up
thy post.—*Soothing pacifies great sins*], pacifies the anger aroused
by great errors. The cause is here put for the effect. Qoheleth's
advice is the wisdom of the under man, but, as Genung says, it
nevertheless has the virtue of the idea, "Blessed are the meek."—
5. *There is an evil*], a favorite expression of Qoheleth's, *cf.* 5¹³ 6¹.
—*Like an unintentional error*], as if it were an unintentional error.
Qoheleth here exhibits some of the pacifying spirit which he has
just advised. He does not excite the anger of a despot by suggest-
ing that his errors are intentional. Underneath his expression we
detect a deeper note, it is revealed in the word "evil." One must
bow to the despot, but the despot is not always right. This is a
blot on the government of the world.—**6.** *He places the fool in high*

positions], another example of the evils of despotic government. Plumtre thinks it a reference to Agathoclea and her brother, who were favorites of Ptolemy Philopator (B.C. 222–205), (Justin, XXX, 1); Haupt, of the officers appointed by Antiochus IV and his successors, who betrayed Jewish interests (1 Mac. 7^9 9^{25} 2 Mac. $4^{8.\ 13.\ 19.\ 25}$). No doubt, many examples of this fault could be found in every period of Oriental government, but the date of the book (see *Introduction*, §13) makes Plumtre's view probable.—*Often*], is a free rendering of the Hebrew, see crit. note.—*The nobles*], literally "the rich," *i.e.*, men of ancestral wealth, who were regarded as the natural associates of kings, and the holders of offices.—

7. *Slaves upon horses*], another example of the way a despot often reverses the natural positions of his subjects. Justin (XLI, 3) tells how, among the Parthians, one could distinguish freemen from slaves by the fact that the former rode on horses, and the latter ran on foot. An instance of the exercise of such arbitrary power in later times is found in the decree of the Fatimite Caliph Hakim, that Christians and Jews should not ride horses, but only mules or asses (see Chronicle of Bar Hebræus, p. 215). As Siegfried points out, the mention of horses here is an index of late date, as in early Israel kings and princes rode on asses or mules, *cf.* Ju. 5^{10} 10^4 2 S. 18^9 1 K. 1^{38} Zc. 9^9. The sentiment corresponds to that of Pr. 19^{10}. Such a result of tyranny reminds Del. (*Hoheslied und Koheleth*, 222) of the career of the Persian Bagoas, in the mind of Graetz it points to the reign of Herod (*cf.* Jos. *Ant.* xvi, 7 and 10), but almost any period of Oriental history must have afforded such examples.

8. *He who digs a pit shall fall into it*]. This is clearly, as Siegfried and McNeile have seen, a proverb introduced by a glossator. It has no connection with the preceding, and occurs in varying forms in Pr. 26^{27} and BS. 27^{26}. The thought of the first half is that a man who digs a pit for another shall fall into it himself, *cf.* Ps. 7^{16} 57^6 BS. 27^{29}.—*He who breaks through a wall*], to rob a garden or a house.—*A serpent shall bite him*]. Serpents in Palestine often lurk in the crannies of a wall, *cf.* Am. 5^{19}.—**9.** *He who quarries stones*]. This is a proverb which has no reference to the preceding. As Sieg. and McN. have seen, it is a gloss introduced by the *Hokma* glossator. Plumtre, in order to find a connection with the preceding, makes the "stones" the stones of landmarks, as he had made the "wall" of the preceding verse, but this arbitrarily reads a meaning into it. It is clearly a common proverbial saying on the danger of the homely occupations of quarrying and wood-cutting. It is perhaps the same proverb which underlies the saying attributed to Jesus in the Oxyrhynchus papyrus,

> Raise the stone and there thou shalt find me,
> Cleave the wood and there am I.

(See Grenfell and Hunt's *Sayings of our Lord*, 1897, p. 12.) The proverb was probably introduced here because, with its mate which follows, it illustrates the value of wisdom.—*He who cleaves wood*]. This may be fire-wood, *cf.* Lv. 1^7 4^{12}.—*Shall be endangered thereby*]. For an illustration of the danger, *cf.* Dt. 19^5.—**10.** *If the iron be dull*], the axe be dull, *cf.* 2 K. 6^5, where RV. translates "iron" by "axe-head."—*And he do not sharpen*]. The "he" is no doubt intended to refer to the wood-chopper of the preceding verse. This gnomic saying was probably introduced by the hand which introduced the preceding.—*Then he must strengthen his force*]. He must accomplish by brute strength what he might have done more easily by the exercise of intelligence.—*The advantage of wisdom is to give success*]. Wisdom, by enabling a man properly to prepare his tools, helps to ensure a successful issue to his work. For the basis of this rendering, see critical note.— **11.** *If the serpent bite for lack of enchantment*]. This is another proverb, introduced by the *Hokma* glossator, because it has a bearing on wisdom, or the use of wisdom. Plumtre thinks that it was suggested by the serpents mentioned in vs. 8.—*There is no advantage to the charmer*]. A charm, in order to protect from a serpent's bite, must be exercised before he bites. If it is not, it is of no value to its owner. The proverb strikes the same note as that of vs. 10. Success depends upon foresight. Wisdom that comes afterward is useless in producing results. Snake-charming is not uncommon in the East, as in ancient Israel, *cf.* Je. 8^{17} Ps. 58^5 BS. 12^{13}.—**12.** *The words of the mouth of the wise are favor*]. As Hit., Gins., and Zö. have noted, they obtain favor (*cf.* Pr. 22^{11}). This proverbial gloss begins by praising the results of effectual wisdom. It teaches positively what the preceding vs. taught negatively.—*The lips of the fool shall destroy him*]. This presents the antithesis. Ineffectual wisdom is equal to folly.—*Him*], the fool.—**13.** The vs. is another proverbial gloss, which interrupts Qoheleth's reflections on rulers.—*The beginning of the words.*] "Beginning" contrasts with "end" in the next clause. The expression is kindred to the English "from beginning to end."—*Of his mouth*], the fool's. The proverbs continue to treat of him.— *Folly . . . wicked madness*]. There is progression even in foolishness, that which begins as mere folly may end in criminal madness. Possibly Qoheleth meant simply grievous madness, for the word employed by him is ambiguous, see critical note.—**14ᵃ.** *The fool multiplies words*]. Empty talk is a characteristic of folly. This is a fragment of another proverb which was introduced by the *Hokma* glossator. The rest of the verse has no connection with it, and evidently the concluding member of the parallelism is lost.

14ᵇ. *Man does not know that which shall be*]. McN. is right in seeing in this a genuine fragment of the thought of Qoheleth, it is so like 6¹² 7¹⁴ and 8⁷. He is also right in regarding it as out of place here, for it interrupts the reflections on the evils of despotic government. Rashi, Ginsburg and Wright take the verse to mean that the fool talks a great deal about the most unknown of subjects—the future; but Ginsburg and Delitzsch are then puzzled to know why an equivalent to "although" is omitted. The solution of McNeile already presented is far more probable. Some glossator clumsily brought disjecta membra together here.

15. *The toil of fools shall weary him, who knows not how to go to town*]. Another proverbial gloss which is very obscure. Ginsburg rendered "because he does not know," and took it to mean that in his doings as well as in his sayings the folly of the fool manifests itself. Ewald thought it a reference to bad government, in which the toil of fools (*i.e.*, heathen rulers) wearied the poor countryman who did not know how to go to the city. Graetz, whom Renan followed, thought it a reference to the Essenes, who lived by themselves, and avoided cities (Jos. *Ant.* xviii, 1⁵). Wildeboer thinks the meaning to be "he who asks the fool the way to the city will be disappointed," and similarly Genung, "one cannot make out of

a fool's voluble talk the way to the nearest town." These varieties
of opinion serve to illustrate the difficulty of the passage.   The
rendering adopted above makes it mean the folly of fools wearies
the most ignorant.   The expression, "does not know the way to
town," was no doubt proverbial like the English, "He doesn't know
enough to come in when it rains," which is frequently applied to
one whom the speaker wishes to stigmatize as especially stupid.
Perhaps the mutilation of the preceding proverb has made this more
obscure.   For other ways of rendering parts of it, see critical note.

16. *Woe to thee, O land*].   This verse should follow 10⁶.   The
original remarks of Qoheleth upon rulers, which the glossator
has interrupted by his interpolations, are now resumed.—*Whose
king is a child*].   This is an expression which was probably called
forth by some bitter experience in Qoheleth's own time.   Hitzig
and Genung think of Ptolemy Epiphanes, who came to the throne
of Egypt in 205 B.C., at the age of five years.   The word used
does not necessarily mean child (see critical note), but was applied to Solomon at his accession (1 K. 3⁷).   It primarily, however, has that meaning as in 1 S. 3¹, etc., and no doubt has it here.
Haupt thinks it refers to Alexander Balas.   See above, on 4¹³ᶠ.
The considerations there adduced lead us to agree with Hitzig.—
Whose princes feast in the morning], an act which both Hebrew
and Roman condemned.   *Cf.* Is. 5¹¹.   Cicero, *Phil.* ii, 41, says,
Ab hora tertia bibebatur, ludebatur, vomebatur.   Juvenal, *Satire*,
i, 49, 50:

> *Exul ab octava Marius bibit et fruitur dis*
> *Iratis.*

Catullus, *Carmen*, xlvii, 5, 6:

> *Vos convivia lauta sumtuose*
> *De die facitis.*

That it was not common to feast in the morning, Acts 2¹⁵, where
it is argued that the Apostles cannot be drunk because it is only
the third hour, shows.   This implication that the "youth" who
is king is given to revelry, strengthens, in Haupt's opinion, the
view that the writer has Alexander Balas in mind, for Justin says
of him, *quem insperatæ opes et alienæ felicitatis ornamenta velut
captum inter scortorum greges desidem in regia tenabant.*   It could,

however, as well apply to courtiers of Ptolemy Epiphanes.—**17**. *Happy art thou . . . whose king is well born*]. The prevailing regime is not only negatively condemned, but by way of contrast an ideal government is pictured. "Well born" is used here as a compliment to the able king in Qoheleth's mind. It does not necessarily imply an ignoble birth for him who is condemned. Perhaps Qoheleth is paying a compliment to Antiochus III, who gained Palestine in 198 B.C., and was enthusiastically received by the Jews. See Jos. *Ant.* xii, 3³.—*Feast at the (proper) time*]. This reminds us of ch. 3¹⁻⁸, where everything is said to have its time.— *For strength and not for drinking*], that they may be real heroes, and not "heroes for mingling strong drink," such as are described in Is. 5²².

18. *Through great idleness the beam-work sinks*]. As Sieg., Ha. and McN. have seen, this is a proverb introduced as a gloss. Doubtless, the glossator intended to hint by it that when the princes of a state gave themselves to revelry, the structure of government would fall into ruin. "Beam-work" is equivalent to "roof," for Palestinian houses are made of stone and, if they contain any wood at all, it is in the roof.—*Falling of hands*], a synonym for idleness, *cf.* Pr. 10⁴.—*The house drips*], the roof leaks. —**19.** *For laughter they make bread*]. McNeile attributes this to the same *Hokma* glossator, but it does not seem like a proverb. It probably comes, however, from the hand of this glossator. "They make bread," seems to refer back to the feasting princes of vs. 16. The phrase is probably not a part of Qoheleth's works, for he would have introduced it immediately after that vs. "Make bread" means to prepare a meal, *cf.* Ez. 4¹⁵.—*And wine to make life glad*]. Many commentators have seen in this the influence of Ps. 104¹⁵. As Delitzsch noted, however, the thought is not like that of the psalm. It is rather similar to vs. 17; they use eating and drinking not to gain strength, but for sport and revelry.— *Money answers both*]. Money is squandered to secure both. The glossator probably intended to suggest that the feasting of the princes of vs. 16 dissipated public funds.

20. *Do not even in thy thought curse the king*]. The genuine words of Qoheleth reappear once more. He counsels caution and self-control as in vvs. 4, 5. His thought is "treason will out."—*Nor in thy bed-chamber*], in thy most private moments. One is reminded of the proverb "walls have ears."—*Curse a rich man*]. It is taken for granted, as in vs. 6, that the wealthy are natural rulers. —*The bird of heaven*]. As in the English saying, "a little bird told me"; the mysterious paths by which secrets travel, are attributed to the agency of birds.

10⁴. [רוח=] "anger" sometimes, *cf.* Ju. 8³ Is. 25⁴ 33¹¹ Zc. 6⁸.—[עלה] is regularly used of anger, *cf.* 2 S. 11²⁰ Ez. 38¹⁸ and Ps. 78²¹·³¹.—[מקומך]= "place" in the sense of "post," *cf.* 1 S. 20²⁷.—[חנח], fr. נוח= "leave," *cf.* BDB. 629a.—[מרפא] means "healing." McN. rightly renders it "soothing." BDB.'s "composure" (p. 951b) does not suit so well. The root is used in Ju. 8³ of assuaging anger.—[יניח]= "quiets" or "relaxes," *cf.* 7¹⁸ 11⁶.—5. [ראיתי], אשר is implied before it.—[־ְכ] was called by the older grammarians "Kaf veritatis." It is in reality= "as," *cf.* Neh. 7² and Ges.ᴷ· §118x.—[שֶׁ־] is omitted by 𝔊, but as Eur. observes, this is probably accidental. Its omission in one authority would be more likely due to accident than its insertion in all the others, to design.—[שגגה]= "unintentional error," *cf.* Lv. 5¹⁸ Nu. 15²⁵.—[יצא], fem. part., instead of יצאה—another example of a ל״א verb, treated by Qoheleth as ל״ה.—6. [נתן], as often means "set," "place," *cf.* Dt. 17¹⁵ Est. 6⁸.—[סֶכֶל], 𝔊, 𝔖, 𝔄, 'A, Σ, all read סָכָל. They, no doubt, had an unpointed text before them. Ra., Gins., Del., and Wr. read סֶכֶל, and explained the abstr. as used for the concrete, but it is better with Eur. and Dr. to read סָכָל.—[מרומים]= "exalted positions" or "posts," *cf.* Is. 24⁴ Job 5¹¹.—[רבים] is an appositive to מרומים= "high positions— many of them." It is rendered freely above to preserve more nearly the metrical form.—[עשירים] was thought by Houb. and Spohn not to form a good contrast, they accordingly emended the text; but, as explained above, it fits both the literary form and the historical fact. Gins. and Del. compare שוע in the sense of "liberal" in Job 36¹⁹ and Is. 32⁵.— 7. [על הארץ] is equal, as Del. noted, to בְּרֶגֶל.

8. [גומץ], an Aramaic loan word, *cf.* Barth, *Nominalbildung*, §45n 1, and Nöldeke, *Mandæan Gram.* §44. The word is used in the Targ. on Pr. 22¹⁴ for the Heb. שוחה. It occurs in the same form in Targ. on Pr. 26²⁷; in Targ. to Is. 24¹⁷·¹⁸ and Je. 48⁴²·⁴³ it is written כימץ, while the Targ. on 2 S. 18¹⁷ writes it קומץ.—[גדר] is not a hedge, it is built of stones, *cf.* Pr. 24³¹. Ha. arbitrarily regards the word as a gl. Not even his metrical theory demands it.—[נשך] is used of the bite of a serpent, *cf.* Gn. 49¹⁷. Wr. and Wild. held that the imperfects here implied simply possibility, but to render "may fall" and "may bite" would rob the couplet of force.—9. [מסיע]= "to break up" or "quarry," *cf.* 1 K.

5³¹ and *BDB*. 652b.—יֵעָצֵב] frequently means "be grieved," as in Gn.
45⁵ 1 S. 20³, but it also means "be pained," as in 1 S. 20³⁴ 2 S. 19³, then
as here "be hurt," *cf. BDB*. 780b.—יִסָּכֶן] was a great perplexity to the
commentators of the first half of the nineteenth century, but as Del.
pointed out, it is a NH. word="be in danger" (*cf. Berakoth*, 1³). It also
occurs in Aram. and is no doubt an Aramaism, *cf. BDB*. 698 and Ja.
991b.—**10**. This is, as Wr. observed, linguistically the most difficult verse
in the book.—קֵהָה] occurs here as Piel—the only instance in BH., it
is found as Kal in Je. 31²⁹· ³⁰ Ez. 18². The Kal is common in NH.,
cf. Ja. 1321b. 𝔊 read נפל, but that gives no sense.—פנים]="face"
or "forepart," here used instead of פה or פי for "edge," *cf. BDB*. 816a.
In Ez. 21²¹ it is also used for the "edge" of a sword.—קלקל], Pilpel of
קלל. *Cf*. נחשת קלל]="polished bronze," Ez. 1⁷ Dn. 10⁶. A "polished
edge" is a "sharpened edge."—חילים יגבר]="to make mighty (one's)
power," see Job 21⁷ and *cf*. 1 Ch. 7⁵· ⁷· ¹¹ and ⁴⁰.—הכשיר חכמה], should
probably with Winck., Ha. and Dr. be transposed, as we have done
above in translating. McN. follows 𝔊, 𝔖 and 𝔚 in reading הכשר=
"the successful man." This has better textual authority, but gives
doubtful sense.—הכשיר], is Hiph. Inf., *cf. BDB*. 506b. Zap. omits חכמה,
to make the metre more symmetrical.—**11**. לחש]="to whisper," used in
Is. 26¹⁶ of a whispered prayer, elsewhere in BH. is used of the whispered
utterances which charm a serpent, *cf*. Je. 8¹⁷ Is. 3³ Ps. 58⁶. The root
has the same meaning in the Talmud, *cf*. Ja. 704 (*i.e.*, J.Ar.), and in
Syr.—בלוא] is used before nouns in the sense of "for lack of," "without"
and in kindred meanings. *Cf*. Is. 55¹· ² Job 15³² and Kö. §402r.—בעל
הלשון]="lord of the tongue," was taken by Hit., on the analogy of בעל
כנף="bird," to mean "a human being," but ישמע לקול מלחשים in
Ps. 58⁶ shows that in "charming" stress was laid on the use of language,
and this, taken in connection with the context here, makes it clear that
Gins., Del. and Wr. were justified in rendering it "enchanter," "wiz-
ard."—**12**. חן], *cf*. Ps. 45³ Pr. 22¹¹. The metaphorical statement makes
the sentence emphatic.—שפתהו], instead of שפתים, is poetical and late,
cf. Is. 59³ Ps. 45³ 59⁸ Ct. 4³· ¹¹ 5¹³.—תבלענה], fem. imperf., the subj.
is שפתות. The suffix refers to כסיל.—**13**. תחלת] occurs only here in
Qo. In 3¹¹ he has ראש and in 7⁸ ראשית. תחלה is, however, good BH.,
cf. Gn. 13³ (RJE.) and Ho. 1².—פיהו] in 13b is used by metonomy for
דָּבָר, or some synonym of it as in Is. 29¹³ Ps. 49¹⁴. Gins. and Sieg. are
wrong in thinking it necessary to supply דִּבְרֵי before it. Q. varied the
expression for the sake of variety.—חוללות], *cf*. on 1¹⁷.—רעה], as Del.
suggests, may have only the force which it has in חלי רעה (6²) and
רעה חולה (5¹²), where it means "disagreeable" or "serious," but it
may also stand for ethical evil as in Dt. 30¹⁵ 2 S. 14¹⁷ Is. 5²⁰ Am. 5¹⁴.
—**14**. ישיהיה]. The versions, except 𝔚, read שהיה, but this was probably because the passage was obscure, and a contrast of tenses seemed to help

I 2

it. Analogy of other passages in Q., where the sentiment occurs, supports MT.—**15.** חיגענו] seems to take עמל as a fem., which is without parallel. This has caused scholars much discussion. The true solution has, however, been found by Albrecht (*ZAW.*, XVI, 113), who emends the verb to ייגענו. This is supported by Kö. (§249m) and Sieg. The suffix גנ֫ ־ is ambiguous. Does it refer to הכסילים, a sing. to a pl., as so often happens in Deut.? So, Hit., Gins. and Wr. Does it refer back to ארם in vs. 14? So, Kö. (§348v). It seems better to make it point forward to the relative.—אשר] is taken by Kn. and Gins. and Gr. = "because." It seems better with Heil. to make it a rel. pro. referring to גנ־.—אל־עיר], a colloquial expression, like the English "to town," for אל העיר. Pl. thinks that it points to a boyhood near Jerusalem. It is probably, however, a proverbial expression, with no local reference.

16. אי], a late form used in the Talm. In BH. usually אוי, as in Is. 6⁵; sometimes הי, as in Ez. 2¹⁰.—שמלכך נער], as Del. observes, would in earlier Heb. be נער מלכה.—נער] אשר was held by Död., Van der P., Spohn and Gr. to = "slave." Gr. believed it to be a reference to Herod the Great, who is called in the Talm. (*Baba Batra*, 3b, and *Ketuboth*, 24) "the slave of the Hasmonæans." If slave had been intended, probably עבד would have been used. נער is not necessarily a child; it is used of Solomon at his accession (1 K. 3⁷) and of Ziba, who had sons and slaves (2 S. 19¹⁸), but nevertheless is often used to mean "child," *cf.* Ex. 2⁶ Ju. 13⁵. ⁷ 1 S. 4²¹.—יאכל] = "eat," but here in the sense of feast, *cf.* Is. 5¹¹.—**17.** אשריך] varies from the ordinary pointing אשריך. Kö. (§321f) says the variation is because it is used here as an interjection.—בן חורים], an Aramaism = בר חרי = "freeman" (*cf.* S. A. Cook, *Glos. of Aram. Inscr.*, 56). Driver (*Introd.* 519n 1) says חרים is an Aram. word used in northern Israel, but never applied to the nobles of Judah except in Je. 27²⁰ 39⁶, passages which are not in 𝕲 and are later than Je.'s time.—בגבורה], on בְ, *cf.* Ges.ᴷ· §119l.—שתי] = "drinking" or "drinking-bout." It is a α.λ. in BH.

18. עצלתים], dual of עַצְלָה. AE., Hit., Ew., Heil., Gins. and Zö. take the dual to refer to a pair of hands. Del., Wr., *BDB.* (p. 782a) and Kö. (§275c) take the dual form as intensive. Bick. emends to עצלות, after Pr. 31²⁷, Sieg. and McN. emend to עַצְלַת ידים. Dr. hesitates between the two emendations. In the text, we have followed Del., Wr., *BDB.* and Kö. The last cites as parallel רשעתים Ju. 3⁸. ¹⁰ and מרחים Je. 50²¹. To these might, perhaps, be added צהרים = "midday," though Ges.ᴷ· (§88c) casts doubt on the reality of such duals, and it may be better to adopt one of the emendations.—ימך], Niph. of מכך. The verb occurs but twice elsewhere in BH., Ps. 106⁴³ in Kal, and Job 24²⁴ in Hoph. The stem occurs in Aram., Syr., and Ar. It is to be regarded as an Aramaism.—המקרה] is a α.λ. The word is usually קרה, *cf.* Gn. 19⁸ and Ct. 1¹⁷, *cf.* also *BDB.* 900a. Baer, p. 68, observes that the מ is here pointed with

Daghesh to distinguish the noun from the part. which occurs in Ps.
104³.—שפלות] is also α.λ., cf. BDB. 1050b. It is used for slackness of
hand like רפיון ידים, Je. 47³. It is the opposite of כף רמיה, Pr. 10⁴.—
ידלף [=דלף="to drip" and so "to leak." It occurs but twice besides
in BH., Job 16²⁰ and Ps. 119²⁸, where it is used figuratively for weeping.
In Aram. it is found in the Targ. to Pr. 19¹³ and also in the Talm. In
the latter it is more often ילף, cf. Ja. 402a.—19. לשחוק], as Del. and Wr.
observe, ל denotes purpose.—עשים לחם]="to prepare a meal" (cf. Ez.
4¹⁵), as אכל לחם means "to eat a meal" (cf. Gn. 31⁵⁴ Ex. 18¹² Je. 41¹).
—וישמה] is difficult. It is better, as McN. has proposed, to follow 𝔊
and emend to לשמח, making it parallel to לשחוק.—הכסף], silver stood for
money throughout the ancient world, except in Egypt in early periods
of its history. The ordinary man saw no gold.— יענה]. As Del. and Wr.
observe, there is no reason with Gins. to regard this as a Hiph. "Money
can procure (answer) to both," is the thought.—הכל]. For this in the sense
of "both," see on 2¹⁴.—20. אל . . . . . גם]=ne quidem, cf. Kö. §341u.— מדע],
"knowledge" is here used for "mind" or "thought." It is a late Ara-
maized form occurring elsewhere in BH. only in 2 Ch. 1¹⁰· ¹¹· ¹² and Dn.
1⁴· ¹⁷. It occurs in the Targ. on Je. 3¹⁵ Ps. 34¹ and Pr. 1⁵. In Aram.
it frequently appears מנדע; cf. Dn. 2²¹ 4³¹· ³³ 5¹² and Targ. to Job 33³.
—מלך] is in Q. definite without the art., cf. 5⁸ 8²·⁴ 9¹⁴ and Kö. §294d.
—בחדרי משכבך], cf. 2 K. 6¹².—עוף ה"] is not individualized, cf. Kö. §254f.—
בעל כנפים], syn. for a bird, cf. בעל כנף, Pr. 1¹⁷. Cf. also בעל קרנים, in
Dn. 8⁶· ²⁰.— יגיד] is one of the few jussives in the book. Why a jussive
should appear here is a puzzle. Kö. (§191a) says the reading is uncertain, and Dr. does not hesitate to read יגיר. Probably this is right,
though Baer (p. 68) adduces a parallel to יגיד (the jussive with cere
followed by י) in ותגיד, Ex. 19³. Ges.ᴷ·, however (§53n), declares
יגיד both here and in Ex. 19³ to be an error. This is probably correct.

11¹–12⁸.—Qoheleth's final advice.

11¹. Cast thy bread on the face of the waters,
   For in many days thou shalt find it.
². Give a portion to seven and also to eight,
   For thou knowest not what evil shall be on the earth.
³. If the clouds are filled with rain,
   They empty it over the earth;
   If wood fall southward or northward,
   The place where wood falls—there it shall be.
⁴. A wind-observer will not sow,
   And a cloud-watcher will not reap.
⁵. As thou knowest not what the path of the wind is.
   Nor the bones in the womb of a pregnant woman,
   So thou mayest not know the work of God,
   Who makes the whole.

⁶. In the morning sow thy seed,
    And till evening rest not thy hand,
    For thou knowest not which shall succeed, this or that,
    Or both alike shall be good.

⁷. The light is sweet, and it is good for the eyes to see the sun.   ⁸. For if a man shall live many years and rejoice in them all, yet let him remember the days of darkness, for they will be many.   All that is coming is vanity.

⁹. Rejoice, O young man, in thy youth,
    And let thy heart cheer thee in the days of thy prime,
    And walk in the ways of thy heart and the sight of thy eyes,

BUT KNOW THAT FOR ALL THESE THINGS GOD WILL BRING THEE INTO JUDGMENT.

¹⁰. Put away vexation from thy heart
    And remove misery from thy flesh,—
    For youth and prime are vanity.

12¹. BUT REMEMBER THY CREATOR IN THE DAYS OF THY PRIME.

While the evil days come not,
    Nor approach the years of which thou shalt say
    I have in them no pleasure;
². While the sun be not darkened,
    Nor the light and moon and stars,
    Nor the clouds return after rain,
³. In the day when the keepers of the house shall tremble
    And the men of valor bend themselves,
    And the grinding-maids cease because they are few,
    And the ladies who look out of the windows are darkened,
⁴. And the doors on the street are shut
    When the sound of the mill is low,
    And he shall rise at the voice of the bird,
    And all the daughters of song are prostrate,—
⁵. Also he is afraid of a height,
    And terror is on the road,
    And the almond-tree blooms,
    And the grasshopper is burdensome,
    And the caper-berry is made ineffectual,
    For the man goes to his eternal house,
    And the mourners go around the street;—
⁶. While the silver cord is not severed,
    Nor the golden bowl broken,
    Nor the water-jar be shattered at the spring,
    Nor the wheel broken at the cistern,
⁷. And the dust shall return to the earth as it was,
    And the spirit shall return unto God who gave it.

⁸. Vanity of vanities, *says Qoheleth*, all is vanity.

11¹–12⁸ contains Qoheleth's final advice. This he utters in full consideration of all that he has said before. The discourse is often enigmatical, but with the exception of two glosses from the hand of the *Chasid* (11⁹ᵇ and 12¹ᵃ), which have given much trouble to interpreters, it flows on uninterruptedly. He urges prudent kindliness and industry, combined with pleasure, before old age makes all impossible.

11¹. *Cast thy bread on the waters*]. This is evidently a figurative expression, but what does the figure mean? At least four interpretations have been suggested. (1) It has been taken by Geier, Mich., Död., Mendelssohn, Hit., Del., Wild., Ha. and McN. to apply to trading. "Commit your goods to the sea and wait for your returns until long voyages are over." (2) Van der P. and Bauer took it to refer to agriculture, meaning "Sow thy seed on moist places near water, and thou wilt obtain a rich harvest." (3) Graetz, in the same way, takes "bread" as equivalent to "seed," but interprets it of the "seed" of human life, and so finds in the verse a maxim bordering on the licentious. (4) It is taken by Kn., Gins., Zö., Wr., No., Sieg. and Marsh. as an exhortation to liberality. Of these interpretations the second and third are undoubtedly wrong, for "bread" never means "seed." The first seems, on the whole, less probable than the fourth, for "bread" does not mean "merchandise." In favor of the fourth explanation is an Arabic proverb, which Heiligstedt, Ginsburg, Plumtre and Wright quote from Diaz' *Denkwürdigkeiten von Asien*. The proverb forms the culmination of a story which relates how Mohammed, son of Hassan, had been daily in the habit of throwing loaves into a river, how the life of an adopted son of Caliph Mutewekkel, who had escaped drowning by climbing upon a rock, was thus preserved, and how Mohammed saw in it the proof of the truth of a proverb he had learned as a boy, "Do good, cast thy bread upon the waters, and one day thou shalt be rewarded." The story suggests that this proverb may be an echo of Qoheleth himself. One may compare another Arabic saying (see Jewett's "Arabic Proverbs," JAOS., XV, p. 68):

The generous man is always lucky.

If this be the meaning of the verse, its thought is kindred to the exhortation of Jesus, "Make to yourselves friends by means of the mammon of unrighteousness," Lk. 16⁹.—**2.** *Give a portion to seven and also to eight*]. There has naturally been given to this verse the same variety of interpretations as to vs. 1, each interpreter explaining the vs. as completing his view of that. The two most popular explanations, however, are (1) that which makes it refer to merchandise, and (2) that which makes it refer to liberality. According to (1), the verse advises the merchant to divide his venture between seven or eight ships, because he does not know which may be overtaken by disaster. According to (2), the giver is advised to give to seven or eight people, because he does not know what evil may overtake him or whom he may need as friends. *Cf.* Lk. 16⁹, last clause. According to the meaning which we found in the first verse, the second of these interpretations seems most probable. Such an arrangement of numbers in a literary figure is frequent in BH. Thus "once" and "twice" occur in Job 33¹⁴ Ps. 62¹¹, "twice" and "thrice" Job 33²⁹, "two" and "three" Is. 17⁶, "three" and "four" Am. 1³. ⁶. ⁹. ¹¹. ¹³ 2¹. ⁴. ⁶ Pr. 30¹⁵. ¹⁸. ²¹ Ex. 20⁵ 34⁷, "four" and "five" Is. 17⁶, "seven" and "eight" Mi. 5⁵. Such figures are vivid ways of conveying the idea of "a few," or "some" or "many."

3. This verse is loosely connected with the closing words of vs. 2, since it shows man's powerlessness in the presence of the laws of fate. Human helplessness is illustrated by two examples,

> If the clouds are filled with rain,
> They empty it over the earth,—

i.e., man is powerless to prevent it. Nature goes on in accordance with inflexible laws, which man cannot alter. This is one example. The other is,

> If wood falls southward or northward,
> The place where wood falls—there it shall be.

The word here rendered "wood" has usually been rendered "tree." It has both meanings. If we understand that a tree is meant, the illustration as McNeile has noticed is a weak one. Man cannot prevent the rain, but, though a tree felled by a tempest may be unable to move itself, man can move it. If this were the meaning, the illustration is inapt, and the verse forms an anticlimax. McNeile's suggestion that the clause refers to divination by means of a rod or staff, such as that to which Ho. 4¹² alludes, has accordingly much to commend it. The half verse would then mean, " If a stick is tossed up in the air, that a man may guide his action by the direction in which it comes to rest, he has no control over the result." This meaning gives a climax and is probably correct.—**4.** *A wind-observer will not sow*]. One who waits till there is no wind to disturb the even scattering of his seed.—*A cloud-watcher will not reap*]. One who wants to be sure that his grain, when cut, will not get wet. The thought of the verse is, " If one waits for ideal conditions, he will lose his opportunity and accomplish nothing." Siegfried objects that this verse could not have been written in Palestine, because it never rains there in harvest-time, and he cites 1 S. 12¹⁷ as proof. The passage in Samuel, however, proves, not that it never rained in harvest, but that rain was sufficiently rare at that time to make people think that when it came, it was sent as a punishment for wickedness. In later times it was regarded as out of place, though not impossible, see Pr. 26¹. Seasons vary greatly, but in years of exceptionally heavy rains it often happens that rain continues to fall well into April, and interferes with the cutting of the earlier-ripening grain. *Cf.* Barton, *A Year's Wandering in Bible Lands*, 185 ; Bacon, *Amer. Jour. of Arch.*, Supplement to Vol. X, p. 34 *ff.*, and Ewing, *Arab and Druze at Home*, 1907, p. 127, *cf.* p. 2 *ff.* and 10 *ff.*—**5.** *Thou knowest not what the path of the wind is*]. Qoheleth now passes on to point out that man does not know and cannot know the ways and works of God. The " path of the wind " reminds one of Jn. 3⁸. This last passage is perhaps a reminiscence of Qoheleth, though the resemblance is too vague to make the reminiscence certain.—*Nor the bones in the womb*]. The mystery of birth filled also a Psalmist —probably of the Maccabæan period—with awe, *cf.* Ps. 139¹³⁻¹⁶.— *So thou mayest not know the work of God*]. Man's inability to penetrate the works of God is a favorite topic with this writer (*cf.* 3¹¹ 8¹⁷ 9¹²). Qoheleth is, however, a theistic agnostic, though his idea of God's goodness is not exalted (*cf.* 3¹¹.—*The whole*]. According to Delitzsch, this does not mean " the universe," but all such things as have been mentioned. The phrase might be rendered "who makes both," *i.e.*, the way of the wind and the bones in the womb, *cf.* critical note on 2¹⁴.

6. *In the morning sow thy seed*]. It is clear that the verse is figurative, but what does the figure mean? Like verse 1 it has received widely different interpretations. (1) Graetz, following a Jewish Midrash and a Talmudic passage (*Yebamoth*, 62b), takes it to mean "Beget children in youth and even to old age, whether in or out of wedlock." Indeed, it is from this verse that he obtains the meaning for vs. 1 noted above. There is no reason, however, for taking "seed" in this sense in either vs. Qoheleth was not averse to such pleasures of sense (*cf.* 2⁸ 9⁹), but he never revels in filth. He is thoroughly healthy-minded. (2) Plumtre takes it to mean that one is to sow the seed of good and kindly deeds, and await the harvest which is hidden from him. This, it is true, would harmonize with the meaning which we have found in vs. 1, but the context indicates that the writer has now passed away from that topic. (3) Most recent interpreters rightly take it to mean that from youth till the evening of life, one is manfully to perform the full round of life's tasks, that he is not to hesitate because of the uncertainties which were set forth in vs. 5, and that he is to take the losses which come in a philosophical spirit.—*Thou knowest not which shall succeed*]. Try your hand at every right task, for you cannot tell in advance which will bring success. As Genung observes, the verse is evidence of Q.'s sturdy sense and manliness.

7. *Light is sweet*]. The pessimistic mood of ch. 4², which had passed away from Qoheleth when he wrote 9⁴, has not returned. He recognizes in this verse the primal delight of mere living.— **8.** *If a man live many years and rejoice*]. Life is good—to behold the sun is sweet, but Qoheleth is oppressed by its brevity and the dread of death, as Horace was (*cf. Odes*, I, 4¹⁵; IV, 7¹⁶).—*Remember*], if used of future things, is equivalent to "ponder," "reflect upon."—*The days of darkness*], *i.e.*, the days in Sheol, which is several times described as the land of darkness, *cf.* Ps. 88¹² 143³ Job 10²¹· ²².—*All that is coming is vanity*], the whole future—the days in Sheol—is an unsubstantial reality. No positive joy can be counted on there.—**9ᵃ.** *Rejoice, O young man, in thy youth*]. As a result of the brevity of life and the darkness of the

future, Qoheleth urges young men to make the most of youth and
of manhood's prime. It is a natural argument which has occurred
to others also. Herodotus (2⁷⁸) tells how the Egyptians at their
feasts had the image of a dead body in a coffin carried about and
shown to each of the company who was addressed thus, "Look on
this, then drink and enjoy yourself, for when dead you will be like
this." That it had also been used by the Babylonians has been
shown in the notes on 9⁷ᴴ.—*Walk in the ways of thy heart*]. Gratify thy desires. From these come all the pleasures man is ever
to receive, so self-denial is self-destruction. *Cf.* 1 Cor. 15³².
This verse is controverted in *Wisdom*, 2⁶.—9ᵇ. *But know that for
all these things God will bring thee into judgment*]. This is so out
of harmony with the context, but so in accord with the *Chasid* point
of view, and especially with 3¹⁷, which we have already recognized
as a *Chasid* gloss, that there is no doubt but that McNeile is right
in regarding this phrase here as the work of the *Chasid* glossator.

10. *Put away vexation from thy heart*]. Take the easiest course
both mentally and physically.—*For youth and prime are vanity*].
Youth and the prime quickly flee. The vs. is a restatement of the
thought of vs. 9a. If we are right in seeing in 12¹ᵃ another *Chasid*
gloss, the argument to make the most of swiftly passing youth is
continued in 12¹ᵇ⁻⁷.

12¹ᵃ. *Remember now thy creator in the days of thy prime*]. This
is as McNeile has pointed out an insertion of the *Chasid* glossator.
As Cheyne has suggested, it contains exhortation based on psy-
chological principles, for as age advances it is less easy to remember one's creator unless it has been done in youth. It is needless
to point out how unlike Qoheleth it is. For efforts to bring it into
harmony with his prevailing thought, see critical note.

1ᵇ. *While the evil days come not*]. This is the continuation 11¹⁰,
from which it has been severed by the gloss inserted in 12¹ᵃ. Qoheleth urged:

> Put away vexation from thy heart
> And remove misery from thy flesh,—
> For youth and prime are vanity,—
> While the evil days come not, etc.

"*The evil days*" do not refer to the days of darkness in Sheol
mentioned in 11⁸, but to the period of old age which he now goes

on to describe. They are "evil" in the sense of "miserable" because less full of pleasure than youth and prime. This is the meaning of *I have no pleasure in them*.

Vvs. **2–6** have been variously interpreted. All have agreed that the passage is allegorical, but as to the details of the allegory there are wide differences of opinion. These opinions may be grouped in seven divisions. (1) The verses are believed to describe the failing of an old man's physical powers, the various figures referring to anatomical details. This was the view of early Jewish commentators beginning with Tobia ben Eliezer, and of many modern ones. (2) The verses represent under the figure of a storm an old man's approaching death. So, Umbreit, Ginsburg and Plumtre. (3) The approach of death is here pictured under the fall of night. Thus, Michaelis, Spohn, Nachtigal and Delitzsch. (4) Marshall thinks it the closing of a house at the approach of a sirocco. (5) The passage is a literal picture of the gloom in a household when the master has just died. So Taylor. (6) The verses are to be explained by the "seven days of death," or days of cold wintry weather, which immediately precede a Palestinian springtime. These days are thus named because they are peculiarly dangerous to aged and sickly persons. This is the view of Wetzstein and Wright. (7) The verses are in general a picture of old age, but one line of thought is not followed throughout. The metaphors change and intermingle in accord with the richness of an Oriental imagination. This is the view of McNeile. The last of these explanations is but a slight modification of the first. It seeks to avoid, by the exercise of a little plain sense, the vagaries to which excessive zeal for anatomical identification has led, and in so doing strikes the right path. Green, *Expositor* (1895), p. 77 *ff.*, points out that in Icelandic poetry the parts of the body are often alluded to under similar figures, and that such allusions are known as *kennings*.

2. *While the sun be not darkened, nor the light and moon and stars*]. This may be taken in two ways: it may either refer to failing eye-sight, so that the lights of all sorts become dim, or it may refer to the fact that, as age advances, the brightness (*i.e.*, the enjoyment) of life becomes less. The context both before and after the phrase favors the latter view. The speaker says, "I have no pleasure in them," because the brightness of his joy is decreasing. The Talmud (*Sabbath*, 152a) explained the "sun" as forehead, "light" as nose, "moon" as soul, and "stars" as cheeks. Haupt explains them thus, "the sun is the sunshine of childhood when everything seems bright and happy, the moon is symbolical of the more tempered light of boyhood and early manhood, while the stars indicate the sporadic moments of happiness in mature age." The anatomical application is so far-fetched as to be absurd, Haupt's explanation seems too esoteric to be probable, and it has the disadvantage of leaving "light" (which Haupt does not erase from the text) unexplained. Earlier interpreters explained this "light" to be "twilight" or "dawn"—a period of light when none of the orbs of light were visible. Such detailed explanations are, however, unnecessary. The poet is describing the lessening brightness of advancing life. Its characteristic is fading light. To express his thought, he has with Oriental richness of imagination and carelessness in exact use of metaphor mingled "light" and the various orbs of light in one figure.—*For the clouds return after rain*]. When clouds follow rain they cut off brightness. The frequency of gloomy storms happily figures the increasing gloom of age. Vaihinger thought it referred to winter, as the rainy time or time of gloom, Palestine having but two seasons, winter and summer. In Palestine the "winter of life" might well be opposed to our "springtime of life."

3. *In the day when*], a fuller way of saying "when," *cf.* Ct. 8⁸. From a general description of the darkening of life's joys in advancing age, the poet now passes on to picture the decay of the body under the picture of a house. The figure is loosely used, perhaps with no thought that all its details were to be literally applied to the members of the body, though the figure itself is, as a whole, appropriate and forcible. Whether the house is portrayed as undergoing the changes described, because of an approaching storm, or because night has come, is open to discussion. Those who favor the storm, find an argument for it in the "clouds" and the obscuring of all the heavenly bodies in vs. 2. It is really unwise to press the figure too far, either as a description of the decay of the body, or the closing of a house. In speaking of the former in terms of the latter, the poet has mingled the features of the two in pleasing and suggestive imagery, which, though poetically vague in details, does not mislead.—*The keepers of the house shall tremble*]. The "keepers" correspond, as Ginsburg saw, to the menials or guards of a palace. When we come to applications to definite parts of the body, there is more difficulty. Rashi thought it meant "ribs" and "loins," Plumtre the "legs," Delitzsch the "arms," Haupt the "hands." The last is probably right.—*The men of valor bend themselves*]. In the figure, as Ginsburg saw, "men of valor" are the superiors of the house, each palace containing masters and servants. In applying the figure to the body, there are again differences. The Targum and Plumtre think of the "arms," Ra., Rashbam, AE., Knobel, Hitzig, Zöckler, Delitzsch, Wright and McNeile of the "legs," "knees," or "feet," Haupt of the "bones," especially the spinal column. The reference is probably to the legs. See the description of the feet of old men in 3 Mac. 4⁵.—*The grinding maids shall cease because they are few*]. It is generally agreed that this refers to the teeth, which are called "maids," because grinding in the East is usually done by women (*cf*. Is. 47² Job 31¹⁰ Mt. 24⁴¹ *Odyssey* 20¹⁰⁵. ¹⁰⁶).—*The ladies who look out of the windows*]. These are with much unanimity taken to be the eyes. For the figure, *cf*. Ju. 5²⁸ᵃ. The figures represent the two classes of women in a house—ladies and serving maids—just as the two classes of men were represented. —*Are darkened*], that is, the eyes lose their lustre and their sight.

4. *The doors on the street are shut*]. In applying this part of the figure, there are again diversities of opinion. The Talmud, Ra. and Rashbam thought the pores of the skin were referred to, the Targum the feet, AE., Död., Ros., Kn., Ew., Hit., Vaih., Zö., Wr. and Sieg. the lips, which, when the teeth are gone, shut more closely; Kimchi, Grotius and Cleric thought of the literal shutting of the street door, so that the old man could not go out; Hengstenberg of the eyes, Lewis of the eyes and ears, Wildeboer of the ears, Haupt of the anus and bladder, the man beginning to suffer from retention (*ischuria*) and intestinal stenosis. It is probable that the reference is to the lips, the figure of a door being elsewhere applied to them (see Mi. 7⁵ Ps. 141²).—*When the sound of the mill is low*]. Again there are differences of opinion. The Talmud, Ra., Rashbam and AE. and Haupt hold it to refer to the impaired digestion; the Targum, to the appetite; Grotius, Döderlein, Knobel and Hitzig to the voice of age, which is broken and quavering; Zöckler and Delitzsch to the rustle of the toothless mouth. The last is, perhaps, right.—*And he shall rise at the voice of the bird*]. This phrase has been variously translated, and even more variously interpreted. Kn., Wr., Wild. and Ha. think that it means that the old man awakes early just as the birds begin to twitter, and so refers to the loss of sleep in old age; Ew., Hit., Heil., Zö., Del. and Pl. hold it to refer to the childish treble of age. Probably the first of these interpretations is the right one.—*The daughters of song are prostrate*]. Kn. and Heil. thought that this refers to the failure of the old man's singing voice, which is lost, though Kn. held that possibly it might refer to the notes of birds, which the old man could not hear. Del., who is followed by Wr., Wild., McN. and Ha., interprets it by 2 S. 19³⁵, where the aged Barzillai can no longer hear the voice of singing men and singing women, and so takes the line to refer to the deafness of age. With this Ges.ᴷ· and Kö. seem to agree, for they show that "daughters of song" mean the various notes of music, these all seem low to the old man. The line accordingly refers to deafness.

5. *Also he is afraid of a height*]. The figure of the house is now dropped, and four additional statements of growing incapacity are added. Interpreters generally agree that the reference here is to the shortness of breath which comes in old age, and makes the ascent of a height difficult. For the rendering "he fears" instead of "they fear," see critical note.—*And terror is on the road*]. This is almost a synonym of the previous clause. A walk is full of terrors, because the old man's limbs are stiff and his breath short. —*And the almond-tree blooms*]. According to Kn., Ew., Zö., Wr., Marsh., Gen., and Ha., it is a poetical reference to the white hair of old age. The almond-tree blooms in January, and at the time it has no leaves. The blooms are pink at the base, but soon turn white at the tips, giving the tree a beautiful white appearance, which makes the landscape in January and February most attractive (see Post, in Hastings' DB., I, 67a). This, then, is a natural symbol of the gray-haired man. It is used allegorically by Philo, *Life of Moses*, 3²². Probably this is the correct interpretation, though others are urged by some. Since the Hebrew word for almond-tree is derived from a stem which means "to waken," and that is the use made of it in Jer. 1¹¹ᵍ, Hengstenberg and Plumtre take it to mean that "sleeplessness flourishes." De Jong, Wildeboer and McNeile render the verb "despised," and take it to refer to the old man's failing appetite, because "the almond is rejected" (see critical note). This view is not so probable.—*The grasshopper is burdensome*]. The rendering "grasshopper" is disputed by some. Delitzsch and Wildeboer, following the Talmud, render it "hips" and the verb "drag themselves along," thinking the phrase a reference to an old man's walk. Kn. rendered "breath," making it refer to labored breathings. Graetz thought it a poetical reference to *coitus*, while Moore (JBL., X, 64) thinks that a melon instead of a grasshopper was intended. Of the interpreters who translate "grasshopper," Heiligstedt understands it to mean that the old man is too weak to cook and masticate the grasshopper for food (*cf.* Mt. 3⁴), Zöckler that the old man's form is emaciated like that of a grasshopper, Plumtre that the grasshopper is an emblem of smallness (Is. 40²² Nu. 13³³), so that the smallest thing becomes burdensome; Wetzstein and Wright, that the grasshopper springs up in the days when spring begins, *i.e.*, just after the seven days of death (see above, after vs. 1), and Genung takes it to refer to the halting walk of age—the old man like a grasshopper halts along. Biblical analogy would lead one to agree with Plumtre and take it as a symbol of smallness, though there is no reason to regard it, as he does, as a Greek symbol, and so to find an example of Greek influence here. The passage then means that the smallest weight is a burden, which the old man drags along.—*The caper-berry is made ineffectual*]. The caper-berry was a plant used to excite sexual appetite. There can be little doubt that the Hebrew word here used refers to it, since it is the singular of the word which designates the same product in the Talmud (see Moore, JBL., X, 55 *ff.*, and Ja. 5b). Most interpreters rightly take it to mean that stimulants to appetite are rendered ineffectual

by the failing of vital power. Graetz, however, takes "caper-
berry" as a figure for the *glans penis*, but, as Renan remarks,
Qohelêth is never obscene. Wetzstein and Haupt, taking a hint
from Σ, connect the word rendered "caper-berry" with the Hebrew
root for "poor," and think it a figurative expression for the soul.
Haupt renders the word for "grasshopper" "chrysalis," making
"inert lies the chrysalis, till the soul emerges." This is very improbable, though beautiful. For the rendering "is made ineffectual," see critical note.—*The man goes to his eternal house*].
Here first the writer speaks of death itself. "Eternal house"
is a reference to the tomb; *cf.* Tobit 3⁶ and the Talmudic and
Coranic usage cited in crit. note.—*Mourners go around the street*].
According to Hebrew custom, *cf.* Am. 5¹⁶ Je. 9¹⁶⁻²⁰.

6. *While*] is a repetition of the opening word of vs. 1b, and like
it connects the thought with 11¹⁰, urging the young man to enjoy
himself.—*While the silver cord is not severed, nor the golden bowl
broken*]. This last is a poetic picture of death, to which the thought
was led in vs. 5b. The imagery by which this is expressed is, as
several critics have seen (Pl., No., Wr., Wild. and McN.), borrowed
from Zc. 4². ³, where a golden bowl fed oil to the seven lamps.
Here, however, the golden bowl is, with that richness of imagery
common to the Orient (*cf.* Pr. 25¹¹), represented as hanging by a
silver cord. The cord is severed, the lamp falls, the bowl is broken
(or more literally crushed, the objection that a golden bowl cannot
be broken, is without force), the oil lost and the light goes out—a
fit emblem of the sudden dissolution of the body and the escape of
the spirit. Probably Qoheleth used this imagery with poetic
freedom without thinking of special applications of details, but it
has been otherwise with his commentators. The Targum makes
the silver cord, the tongue; the golden bowl, the head; Del. makes
them, respectively, the soul and the head; Haupt, the spinal column
and the brain.—*And the water-jar be shattered at the spring*]. By
another common figure life is likened to a fountain (*cf.* Ps. 36⁹).
That figure is now employed. The individual body is made the
water-jar, such as women in the East still use in carrying water
home (*cf.* Gn. 24¹⁴. ¹⁷. ⁴³ Ju. 7¹⁶. ¹⁹. ²⁰); when the jar is broken it can
contain no more water, and so the life ends.—While this meaning

is clear, some contend that the bucket does not represent the whole body, but some special organ, Del., Sieg. and Ha. think of the heart. —*The wheel broken at the cistern*]. This is another application of the same figure. Some wells are fitted up with a wheel to assist in drawing water. Sometimes this is small and can be worked by hand, as that seen to-day at "Jacob's well," near Nablous, or on one of the wells at Beersheba, sometimes large enough to be worked by a camel or a donkey, like that pictured in Barton's *A Year's Wanderings in Bible Lands*, p. 205. When the wheel is broken, the water can no longer be drawn. The "wheel" in this line is again a metaphor for the whole body. Some, however, make a special application of the "wheel," Del. and Sieg. regarding it as symbolizing the breathing process. Haupt thinks its "breaking" refers to paralysis of the heart. All the symbols of the verse picture death as coming suddenly—the lamp is crushed, the jar shattered, or the wheel broken.—**7.** *The dust shall return to the earth as it was, and the spirit shall return to God who gave it*]. As Tobia Ben Eleazar in the eleventh century and, in modern times, Plumtre and Wildeboer have noted, this is a definite reference to Gn. 2^7. Qoheleth pictures death as undoing what the creative act of God had accomplished. Siegfried holds that the first clause cannot come from Q^1,—the pessimist,—for he believed the spirit of a man to be no more immortal than that of a beast ($3^{19.\ 20}$); he therefore assigns 7a to Q^2; 7b he denies to Q^2 because that writer did not trouble himself about the dead, but rejoiced in life ($5^{17}\ 9^{4.\ 7\text{-}12}\ 11^{7\text{ff}}$), and assigns it to Q^4, the *Chasid* glossator. Such an analysis makes no allowance, however, for the moods of human nature. No man's thought—especially the thought of an Oriental—is as clear-cut as Siegfried supposes. One may have his pessimistic moods in which he questions whether anybody knows whether a man's spirit differs from a beast's; he may hold that man's only good comes from enjoying the sunshine of this physical existence, brief though it be, and still, holding Qoheleth's idea of God (see *e.g.*, on 9^1), write "the spirit shall return to God who gave it." Even a pessimist may quote Scripture without reading into it all the hopes of an optimist. Qoheleth's thought is not out of harmony with the later development of OT. Judaism on this subject (see Schwally, *Leben nach dem Tode*, 104 *ff*.).—**8.** *Vanity of vanities*]. The book concludes with the dirge with which it opened. Qoheleth's concluding sentence reiterates his opening declaration. He has, from his point of view, proved his thesis and closes by reiterating the sad words with which he began: *All is vanity.—Saith Qoheleth*] is probably an insertion of the late editor, who added vvs. 9, 10, and who praises Qoheleth.

11¹. Sieg. arbitrarily denies the vs., as he does those which follow, to Q. The appropriateness of the whole passage, with the exception of 11⁹ᵇ and 12¹ᵃ to Q.'s thought, is too evident to need demonstration.—**2.** [חלק], probably אֶכָל is to be supplied, *cf.* BDB. 324a.—[לשבעה וגם לשמונה], on such rhetorical use of numbers, *cf.* Ges.ᴷ· §134s.—[מה יהיה רעה], on the form of expression, *cf.* Kö. §414q.

3. [יִמָּלְאוּ], Niph., *cf.* BDB. 570a.—[נשם] is to be taken with ימלאו as acc. of material (so Wild.), not with יריקו (Ha.).—[העבים], the mistake in the accent of this word in the older printed Bibles, to which Del. called attention, has been corrected in the texts of Baer, Kittel (Driver), and Ginsburg.—[ררום], *cf.* on 1⁶.—[מקום]=*loco*, *cf.* Kö. §330ky and 337g.—[מקום־ש׳], *cf.* מקום אשר, Ez. 6¹³ Est. 4³ 8¹⁷.—[והוא], on the root, see above on 2²². The root is הוה, used here as a synonym of היה. The א has caused trouble. Wr. regarded it as an orthographic addition such as in certain cases is found in Arabic, Ges.ᴷ· (§75s) would emend to יהִי (=יהי), while Bick. and Sieg. would emend to הוא. One of these emendations appears to be necessary. It will be noticed that in both the conditional sentences in this vs. the imperf. is employed in both protasis and apodosis. This points to יהו rather than הוא as the true reading of the final word. Del. notes that in the earlier language such conditions would have employed the perfect in both clauses, *cf.* Dr. §12. —**4.** [שֹׁמֵר], this part. and רֹאֶה express the continuity of the action="he who habitually watches" . . . "he who habitually looks."—**5.** [כאשר] begins a correlative sentence as in Je. 19¹¹, *cf.* Kö. §371f. 𝕲 and 𝕾 read כאשר, but that is evidently a mistake.—[כעצמים בבטן המלאה] is an abbreviated comparison="as thou art ignorant of the formation of the bones in the womb," etc. For a fully expressed comparison, see Dt. 32².—[המלאה], in the sense of pregnant woman, occurs nowhere else in BH., though found once in the Mishna (*Yebamoth*, 16¹). Assyrian had the same usage, thus *ilu Istar kima maliti*="Ishtar like a pregnant woman" (*cf.* Haupt, *Nimrod Epos*, p. 139, line 117, variant). In Latin *Plena* was sometimes used in the same sense, see Ovid, *Metam.* x, 465 Zap., for metrical reasons, would erase the word as a gloss.—[יודע . . . . . תרע], note the delicate use of the part. and imperf.="as thou continuously dost not know . . . so thou mayest not know."—[כעצמים], 40 MSS. and

ᵷ read בעצמים, but that is an error.—[אשר יעשה את כל reminds one
of Am. 3⁶, but the context shows that the thought is not so general as
that of Amos.—**6.** [בבקר is not used with ערב as Kn. thought poetically to
include all time, but figuratively for youth.—[ולערב, not בערב, as some
MSS. of ᵷ. Q. does not advise working "in evening," for that was
resting-time (cf. Ps. 104²³), but rather "till evening," cf. Job 4²⁰.—[הנח,
cf. the use of this verb in 7⁹. Cf. also אל תרף ידיך in Jos. 10⁶.—[אי זה =
"which of two" or more—a late usage confined to Q. (2³ only besides
this vs.), cf. BDB. 32a.—[הזה או זה, on this disjunctive question, cf.
Kö. §379b. Ha., for metrical reasons, erases the words as a gloss. It
is here a tempting emendation.—[כאחד occurs only in late books, as
Is. 65²⁵ 2 Ch. 5¹³ Ezr. 2⁶⁴ 3⁹ 6²⁰ Ne. 7⁶⁶. It is an Aramaism, occurring
in Dn. 2³⁵, ᵷ on Gn. 13⁶ and on Job 31³⁸.

7. [מתוק is used of material substances like honey (Ju. 14¹⁴ Pr. 24¹³)
and then figuratively as here and 5¹¹, where it is applied to sleep.—
[האור, not the "light of life" as Kn. held, but the ordinary light of day.
The expression is almost identical with ἡδὺ γὰρ τὸ φῶς (Euripides,
Iphig. in Aulis, 1219).—[לעינים, ל is here (as in 1 S. 16⁷) pointed with
= as though ע received Daghesh forte implicitum, but in Gn. 3⁶ and Pr.
10²⁶ it is pointed with ֵ, cf. Baer, p. 68.—**8.** [כי is not here to be construed with אם, as in 3¹² and 8¹⁵, but is = "for," and gives the reason for
the preceding statement (so Hit. and Del.).—[הרבה, an adv. See on
1¹⁶ and cf. Kö. §318e.—[כל־שבא, Del. compares the expression מכאן ולהבא
= "from the present even to the future" (*Sanhedrin*, 27a), used for the
more frequent לעתיד לבא.—**9.** [בחור = "chosen one," regularly used for
a young man in the prime of manhood, cf. BDB. 104b.—[ילדות, a late
form which occurs but three times in BH., here, in vs. 10, and in Ps.
110³. It occurs also several times in the Talm., cf. Ja. 578b. According to its etymology it should mean "childhood," but it is clearly here
employed of the time of life called בחור, and accordingly = "youth."
—[ויטיבך לבך, Del. observes that ויטיב לבך would have expressed the
thought. The pleonastic expression is a sign of lateness.—[בחורות,
for the ordinary בחורים. The ending ־ות is found in BH. only here
and in 12¹. Has it not been approximated to the Aram. בחרות =
"youth" (cf. Dalman, *Aram.-Neuhebr. Wörterbuch*, 49b)? Perhaps it
should be pointed בחורות.—[הלך, the Piel is not uncommon, cf. Ps.
131¹.—[במראי, the Qr. and some 100 MSS. read במראה. It is difficult
to decide between the two readings. מראה occurs in 6⁹, and it may be
argued with Gins. that it has been changed to a plural here to make
it conform to דרכי. On the other hand, the plural occurs in Ct. 2¹⁴ and
Dn. 1¹⁵, and it may be argued with Eur. that that was the original reading,
because מראה is so natural that, if that had stood there, no one would
have thought of changing it.

10. [כעס, see on 1¹⁸.—[רעה, here not ethical, but physical evil, hence "misery" or "wretchedness."—שְׁחֲרוּת], not as Kn. and Hit. held from שַׁחַר, dawn (*cf.* מִשְׁחָר = "morning," Ps. 110³), but a NH. word, from שָׁחַר, "be black." Such a root occurs in Job 30³⁰ and in BS. 25¹⁶. It occurs in the Talm. (*cf.* Ja. 1551), in Syr. with the meaning = "coal," and in As. as *šûru* = "coal." This view is probably represented by 𝔊, 𝔖, 𝔙, was held by Ra., Rashbam, and AE., and among recent interpreters is upheld by Gins., Del., Wr., Eur., Wild., Ha. and McN. שַׁחֲרוּת on this view = "time of black hair," as opposed to שֵׂיבָה, "the time of gray hair" or "old age." Wild. compares the Ar. *šârih* = "youth," in which the last two radicals are reversed.—חבל], *cf.* on 1².

12¹. בּוֹרְאֶיךָ], many interpreters—Kn., Hit., Gins., Del., Pl. and Wr.—held this to be a *pl. majestatis* like אלהים, קרשים, etc. The Versions read it as sing., and Baer, Eur., Ges.ᴷ· (§124k) and Sieg. so read it, though Dr. and Gins. still keep the pl. in their editions of the text. The sing. is to be preferred. Gr., who is followed by Bick., Che. and Haupt, emends בוראך to בורך = "cistern," and by comparison with Pr. 5¹⁸ takes it to refer to one's wife. On this view the exhortation is "Do not neglect thy lawful wife." The emendation, however, reads into the book a lower note, Davidson has observed (*Eccl.* in EB.), than any which the book touches. The one passage (9⁹) which seems to contradict Davidson's view, was influenced by the Babylonian epic. Gr.'s theory does not commend itself.

2. עַד אֲשֶׁר לֹא], *cf.* עַד לֹא, Pr. 8²⁶. The phrase of Q. borders on the idiom of the Mishna, *cf.* עַד שֶׁלֹּא, *Berakoth*, 3⁵. *Cf.* Kö. §3870.—**3.** זוע] = "tremble," "shake," occurs but twice beside this in BH., Est. 5⁹ and Hb. 2⁷. It occurs frequently in Aram., *cf.* Dn. 5¹⁹ 6²⁷. For Talmudic references, see Ja. 388a.—הִתְעַוְּתוּ], *cf.* on 7¹³.—בטל], a pure Aram. word occurring nowhere else in BH. It is found in the Mishna (*Botah*, 9⁹), in the Aram. of Ezr. 4²³· ²⁴ 5⁵. For Talmudic references, see Ja. 157. *Cf.* also S. A. Cook, *Glos. of Aram. Inscr.*, p. 29, and G. A. Cooke, *North Sem. Inscr.*, p. 335.—מעטו], Bick. and Sieg. erase without sufficient reason. The Piel occurs only here, but with an intransitive force, *cf.* Ges.ᴷ· §52k.—**4.** בִּנְשֹׁפל], the inf. with בְּ, is taken by Gins. and Wr. as temporal, but Kö. (§403a) regards it as causal. Either gives a good meaning.—ויקום], a jussive form without a jussive force, *cf.* Ges.ᴷ· § 72t.—לְקוֹל], ל is temporal = "at the time of the bird's voice," *cf.* Kö. §331f.—הצפר], the particular for the general, *cf.* Kö. §254f.—בנות השיר], probably the "notes of song." For many examples of the figurative uses of בן and בת, see Ges.ᴷ· §128v and Kö. §306m.—**5.** וְיָבֵּא] is a noun, *cf.* 1 S. 16⁷ (so Del.).—וייראו], the pl. is unexpected. Kn. regarded it as an example of the ease with which the Heb. passes from the sing. to the pl. Dr. and McN. suggest that the י is a dittograph of the following ו ⁻ a probable explanation.—וחתחתים], this noun is reduplicated from the stem חתת. The formation is similar to עפעפים =

eyelids. סלסלות=baskets, תלחלים=palm-branches, קשקשים=scales.—
וינאר], the stem נאץ="reject," does not, in the opinion of most interpreters, give a satisfactory meaning. Ki. regarded the א as quiescent
(see Baer, p. 69). Del. held it to be an orthographic variation for
וינץ, as קאם is for קם in Ho. 10¹⁴ and ראש for רש Pr. 13²³, and in this
he is followed by Ges.ᴷ· §73g and BDB., 665a. Dr. would correct the
reading to וינץ.—חגב], Kn. connected with the Ar. ḥagaba, "to breathe,"
Del. and Wild., following the Talm., with the Ar. ḥagabat=caput femoris,
or hip; Moore (JBL., X, 64) connects with Ar. ḥagb, a "kind of
melon," but most interpreters take it for grasshopper, as in Is. 40²².—
ויסתבל], 28 MSS. read ויסתכל. Cf. Dr.—ותפר], some emendation is
necessary. The simplest is to follow the Versions, and make it a
Hophal, as BDB. (p. 830b), Dr. and McN. do. This has been done
above. Moore objects that פרר in BH. is always used of making covenants or judgments ineffectual, and never, in a physical sense; he would
accordingly follow 'A and take it from the root כרה. In a late writer, like
Q., however, earlier usage may have been violated.—האביונה]="caper-
berry," the sing. of אביונות, which occurs in the Mishna and Talmud
(see e.g., Ma'aseroth, 4⁶). So Moore, JBL., X, 55 ff. and Ja. 5b. For
a description of the fruit, see Moore. Wetz. and Ha. point אביונה=
"poor" and understand it as an epithet of נפש. Vrss., with the possible
exception of Σ, 𝕿, support "caper-berry."—בית עולם], cf. Sanhedrin,
19a, where a cemetery is בית עלמין and dār ul-ḥuldi, Qur'an, 41²⁸.—
הסופרים] might be men as in Am. 5¹⁶, or women as in Je. 9¹⁶⁻²⁰.—
6. עד אשר לא], cf. on 12¹.—ירחק], the Kt.="be put far away."—ירתק, the
Qr.="to close up," or "bind," neither of which gives a satisfactory
meaning. 𝕲, 𝔖, 𝕳, Σ, read ינתק, which is adopted by Ges., Ew., Eur.,
Sieg., Wild. and McN., and has been adopted in the rendering given
above.—הריץ], acc. to Del., a metaplastic form of the imperf. of רץץ=
"break" (cf. Ges.ᴷ· §§67q, 67t and BDB. 954b). Sieg., Wild. and McN.
emend to ותריץ.—נלת], the very word used in Zc. 4². ³. Gins. and Zö.
would make it mean fountain (cf. נלה Jos. 15¹⁹ Ju. 1¹⁵, and נל Ct. 4¹²),
but later interpreters have rightly rejected this.—כר], a fem. sing., with
pl. in דים, cf. Kö. §252k.—מבוע]="a fountain opened in the desert"—a
rare word occurring, besides in BH., only in Is. 35⁷ and 49¹⁰. It is found
also in J.Ar., cf. Ja. 725a.—7. וישב], a jussive form, according to
Del. it is suited to עד אשר לא of vs. 6 as a subjunctive, according to
Ges.ᴷ· §109k and Kö. §366u it does not differ in force from the ordinary
imperf.—הרוח]=נפש or נשמה, cf. Gn. 2⁷ Is. 42⁵ Job 33⁴.—על.....אל] in
late writing are used interchangeably. Vs. 6 furnished an example of
this also. 8. הכל הבלים], cf. on 1².—אמר הקהלת] some would emend
to אמרה קהלת after 7²⁷, but probably that passage should be emended
to this. On קהלת, see on 1¹.

12⁹⁻¹².—A late editor's praise of Qoheleth, and of Hebrew Wisdom, to which is added a Chasid's last gloss (12¹³⁻ ¹⁴).

12⁹. *And besides that Qoheleth was wise, he still taught the people knowledge, and tested and examined and arranged many proverbs.* ¹⁰. *Qoheleth sought to find pleasant words, but he wrote uprightly words of truth.* ¹¹. *The words of the wise are as goads, and as driven nails are the members of collections; they are given by one shepherd.* ¹². *And besides these, my son, be warned. Of making many books there is no end, and much study is a weariness of the flesh.* ¹³. *End of discourse. All has been heard.*

FEAR GOD AND KEEP HIS COMMANDMENTS, FOR THIS IS EVERY MAN. ¹⁴. FOR EVERY WORK GOD WILL BRING INTO THE JUDGMENT CONCERNING EVERY SECRET THING, WHETHER GOOD OR BAD.

12⁹. *Besides that Qoheleth was wise*].   This praise of Qoheleth is unlike anything in the book, and sounds as many interpreters, from Döderlein down, have noted, like a later editor.   The language in which this editorial addition is written differs, if possible, even more widely from Biblical Hebrew (see critical notes) than the language of Qoheleth.—*Still taught the people knowledge*], through his wise writings.—*And tested and examined and arranged many proverbs*].   Probably, as Hitzig and Wildeboer say, this is a reference to our book of Proverbs, which the editor attributed to Qoheleth, whom he identified with Solomon.—**10.** *Qoheleth sought to find pleasant words*].   He tried to give his composition a pleasing or elegant form.   This is also a part of the editor's testimony to Qoheleth-Solomon.   He claims that Qoheleth sought to give literary finish to his compositions.—*But he wrote uprightly words of truth*].   He never sacrificed matter to form.   Perhaps this is the editor's apology for some of the statements in the book before us. For a justification of the above translation, see critical note.— **11.** *The words of the wise are as goads*].   They prick and stimulate to activity.   Plumtre recalls that the words of Pericles were said to have a sting.—*As driven nails*].   It is difficult to tell whether the editor is thinking of the appearance of written words in a row, like a row of driven nails, as Delitzsch suggests, or whether he is thinking of the permanent effect of a written word embodied in a collection in comparison with the goad-like effect of a spoken word.   The latter seems the more probable.   Haupt contends that

the contrast here is between disjointed sayings, such as the book
of Proverbs, and more connected thought such as is contained in
Qoheleth's book—a less probable view.—*Members of collections*].
Utterances that have been embodied in a collection of sayings. For
the translation and for different renderings, see the crit. note.—
They are given by one shepherd]. Haupt, for metrical reasons, regards these words as a gloss, but there is no proof that the editor
attempted to write poetry, and the words seem a natural part of his
thought. The "one shepherd" was thought by Heiligstedt to refer
to Qoheleth, and by Delitzsch and McNeile to Solomon. This
makes it an assertion that all the contents of the preceding book (or
books) come really from Solomon. As Knobel, Ginsburg, Plumtre,
Wright and Wildeboer have seen, "Shepherd" in the OT. is usually
an epithet of God (Ps. 23¹ 80¹ 95⁷, *cf.* Is. 40¹¹ Ez. 33¹⁵), and is probably so here. On this view the editor means to say, the words of
the wise may be uttered by different men, but they all come
from God. Krochmal, who is followed by Graetz, thought that
the last three verses of the book applied not to Qoheleth alone, but
were the closing words of the whole Hagiographa, dating from the
council of Jabne, A.D. 90. If this were true, one would be tempted
to include the book of Job in the "words of the wise," to which
allusion is made here, but external evidence proves Krochmal's
view to be impossible, see above, *Introduction*, §§11, 13.—**12.** *And
besides these*]. Besides these inspired words of the wise, just referred to in the preceding vs.—*My son*], a common address to a
pupil in the Wisdom literature, see Pr. 1⁸· ¹⁰· ¹⁵ 2¹ 3¹· ¹¹· ²¹ 4¹.—*Be
warned*]. This refers, as the following clause proves, to other collections of books than "the words of the wise," described in the
preceding vs. Interpreters differ as to whether the editor was
warning against heathen writings (so Plumtre), or against rival
Jewish writings, such as Ecclesiasticus (so Wright), or the Wisdom of Solomon. If our view of the history of Qoheleth's writing
be true (see above, *Introduction*, §§7, 11), references to BS. and
Wisdom would be here impossible.—*Of making many books there
is no end*]; a continuation of the warning against other literature.
Possibly the writer was thinking of heathen libraries when he composed this hyperbolical statement.—*Much study is a weariness*

of the flesh]. This is, perhaps, suggested by Qoheleth's own words in 1¹⁸. The editor would deter his pupil from unorthodox or heathen literature by the thought of the weariness of study. **13ᵃ**. *End of discourse*], the end of the book.—*All has been heard*]. These words probably formed the conclusion of the editor's work, and once formed the end of the book.

13ᵇ. *Fear God and keep his commandments*]. These begin the *Chasid* glossator's final addition. It is in harmony with his previous insertions, *cf.* 3¹⁷ 8⁶ 11⁹ᵇ. *This is every man*]. A Hebrew metaphorical way of saying, "this is what every man is destined for and should be wholly absorbed in." For parallels, see crit. note.—**14**. *For every work God will bring into the judgment concerning every secret thing*]. This echoes the words of the *Chasid* in 11⁹. With this note of judgment the book, as the *Chasid* left it, closes. The Massorets thought the ending too harsh, and accordingly repeated vs. 13 after it, to make the book close with a more pleasant thought. They made similar repetitions at the end of Isaiah, the Minor Prophets and Lamentations.

12⁹. וְיֹתֵר] was taken by Heil., Zö. and Dale to mean "as to the rest," or "it remains" (to speak of). The word is, however, an adv. as in 2¹⁵ 7¹⁶. In those passages it means "excessively," here, "besides," *cf. B*DB. 452b. This approaches the Mishnic meaning of "additional," given to a kindred form, see Ja. 605a.—לִמֵּד] Piel with causative force of למד = "to learn," *cf.* BD*B*. It takes two objects, *cf.* Kö. §327r.—חעם]. &, A, read חאדם, which Gr. preferred.—אִזֵּן] was connected by the Versions with אֹזֶן = "ear," either as noun or verb. It is in reality the only survival in BH. of אזן = "to weigh" (*cf.* Ar. *wazan*), from which comes מאזנים = "scales." Here it seems to mean "weigh" in the sense of "test" (*cf.* Ges.ᴮᵘ· p. 23a and *B*DB. 24b).—חִקֵּר] = "to search out," occurs in Piel only here. Zap. would erase it on metrical grounds as a gl.—הִקֵּן] is used by Q. only in the sense of "making straight the crooked," *cf.* 1¹⁵ 7¹³. Here it means "set in order," "arranged," as in the Targ. and Tal. (*cf.* Ja. 1692). This difference from the usage of Qoheleth confirms our suspicion that the verse is from a later editor. —הרבה], on the use of this word with nouns, see Kö. §318e. & takes it with the following vs.—**10**. דברי חפץ] = "words of pleasure," *i.e.*, that give pleasure. Ha. is right in thinking that it refers to elegance of form. Marsh.'s rendering, "words of fact," on the ground that חפץ in Q. = "matter," "business," overlooks the fact that in this very chap. (12¹) חפץ = "pleasure."—וְכָתוּב] &= καὶ γεγραμμένον, supports this reading.

Ginsburg held that the pass. part., when it follows a finite vb., has the distinction of that vb. implied. Del., Pl., Wr., held to the text, taking it in the sense of "writing" as in 2 Ch. 30⁵, but this makes a harsh and awkward sentence. Hit. emended to כָּתוּב, and thought the inf. abs. was used like inf. const. after בקש; Bick. and Sieg. emend to=וְלִכְתּוֹב, making it parallel to לִמְצֹא in form as Hit. did in thought. McN. emends to וּכְתוֹב, taking it as "writing." 𝕊, 𝕿, ᾿A, 𝕳, read כָּתוּב (hist. inf.) or, as 5 MSS. read, כְּתָב, to one of which we should, with Dr., emend the text.—יֹשֶׁר], as Wr. and Wild. have seen, is an adverbial acc., cf. Ges.ᴷ· §118m.—אֱמֶת], cf. for the meaning Ps. 132¹¹.—11. דָּרְבֹנוֹת] oc- curs only once besides in BH., that in 1 S. 13²¹, a hopelessly corrupt passage (cf. Budde, SBOT., and Smith, Inter. Crit. Com.). As this last occurrence may be due to late editing in S., and as the word is fairly common in Aram. (cf. Ja. 320b), and the formation is an Aram. one, the word is probably an Aram. loan word (see BDB. 201b). It is from דרב="to train" (cf. Ar. dariba, Eth. darbaya). מלמד, from למד, is often used in Heb. for "goad."—מִשְׂמְרוֹת] is spelled elsewhere מסמרות, cf. Je. 10⁴ 2 Ch. 3⁹ and מסמרים Is. 41⁷ 1 Ch. 22³, sing. מַשְׂמֵר, see Sabbath, 6¹⁰, Kelim, 12⁴, and the references in Ja. 809a. Wild. regards it as an Aram. loan word, but inasmuch as it is found in Je. and Is.², that can hardly be. —נטוע], usually "plant," as of trees, etc., but in Dn. 11⁴⁵ of tent-pegs, as here of nails.—בעלי], not "masters (of assemblies)," nor "masters (of collections)," but as Del. pointed out="a participant of," as in Gn. 14¹³ and Ne. 6¹⁸, cf. Kö. §306g. As. has the same use of the word, cf. bel adi u mamit ša ᵐᵃᵗᵘAššurᵏⁱ= "participator in the covenant and oath of Assyria," Sennacherib, Taylor, Cyl. II. 70.—אֲסֻפּוֹת], a late word found elsewhere only in Ne. 12²⁵ and 1 Ch. 26¹⁵·¹⁷, and there masc. In those passages it refers to collections of people; here, according to Heil., Del., Wr., Gen., Ha. and McN., to a collection of sayings or a written work. Sieg. still holds to the older and less probable view that it refers to an assembly of people.—12. יֹתֵר], adv. as in vs. 9, but here with the addition of מִן=English: "in addition to these." According to Kö. (§308f) it is =plus quam.—עֲשׂוֹה], with its object, is the subject of the sentence, cf. Kö. §233d. 𝕮 apparently read אֵין קֵץ.—לַעֲשׂוֹת] is virtually an adj.= "endless," like אֵין עֲיֵל in Dt. 32⁴, so Del.—לַהַג]=with הרבה, to "de- vote oneself to prolonged study," is α.λ. Analogy is found only in the Ar. lahiga="be devoted (or attached) to a thing." Cf. No., ad. loc. and BDB. 529b.—13ᵃ. סוֹף דָּבָר] is an Aramaism. Cf. סוֹף פָּסוּק. סוֹף oc- curs in a few late writings—Jo. (2²⁰), Chronicles and Qoheleth in the sense of קֵץ (cf. BDB. 693a), but is the regular word in J.Ar. (cf. Dn. 4⁸·¹⁹ 7²⁸, and for post-Biblical references, Ja. 968a). The use of דבר without the art. shows that we cannot here translate "the end (or con- clusion) of the matter." It is probably a technical expression like סוֹף פסוק, with which the editor marked the end of his work. This

expression makes the impression that when these words were penned, the
Chasid's gloss had not been added, and these words formed the conclusion of Qoheleth. *Cf.* Kö. §277v.—נשמע]. Gr. and Sieg. hold that
ﬡ read שָׁמֵעַ, and Sieg. would so emend the text, but Eur. points out
that ἀκούε may be an itacism for ἀκούεται, so that no other reading is
necessarily pre-supposed. נשמע is taken by Gins., Del., Wr., Marsh.,
and McN. as perf. Niph., Kameç being due to the Athnah. Wild.
and Ha., among recent interpreters, still regard it as an imperf. first pers.
cohortative. There is an evident reference to this final word of Qo.'s
editor in BS. 43²⁷: עוד כאלה לא נוסף וקץ דבר הוא הכל. This quotation
confirms our view that when it was made the *Chasid* gl. had not yet
been added.

13ᵇ. זה כל האדם], as Del., No., Wr. and McN. have seen, can only mean
"this is every man." As Del. pointed out, it is a bold metaphor like
עמך נרבת="thy people are a free-will offering," Ps. 110³, אני תפלה=
"I am prayer," Ps. 109⁴, and מקרה בני האדם="fate are the children of
men," Qo. 3¹⁹.—כל האדם can only mean "every man," *cf.* 3¹⁸ 5¹⁸ 7².—
14. יבא במשפט] are the very words used by the *Chasid* in 11⁹.—במשפט],
without the article, as Gins. saw, is further defined by על כל נ'="the
judgment concerning every secret thing." (So Del., Wr. and McN.)
Cf. Je. 2³⁵.—וְעֶלֶם], McN. observes, has Daghesh in ל to insure the pronunciation of the quiescent guttural; it occurs, however, in 1 K. 10³
without Daghesh. On אם .... אם], *cf.* Kö. §371r.

INDEXES.

INDEXES.

I. HEBREW INDEX.

אבר, 104.
אבל,142.
אביונה, 52, 196.
אדם, 33, 148, 167.
אהב כסף, 33, 131.
אור, 194.
אז, 93.
אז יתר, 32.
אֵיֶן, 199.
אחר, 93, 118.
אחז, 89.
אחז ב־, 144.
אחכמה, 147.
אחרית, 142.
אחרנים, 76, 122.
אי, 52, 178.
אי זה, 194.
אֵיך, 94.
אילו, 118.
אין, 106, 145.
אין כל חדש, 75.
אין קץ, 200.
אִיש זה, 53.
אכל בחשך, 132.
אכל בשר, 117.
אלו, 135.
אל לב, 141.
אל עיר, 178.
אל תאחר, 125.
אל מקום, 73.
אל מתים, 160.
אם, 134.
אמר, 88, 111, 148.
אמר ל־, 158, 169, 196.

אמת, 200.
אני, 86, 88, 92, 152.
אסורים, 121.
אֲסֵפות, 200.
אף, 92.
ארך רוח, 142.
ארך ימים, 145.
אשר, 53, 89, 117, 137, 138, 150, 166, 178.
אשר לא, 145.
אשר להיות, 107.
אשרי, 178.

בְּ־, 125, 131, 132, 143, 178, 196.
בא, 73.
באש, 168.
באשר, 141, 152, 160.
בהל, 152.
בוא, 113, 201.
בוראיך, 195.
בזויה, 168.
בחור, 194.
בטחון, 161.
בטל, 195.
בית עולם, 196.
בכן, 155.
בלכי, 88.
בלוא, 177.
בלע, 177.
בנות השיר, 195.
בן חורים, 178.
בני ביה, 90.

בעל, 131, 132, 177, 179, 200.
בעלי, 200.
בצל, 143.
בקש, 104.
בקר, 194.
ברכות, 89.
בֹּשֶׁ־, 53, 94.
בשל אשר, 158.
בתים, 89.

גֵּבֶה, 142.
גבהים, 130.
גֵּבֶר, 178.
גרר, 176.
גופֶץ, 52, 176.
גֵּזֶל, 130.
גָּלֻח, 196.
גם, 93, 118, 122, 135, 145, 169.
גם ...... אל, 179.
גם אם, 158.
גם אני, 93.
גן, 89.
גערת, 142.
גרע, 106.

דבר, 75, 142.
דָּבָּר, 75, 145.
דברי חפץ, 199.
דברים, 137.
דבר רע, 152.
דברתי עם לב, 86.
רין, 137.

II. INDEX OF PERSONS.

III. INDEX OF SUBJECTS.